THE BRITISH TAKEOVER OF ASSAM

THE BRITISH TAKEOVER OF ASSAM

Tea, Hill Tribes and Transportation in the Nineteenth Century

CAROLINE KEEN

AMBERLEY

First published 2024

Amberley Publishing
The Hill, Stroud
Gloucestershire, GL5 4EP

www.amberley-books.com

Copyright © Caroline Keen, 2024

The right of Caroline Keen to be identified as the Author of this work has been asserted in accordance with the Copyright, Designs and Patents Act 1988.

All rights reserved. No part of this book may be reprinted or reproduced or utilised in any form or by any electronic, mechanical or other means, now known or hereafter invented, including photocopying and recording, or in any information storage or retrieval system, without the permission in writing from the Publishers.

British Library Cataloguing in Publication Data.
A catalogue record for this book is available from the British Library.

ISBN 978 1 3981 2272 7 (hardback)
ISBN 978 1 3981 2273 4 (ebook)

1 2 3 4 5 6 7 8 9 10

Typesetting by SJmagic DESIGN SERVICES, India.
Printed in the UK.

Contents

Introduction	9
1 History	**15**
Ahom Rule	15
The Burmese War of 1824–26	17
Annexation	22
Post 1857	28
Twentieth Century	33
2 Geography	**35**
3 Hill Tribes	**51**
The Bhutanese	55
The Akas	58
The Daflas	61
The Miris	62
The Abors	64
The Mishmis	68
The Khamtis	72
The Singphos	74
The Nagas	76
The Mikirs	84
The Jaintias and Khasis	85
The Garos	88
The Lushais	90
The Cacharis	93
Government Policy towards Tribal People	95

4 Trade and Industry	**102**
Tea	105
The Tea Trade	105
The Tea Garden	112
The Tea Planter	117
Tea Workers	126
Mining	139
Gold	140
Oil	141
Coal	147
Iron	154
Transportation	157
Railways	157
Waterways	165
Roadways	174
Forestry	183
Agriculture	189
Agro-Industries	192
Rubber	192
Jute and Rhea	197
Silk	200
Cotton	204
Lac	206
Sugar and Mustard	207
5 Education	**210**
Primary and Secondary Education	210
Higher Education	220
Female Education	221
Missions	224
Epilogue	236
Endnotes	244
Bibliography	277
Index	290

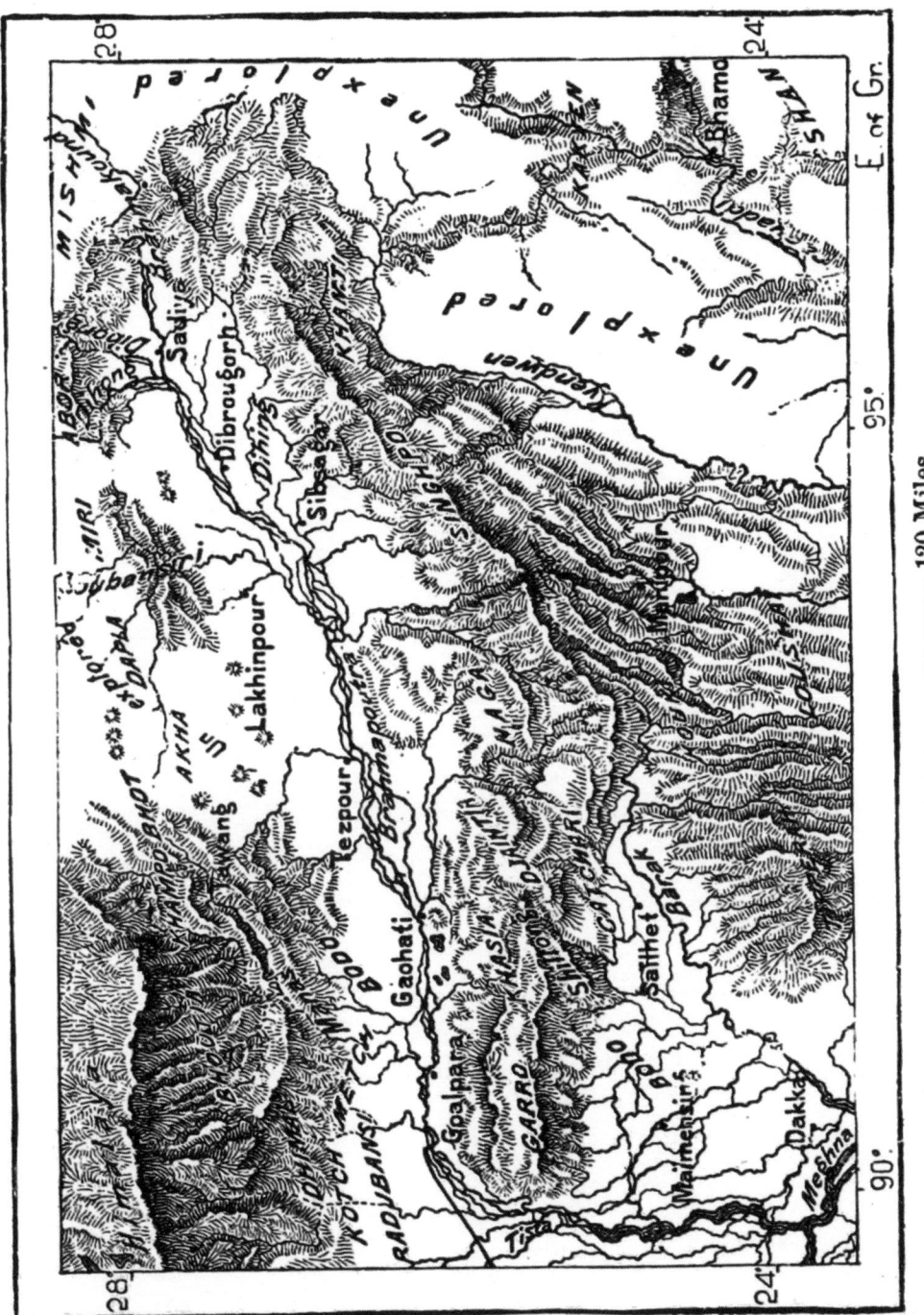

Above: A map showing the distribution of the peoples of Assam. (From *The Earth and Its Inhabitants*, 1882, courtesy of the Princeton Theological Seminary Library)

Overleaf: A map of Assam incorporating the tea and jute plantations and coalfields present in 1873. (W. & A. K. Johnston)

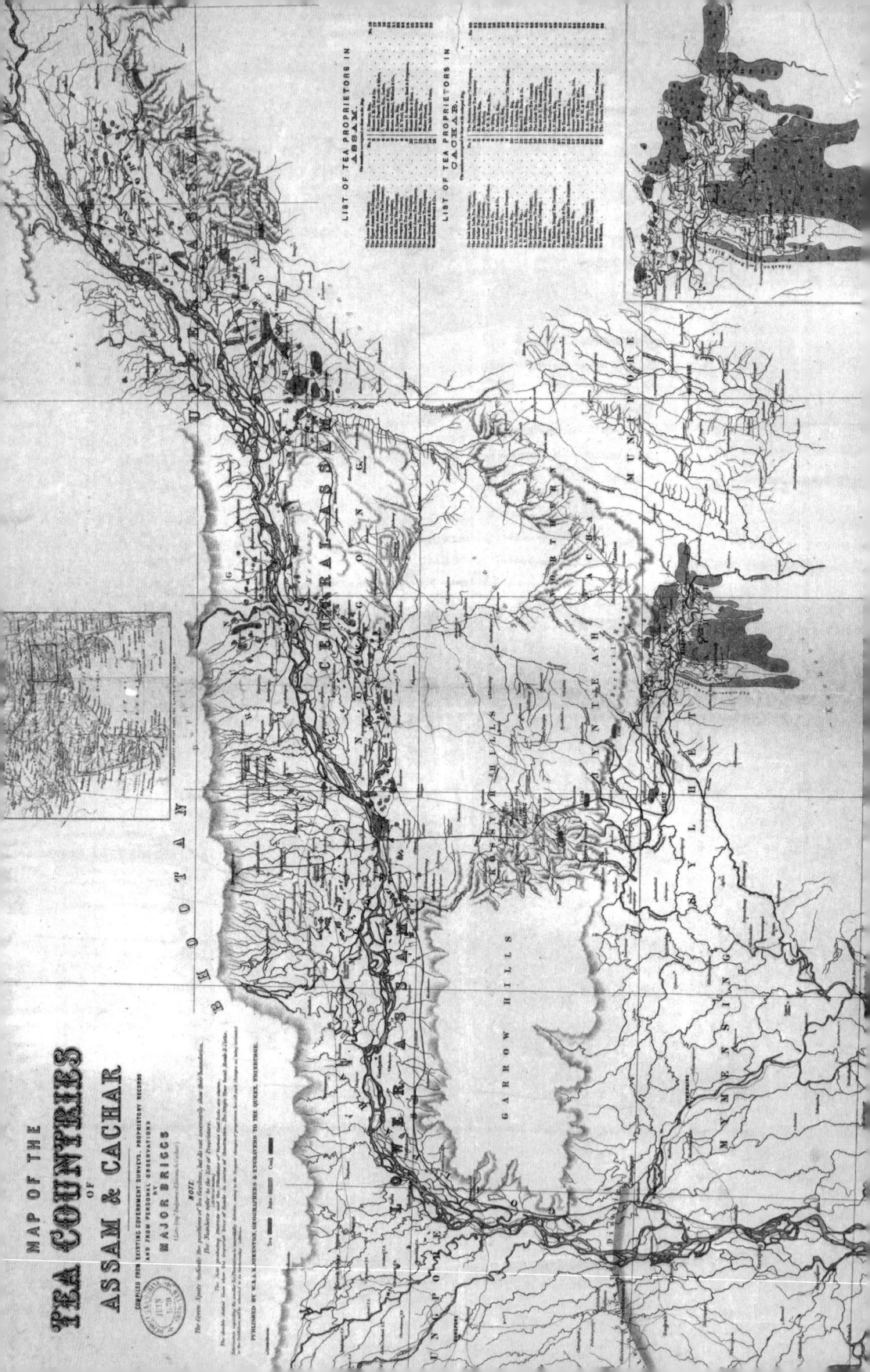

Introduction

In 1838, as an unanticipated consequence of the British military success over Burma and the subsequent acquisition of a number of princely territories, the Ahom kingdom of Assam was annexed to the presidency of Bengal. The few previous British encounters with Assam had resulted in a considerable lack of enthusiasm, with one description of the wild, uncharted territory as a 'profitless ... primeval jungle'.[1] Obtained as the by-product of an unplanned war, Assam's exact place in the changing imperial system was uncertain and immediately after its addition the region was seen of little value. Such a negative perception of Assam's potential stemmed partly from the evidence of internal political turmoil but, as Jayeeta Sharma suggests, to a large extent doubts were based on 'the nature of the partially monetized, subsistence-peasant economy of the area and its relative lack of urbanisation and commercialisation'. Differing from the nucleated village pattern of other areas of South Asia with specialised agricultural and artisanal groups, the Brahmaputra Valley was characterised by small hamlets clustered along the riverbanks, interspersed with urban settlements such as Gauhati and Sibsagar, the largest possessing only a few thousand inhabitants. These towns were a far cry from the great cities of Lucknow or Calcutta, or the thriving bazaars of North India which served the East India Company so well.[2]

In the eighteenth century, Bengal trade with Assam had undoubtedly flourished for both Indian and European traders, with salt as the major export in exchange for imports of *muga* silk, mustard seed, ivory, gold and slaves from Assam. However, the limited extent of this external trade meant that the Ahom rulers were able to prohibit the admission of foreign traders when they felt threatened by the politics on their borders. Such commercial disruption created few problems given the nature of the local commerce, where it was the inter-regional relationships and the connection with Assam's eastern neighbours which were essential to the success of the Assamese economy. Cotton, forest products, oranges, rock salt and iron from the hills were bartered for rice, dried fish, silk and cotton cloth from the valley at markets and fairs held periodically in the foothills. Similar patterns of exchange existed through the caravan routes linking the Assam hills with Bhutan, Manipur, Tibet and Yunnan. However, despite the considerable length of the Brahmaputra and its tributaries, turbulent currents limited the river's navigational possibilities and accounted for the relatively few commercial and administrative links with the rest of South Asia. As a result, at the time of the Burmese defeat the only promise that the new British acquisition of Assam seemed to possess was as a contact point for western expansion into Southeast and East Asia.[3]

Although East India Company growth usually occurred in a piecemeal and unplanned manner, often driven by the short-term opportunism of the men on the spot, the future of Assam was determined by consistent government involvement in the newly discovered financial prospects for the region. Of these the most significant was the scientific recognition of a wild bush growing in upper Assam as a close relative of the Chinese tea plant, laying the foundations for a highly lucrative industry which, with the identification of rich mineral resources, would during the nineteenth century open the province to extensive movements of capital, goods and people. Prior to the emergence of tea cultivation in Assam, British merchants had purchased almost all their tea from China. However, an insatiable demand for this exotic and expensive product at home resulted in an imbalance of payments (made in silver bullion) between Britain and China, stimulating the East India Company's efforts to establish a market for opium in China. Tea grown by the British in Assam from the late 1830s catered to the domestic tea demand and remedied the trade imbalance

Introduction

with China, while also contributing to tea consumption at a global level. As a result, the industry became a crucial component of the imperial economy, requiring a large influx of indentured labour to man the tea estates. The subsequent discovery of petroleum and coal was accompanied by the establishment of regular river traffic on the Brahmaputra and the growth of the railway network, necessitating an increase in imported iron and steel. The rapidity of the investment in tea plantations and mines and the resulting structural changes dramatically affected not only the local economy but also the pattern of social, political, administrative and cultural life.

The introduction of river and rail traffic accompanying the new colonial commercial drive radically changed Assam's trade relations with the bordering regions. While trade with Bengal took on new dimensions, there were closures on other fronts. As the railway dramatically reduced the distance between Assam and Bengal, the province's ties with its eastern and northern neighbours became increasingly marginal. The commerce with Bhutan and Tibet declined markedly, and by the first decade of the twentieth century British officials dismissed this frontier as being of little importance.[4] Deprived of their traditional trade, for the people of the region there was little benefit from the colonial 'enclave' economy that was developed in Assam by the British. The extracted surplus from the tea industry plus a substantial portion of the wage bills disappeared outside the province and a serious imbalance emerged between the growing modern sector, comprising the tea plantations, coalmines, oilfields and associated infrastructure, and the near-stagnant traditional agriculture.[5] With the majority of commercial head offices located in London and Calcutta, the major transportation companies based in Bengal and the manufacture of industrial equipment carried out in Britain, the indigenous sector of the economy benefited marginally from colonial development. In addition, under British rule migration routes were opened up from East Bengal and Assam's demographic profile underwent a major change. In the twentieth century, Assamese ethnic fears of being reduced to a minority were voiced and serious ethno-linguistic rivalries began to surface, having an impact on Assam's relationship with both Bengal and other regions.

With the new financial potential of the region, security for people and goods became an essential requirement. Much of the British contempt for the Ahom rulers had rested upon the view that the Assam Valley was 'surrounded north, east and south by numerous savage and warlike tribes' whom 'the decaying authority of the Assam dynasty had failed of late years to control and whom the disturbed condition of the province had incited to encroachment'.[6] This idea of the Assam hill groups as 'savage and warlike' not only resulted in a policy of segregation, but also provided fertile ground for the current colonial ethnographic interest in the indigenous peoples of the subcontinent whom the British separated into castes and tribes for further analysis. Societies were ranked in relation to each other, and their degree of 'advancement' was measured by various criteria, ranging from technology, habitat and methods of subsistence to climate variations and racial types. With information acquired from British expeditions surveying the hills (often of a military nature to deal with the recalcitrant tribal population), the extraordinarily diverse ethnic populace of upper Assam provided an array of additions to the Indian ethnographic collection and the people of the region were categorised into a continuum ranging from the 'civilised' caste Hindu to the 'savage' headhunter.

Following continuous violent incursions by the hill peoples into the plains, a policy of containment was adopted, resulting in the Bengal Eastern Frontier Regulation of 1873. A new internal frontier for British India was created, beyond which excluded areas were designated into which no British subject or foreign citizen could enter without permission. This measure was ostensibly to allow the inhabitants of the tracts beyond the exclusion zone to 'manage their own affairs with only such interference on the part of the frontier officers in their political capacity as may be considered advisable with the view to establishing a personal influence for good among the chiefs and the tribes',[7] but was in fact established to control and protect 'the commercial relations of our own subjects with the frontier tribes'.[8]

For the hill tribes, as for much of the plains' population of Assam in the nineteenth century, there was an inextricable link with the economic activity which drove the development of the region. This book is concerned with the work of the British individuals involved in opening up the northeast, either in commercial ventures of one sort or another or in expeditions to the hills to procure valuable information on the unknown quantity of the hill tribes and the possible threat they posed to British trade and industry in the Brahmaputra Valley. It attempts to throw light on the opinions and motivations of these men which, although they can be qualified to some extent as reflections of their time, do not necessarily provide easy reading. Other than missionaries, the majority of the British in Assam treated the native occupants of the northeast with undeniable contempt as, under the assumption that they were armed with a colonial right to the use of people and land, they set about maximising the potential of the province. Following the Burmese war there was certainly a commitment on the part of a series of senior British officials to improve the governance and safety of Assam by the imposition of the rule of law through an enhanced police presence and the establishment of impartial upper and lower courts of justice. Moreover, although the development of the communication network in Assam was limited in its availability and extent, as was the growth of medical facilities, the local people did derive certain benefits from these advances. However, there was little evidence of any commitment on the part of the British to ensure the right of the Assamese individual to a share in the proceeds of the local economy, even though elsewhere in India a powerful strand of paternalistic thought maintained that even a colonial state should further the cause of Indian citizens as individuals, rather than exploit India and its people as a resource.[9]

Greater Assamese participation in both government and economy could have been achieved with a dedicated commitment to the education of the inhabitants of the province, but British efforts lacked the urgency to provide adequate resources for the size of the population. Moreover, during the second half of the nineteenth century progress was severely hindered by a series of changes in official policy under which the government of Assam increasingly distanced itself from primary and secondary education. From the 1860s, full state support to schools was replaced by partial monetary assistance to support private endeavours. While this strategy was being simultaneously implemented in the rest of India in accordance with the Wood despatch of 1854 and was successful in stimulating private initiatives in areas such as Bengal, in Assam the approach predictably failed due to a lack of financial involvement on the part of the hard-pressed native population. Although it was officially admitted that such a scheme was not tenable in a relatively impoverished province like Assam, where the traditional elite had lost its place of eminence and a flourishing bourgeoisie was yet to emerge, there is no evidence to indicate that the government attempted to expand its limited patronage in the light of the evident failure to make any great improvement to educational standards.

As with education, it was unlikely that there would be significant local financial participation in the economy. After the severe internal problems during the latter stages of Ahom rule, there was no accumulation of wealth in the region and few Assamese could be regarded as even moderately affluent. Hence, even when the opportunity for investment presented itself, only a negligible minority could take advantage of it. By the end of the nineteenth century, the capital flowing into industry was almost entirely British, and Assam had become predominantly a supplier of raw materials and a market for British industrial goods, made possible by colonial control of both major and minor industrial activity in the region. The British not only owned but also managed a large part of the economy with labour and middlemen recruited from other Indian provinces. The sole contribution of most Assamese was to create some additional manpower in the form of unskilled labour, acting, according to Dadabhai Naoroji, 'as mere slaves to slave upon their own land and their own resources in order to give away the products to the British capitalists'.[10] The shadow of the huge colonial manufacturing drive in Assam tended to eclipse any moral imperative to substantially improve the well-being of the local people. By the beginning of the twentieth century, capital, labour, enterprise, trade and craft were all represented by outsiders.

1
History

Ahom Rule

The early history of Assam is obscure, although there are numerous references in the Mahabharata, the Puranas and the Tantras of a great kingdom known as Kamrupa, which existed from AD 350 to 1140 and encompassed the Brahmaputra Valley, Bhutan, Cooch Behar, and the Rangpur region of Eastern Bengal. Among the early sources of the history of Assam are the writings of the Chinese pilgrim Xuanzang, who in AD 640 attended the court of the ruler of Kamrupa, King Bhaskar Barman, and later stone and copper inscriptions dating from the seventh to the twelfth century indicate a succession of Hindu dynasties. However, by the early thirteenth century any semblance of a centralized kingship in the region had collapsed into a fragmented system of tribal politics and loose confederacies of petty Hindu rajas, or *bhuyans*. The Ahoms, a Shan tribe from which the name Assam is possibly derived, crossed the Patkai mountains on India's northeastern border with Burma in AD 1228. By the sixteenth century they had absorbed the Chutiya and Cachari kingdoms of the upper Brahmaputra which had developed in the wake of Kamrupa rule, subdued the neighbouring hill tribes and integrated the *bhuyans* into the administrative apparatus of a feudalistic state. During the first half of the sixteenth century, the revered *gossain* (teacher/saint) and Assamese cultural hero Shankara Deva inspired a popular Vaishnavite movement which attempted to reform the esoteric practices of Tantric Hinduism and to limit the prerogatives of the Brahmins attached to the Ahom court. The Ahom rulers sponsored an extensive network of Vaishnavite monasteries, whose monks played an important role in the reclamation of wastelands for wet-rice cultivation throughout the Brahmaputra Valley.[1]

During the latter part of the sixteenth and much of the seventeenth century, the Ahom repulsed a succession of Mughal invasions from Bengal and started to annex the eastern portion of the powerful Koch[2] kingdom in 1682 to consolidate their control over the entire Brahmaputra Valley. Full accounts of the invasions come down from both Ahom and Muslim sources and are valuable in the information they provide on old methods of warfare and how little could be achieved by superior arms and numbers when faced with the difficulties of communication, inadequate supplies and an unhealthy climate.[3] The kingdom of the Ahom reached its zenith under Rudra Singha (r. 1696–1714), the renowned military strategist and patron of the *buranji*, or Ahom chronicles. Although during the nineteenth century the country was sparsely populated, there is evidence that the region had earlier supported a large population and kings and nobles of great wealth. In Gauhati, Tezpur and many other places in upper Assam large granite pillars, stone blocks and slabs, elaborately carved with scrolls and figures in relief, were found half buried or scattered about in great numbers. Massive brick palaces and theatres were hidden in jungle, and gold ornaments and dishes were exhumed from ancient tombs. Many of the old royal roads were reclaimed, proving to be the best thoroughfares in the country, and the old bridges that had been built over nullahs and ditches were so substantially constructed that they were still in a sound, reliable condition.[4]

From 1769 a disaffected section of the population, the Moamarias, under the leadership of their Vaishnavite *mahantas* (religious leaders), took part in a series of uprisings against Ahom rule which devastated upper Assam. According to the soldier and military historian Leslie Shakespear, 'the country became filled with the turbulent ruffianism of the great bazaars in Bengal, with disbanded soldiery and fighting fanatics, who pillaged villages and laid waste the fields, reducing the country to ruin'.[5] At the request of King Gaurinath Singha (r. 1780–95), the governor-general of India, Sir John Shore, despatched a mission under Captain Thomas Welsh of the Bengal Army to Rangpur, the Ahom capital, temporarily restoring peace to the kingdom. It was clear that at this stage the East India Company did not intend to conquer Assam or extend its political influence within the kingdom and, under the orders of the governor-general, Welsh withdrew his forces despite Gaurinath's appeal to him to remain. Thereafter, during the period 1786–1822 there was a refusal by all governors-general to interfere in the affairs of the Ahom kingdom. However, after the departure of Welsh, civil unrest continued.

The Burmese War of 1824–26

In 1817 the Burmese took advantage of the rifts among the Ahom nobility and, with the help of military commander Badan Chandra, were able to enter the Brahmaputra Valley where they defeated Purander Singh, the current Ahom ruler, installing his princely rival, Chandrakanta, as the new monarch. With a healthy contempt for the British (engendered partly by the paucity of British troops along the frontier and the proved inefficiency of the Ahom standing army, which was dressed and drilled on the model of the East India Company's sepoys), the Burmese began to take aggressive action not only along the northern frontier of Bengal but also near the port of Chittagong on the Bay of Bengal. Such action threatened Britain's commercial activity with frontier kingdoms, and it was feared that Burmese supremacy over the river routes of Assam would also put the Company's Bengal interests in serious jeopardy. Protestations were made by the governor-general with no effect and a formal declaration of war was issued on 5 March 1824.[1]

The British Takeover of Assam

In anticipation of active operations, a British force of about 3,000 men with several cannon and a gunboat flotilla were assembled at the station of Goalpara on the frontier of the old Ahom kingdom, with the goal of turning the Burmese out of the Brahmaputra Valley. After a demanding journey of fifteen days through jungle and trackless swamps between Goalpara and Gauhati, the force reached Gauhati on 28 March. The Burmese had erected strong stockades in the area, but their numbers had been greatly reduced by desertions, the withdrawal of troops for service in Burma itself and operations in the region of Cachar. As a result, they retired to upper Assam. Had more action been taken at this stage it is probable that the entire valley could have been cleared of the Burmese before the start of the rainy season. But in the absence of information regarding the state of the roads, the possibility of obtaining supplies or the attitude of the local inhabitants, the British force made a long halt at Gauhati.

Meanwhile, insisting that 'we are not led into your [Ahom] country by the thirst of conquest; but are forced in our defence to deprive our enemy of the means of annoying us',[2] David Scott, agent to the governor-general for the eastern frontier, crossed over the Jaintia Hills with three companies of the 23rd Native Infantry to join the British force in the Brahmaputra Valley and travelled south of the river before marching westwards to Gauhati, leaving his escort to hold the town of Nowgong. Colonel Alfred Richards, the British commander, established his headquarters at the neighbouring town of Koliabar, but when the rains set in the difficulty of procuring supplies forced him to return to Gauhati. The Burmese then occupied not only Koliabar but also Nowgong, and, in revenge for the friendship which the Assamese had shown towards the British troops, pillaged the surrounding country and committed appalling atrocities.[3] Some inhabitants were flayed alive, some burnt in oil and others driven in crowds into the village prayer houses which were then set on fire.[4] As a result many thousands of people fled into the hills and jungle to the south, where a large number died of disease or starvation.

When the rains were over, arrangements were made for a fresh advance of British troops. The only practicable means of transport was by boats towed laboriously against the strong current of the river and the rate of progress was very slow. Two divisions were dispatched at the end of October, one by the Kallang River and the other up the mainstream of the Brahmaputra, and when Koliabar had been secured the rest of the troops were gradually transported to the area. They operated with great success against various stockades held by the Burmese, who were forced to concentrate their forces in Jorhat, leaving the road open for the British advance. Although hampered by heavy rain, the British reached Jorhat on 17 January 1825. The commissariat flotilla with its escort of gunboats, unable to ascend the shallow stream of the Dikhu River, halted at its mouth and from this point all supplies had to be transported by road. On the morning of 27 January, the Burmese attacked an advance post of the British encampment. Supports were moved up quickly and to encourage the Burmese to reveal their position a retreat from the bridge was feigned. The Burmese fell into the trap and were routed with heavy losses. Having been joined by the requisite reinforcement of guns, Colonel Richards resumed his march towards Rangpur on the morning of the 29th and, following two armed engagements, was able to occupy the capital on terms agreed with the Burmese.[5]

The surrender of Rangpur and the ejection of the Burmese terminated the main campaign, but the state of anarchy into which the Brahmaputra Valley had fallen, combined with the lawless conduct of the frontier tribes, was still highly demanding for the British forces. The Singpho tribe in northeast Assam had proved particularly troublesome and during the Burmese occupation had made constant raids on the Assamese, carrying off thousands as slaves and reducing the eastern part of the country to a state of almost total depopulation.[6] When in June 1825 about 600 Burmese linked up with the Singpho rebels, a party of the 57th Native Infantry led by Captain John Bryan Neufville was immediately transferred up the Noa Dihing River and in a series of brave assaults defeated the Burmese and expelled them from the Singpho villages.

The Singphos then surrendered and the Burmese made their final exit from that part of Assam. In the course of these operations, it is said that no fewer than 6,000 Assamese captives were restored to freedom. The ease with which the Burmese had been ejected from the upper valley was of little surprise to the officers on the spot due to the lack of Burmese military cohesion. Before the outbreak of hostilities, David Scott had written to the government saying that 'their expulsion would be a matter of no difficulty', although maintaining at that time that 'the unhealthiness of the country would make its permanent occupation by us a matter of regret in some respects'.[7]

However, fresh operations were needed in Cachar and the princely state of Manipur where the Burmese, encouraged by the withdrawal of the main body of British troops, were renewing their military action. Great efforts were made by a force of 700 men to make a road through to Manipur, but serious obstacles were met in the mountainous country with the demanding nature of the clay soil and unusually heavy rainfall. Large numbers of elephants, bullocks and other transport animals were lost, and eventually the attempt was abandoned and the force was broken up. The final expulsion of the Burmese was achieved with the help of the ruler of Manipur, Raja Gambhir Singh, who had accompanied the troops with an irregular levy of 500 Manipuris and Cacharis. These men had been provided with arms by the British commander but were wholly undisciplined, and it was only at Gambhir Singh's urgent request that he and his men were allowed to advance with the British to Manipur. He left Sylhet in the Bengal presidency on 17 May 1825 accompanied by Lt Robert Pemberton,[8] who had volunteered for the expedition, and after a march of great difficulty and privation, often through torrents of rain, the party arrived in the Manipur Valley on 10 June. The Burmese retreated from the capital, Imphal, and the adjoining villages to Undra, about 10 miles to the south. Here also they made no stand, fleeing the area as soon as the advance was resumed. The inclemency of the season and the dearth of supplies made it impossible for the whole force to remain in Manipur and Gambhir Singh returned with the bulk of his followers to Sylhet, leaving a small detachment. On 4 December the raja again set out for Manipur and reached the capital in a fortnight. There were no Burmese in the city, but a considerable number occupied a stockade in Tammu in the southeast corner of the valley. Singh had no guns and the loss in a direct attack would undoubtedly have been great. He therefore cut off the water supply, forcing the Burmese to retreat. The capture of a second stockade on the bank of the Ningthi (Chindwin) River freed the entire state from the Burmese. Here and elsewhere freedom was restored to many Manipuris who had been taken by the Burmese as slaves.[9]

The operations of the British in Burma itself had also been successful, and the king of Ava was at last reluctantly forced to accept the terms of peace which were offered to him. By the Treaty of Yandabo, signed on 24 February 1826, the king agreed among other things to abstain from all interference in the territories which subsequently constituted the province of Assam and to recognize Gambhir Singh as raja of Manipur. The condition of the Brahmaputra Valley at the time of the expulsion of the Burmese was deplorable. No fewer than 30,000 Assamese had been removed as slaves and it was estimated that the invaders had destroyed more than half of the population, which had already been depleted by internal unrest and repeated civil war.[10] Those who survived had been so harassed by the continuing hostilities and recurrent acts of repression that they had almost given up cultivation and lived chiefly on jungle roots and plants. Famine and pestilence killed many of those who had escaped a violent death and captivity. With few exceptions, the remaining nobles of the ancient Ahom dynasty and the great *gossains* had retired to Goalpara after losing the whole or the bulk of their property and were followed by large numbers of commoners. The former eventually returned to their homes but the poorer refugees remained, where their descendants formed a great proportion of the inhabitants of the eastern part of Goalpara.[11]

Annexation

The Burmese had been finally ejected from Assam, but it still remained to be decided how the northeast of India should be divided. Manipur was restored to Gambhir Singh, who had been the primary mover in driving out the Burmese and was considered to have a better claim to the throne than either of his brothers. The raja of Jaintia, Ram Singh, was confirmed in his possessions, both in the hills and in the submontane tract on the north bank of the Surma River. The raja of Cachar, Gobind Chandra, was reinstated and, by a treaty signed at Badarpur on 6 March 1824, acknowledged his allegiance to the East India Company, paying an annual tribute of Rs 10,000 a year and submitting to the Company's arbitration in the case of disputes with other rulers. On their part the Company undertook to protect him from external aggression, to leave him to manage his own internal affairs and to make provision for the Manipuri princes who had recently occupied his country.

The problem in the Brahmaputra Valley was more difficult. During the several years that the Burmese had been in control, most of the old administrative measures had been abandoned and the people split up into many conflicting parties. The elevation of any one pretender to the throne would have resulted, as soon as British troops were withdrawn, in a renewal of the civil dissension which had existed for many years before the Burmese occupation. Moreover, certain members of the former royal family and nobility had conspired to oust the British from central Assam. As a result, there was no intention to restore an Ahom prince to the throne of Assam.[1]

Other than two tracts in upper Assam – Sadiya and Matak – it was decided, for a time at least, to administer the country as a British province. Its management was entrusted in November 1823 to David Scott, whose administrative remit covered the entire northeastern frontier from Cachar and Sylhet in the south to Sikkim in the north. He was at the same time special civil commissioner of northeast Rangpur, consisting of Goalpara and the Garo Hills, and judge of circuit and appeal in the Bengal district of Sylhet. Despite his many duties and inadequate staff, he was highly conscientious in his efforts to correct the worst abuses such as the widespread system of slavery, releasing 12,000 individuals from 'hopeless bondage'. Scott's goal was to retain the previous system and the employment of local citizens as far as possible and, according to the educationalist William Robinson, his introduction of the new regime was both efficient and sensitive.[2] The ordinary criminal and civil duties were performed by councils of the local gentry, designated *panchayats*. More severe cases were tried by the commissioner's assistants, who also dealt with appeals from the *panchayats* and from whose decisions, both appellate and original, lay a further appeal to the commissioner himself. To maintain law and order the British police system was introduced and the number of *thanas* (police stations) was dramatically increased.[3]

In lower Assam it was thought inadvisable to make any radical change to revenue administration until the future of the country was clear. The only important alteration adopted was the imposition of a poll tax of 3 rupees per *paik*, or *corvee* labourer, in lieu of the old liability for personal service for three or four months a year.[4] However, the different *khels*, or groupings of *paiks*, had become so scattered during the recent turmoil that the raising of government dues was both tedious and uncertain, and the amounts which were eventually paid into the treasury were ridiculously small. The method of collection was therefore changed from a personal to a territorial system. The whole area of a district was parcelled out into blocks called *mausas* or *mahals* and an overseeing officer collected the dues from all residents of a given *mahal*. This poll tax was soon abandoned in favour of a regular assessment of the land based on actual measurement.[5]

Following David Scott's death in 1831, the question of restoring the other parts of the Brahmaputra Valley to native rule continued to be discussed. It was apparent that it would not be wise to withdraw the British troops altogether, as this would undoubtedly lead to a revival of the previous fractional rivalry. However, at that time the economic potential of the region was not yet evident, and it was deemed desirable to avoid permanent annexation. The decision was made to install native rule in one part of the province and to retain the other region in British hands as a means of providing the revenue for the maintenance of an adequate garrison. Unsurprisingly it was lower Assam which was retained by the British, where at that stage the revenue prospects were considerably brighter than those in upper Assam. Scott, to pacify the people, had examined a project for reinstating Purander Singh (who was seen as the most pliable of the rival candidates from the royal family) in the country east of the Dhansiri River. This plan was presented to the Government of India by Scott's successor, Thomas Campbell Robertson (who subsequently became deputy governor of Bengal), and early in 1833 the whole of upper Assam, except the territories of Sadiya and Matak, was formally made over to the prince.

By a treaty entered into at the time of his installation, Purander Singh was placed on the same footing as protected princes elsewhere in India: the entire civil administration was left in his hands and his territory was secured from the attacks of hostile states on condition of his payment of a yearly tribute of a sizeable Rs 50,000 out of an estimated revenue of Rs 120,000. In addition, he was bound to obey the orders of the British political agent and administer justice on the principles generally prevailing in Company territories.[6] The British government still maintained direct political relations with the rulers of Matak and Sadiya and the surrounding hill tribes, and continued to keep a garrison and a political officer at Sadiya. Jorhat was made the capital of the new upper Assam state and the headquarters of the political agent, while the Assam Light Infantry was transferred to Biswanath. A detachment of the infantry was left at Jorhat for the protection of the raja and the preservation of peace. In 1834 Robertson was succeeded as commissioner and agent to the governor-general by Captain (later General) Francis Jenkins. At this time the British portion of the valley was divided into four districts: Darrang (including Biswanath), Nowgong, Kamrup and Goalpara. In 1835 the population of the entire valley, based upon land revenue assessment, was estimated to be 799,519: the native states in upper Assam 220,000, Darrang 89,519, Nowgong 90,000, Kamrup 300,000 and Goalpara 100,000.[7]

The arrival of peace and settled government soon led to a marked improvement in the condition of the cultivator, although records of the Jenkins era reveal a significant concern about the use of local land for a combination of shifting and itinerant cultivation. The colonial land settlement policy was premised on the idea of the superior merits of long-term hereditary and transferable rights in land typified by sedentary agriculture. The Assamese peasants, on the other hand, were averse to long-term tenurial agreements and preferred to vacate property after several harvests regardless of the terms of the settlement. Not conversant with local norms, British state officials tended to attribute the surrender of land to the indolence of the cultivators once the household consumption level had been reached. A great quantity of land was given up in this manner each year, but the practice could not be forcibly banned in case it encouraged the peasants to leave the land altogether. Nevertheless, left to their own devices the cultivators fared better under British control, whereas the state of the aristocracy had seriously deteriorated. Their slaves had been emancipated and they had lost the services of the *paiks* formerly assigned to them. No longer able to cultivate their estates, they either abandoned them or, due to arrears of revenue or debt, allowed them to be sold. Some members of the late ruling family were in receipt of pensions from the British government and others held land granted to them by former rulers, either rent-free or at half rate, but with these exceptions the erstwhile nobles found themselves deprived of their old sources of livelihood and forced either to take minor appointments under the British government or to sink to the level of ordinary cultivators.[8]

In Cachar the raja, Gobind Chandra, almost killed the trade between Manipur and Sylhet by imposing draconian transit duties on all articles of merchandise. He also behaved tyrannically towards the Manipuris who had settled in his territory and his tribute fell into arrears. Before matters reached a climax, he died at the hand of a Manipuri assassin, leaving no descendants either lineal or adopted. Following the controversial policy of British rule adopted by the court of directors of the East India Company, the Doctrine of Lapse (under which a princely state or territory would automatically be annexed if the ruler were either 'manifestly incompetent or died without a male heir'), the region was annexed by a proclamation dated 14 August 1832 'with the request and earnestly expressed wishes of the people'.[9] The acquisition of Cachar was without doubt highly desirable for the British with its strategic location in the face of further Burmese hostilities and its potential as the 'granary' for surrounding regions. On its annexation, Cachar was formed into a district with headquarters at Silchar and placed in the charge of a superintendent subordinate to the commissioner of Assam. The procurement of the territory was to be the start of a systematic incorporation of minor fiefdoms into British control.

In March 1835, following a series of warnings to the raja of Jaintia and the raja of Gobha (to the west of Nowgong) in the wake of attacks on British personnel and continuing evidence of human sacrifice, two companies of the Sylhet Light Infantry took formal possession of Jaintiapur.[10] A few weeks later a detachment of the Assam Light Infantry took over Gobha, placing it under the jurisdiction of Nowgong. In the adjoining territory, the Khasi tribe to the south of Kamrup had gradually established themselves in the plain where the local chiefs became virtually independent, exercising criminal jurisdiction and making war on each other with impunity. This lawlessness was checked by the British but, to conciliate the chiefs as far as possible, a separate court was established for the trial of civil and criminal cases, composed of the chiefs themselves and several of their principal officers. In lieu of feudal service, and of the charges formerly paid by new chiefs at the time of their accession, a moderate land assessment was introduced. The settlement was made with the chiefs, who were given a large share of the net profits (amounting in some cases to 50 per cent). However, few possessed any aptitude for business and they soon fell into arrears in their dues. This led eventually to the sequestration of their estates and the special court was abolished after the extension of the Criminal Procedure Code to the region.[11] A British agency was established in February 1835, the remit of which was extended by the annexation of the Jaintia Hills, placing the area under British jurisdiction.

The writing was on the wall for the remaining rulers in the region. In upper Assam Purander Singh began in less than three years to default in his payments due to mismanagement and the general system of corruption which he had apparently encouraged, and he begged for a considerable reduction in his yearly tribute of half a lakh of rupees. Since it was evident that his administration had proved a considerable failure due largely to his own 'avaricious habits',[12] he was deposed and pensioned off in October 1838 and his territories were placed once more under the direct administration of British officers. They were formed into two districts: Sibsagar, which included the tract south of the old course of the Brahmaputra; and Lakhimpur to the north. In Sadiya the aged ruler, the Khowa Gobain, died in 1835 and was succeeded by his son. Following the forcible possession of a disputed tract of land by the new Khowa Gobain, his title was abolished and he was removed to another part of the province. The Bar Senapati, or chief of the Matak country, after nominating his second son to succeed him, died in 1839 and the favourable arrangements sanctioned by the British government for the term of his life came to an end. New terms were offered to his heir and other members of his family, who refused to accept them, whereupon Captain Hamilton Vetch, political agent in upper Assam, assumed direct management of the whole region. In 1842 a proclamation was issued announcing the incorporation of Matak and Sadiya into British territory.[13] Both tracts were added to the Lakhimpur district with headquarters in Dibrugarh.

As a result of the substantial annexation of territory during the preceding decade, in 1838 Assam was absorbed into the Bengal presidency of British India. By 1840 British residences, a church and some municipal buildings had sprung up in Gauhati, which became the headquarters of the new Assam government. For more than ten years after the annexation, Assamese was the language of the courts in the Brahmaputra Valley, but it was superseded by Bengali which also became the medium of instruction in the schools and a great cause of dissension.¹⁴ There were three regiments in the Brahmaputra Valley: the Assam Light Infantry, with headquarters at Sibsagar, and the two Sebundy corps, which were stationed at Gauhati and Ranpur respectively. In 1844 the lower Assam Sebundy corps was transferred into a regular regiment known as the 2nd Assam Light Infantry, and later the 43rd Gurkha Rifles. The 1st Assam Light Infantry, which was afterwards moved to Dibrugarh, became the 42nd Gurkha Rifles, and the Sylhet Light Infantry became the 44th.¹⁵

Post 1857

The Revolt of 1857 left Assam almost untouched, although exaggerated stories of the loss of British power caused some excitement among some of the Khasi chiefs with whom the ex-raja of Jaintia attempted to conspire to recover his lost possessions. In September 1857 there was unease among the men of the Dibrugarh regiment due to letters received by some of the Hindu sepoys from Shahabad, where many of them had been recruited. Some of these men were found to have entered into a conspiracy with the Saring Raja, Kandarpeswar Singh (the grandson of the deposed Purander Singh), who was based in Jorhat. The raja and a few supporters plotted the murder of local English officers to regain authority, but the plan was revealed to the deputy commissioner of Sibsagar, Colonel Charles Holroyd, 'just in time to prevent Cawnpore horror from being enacted in Assam'.¹ Holroyd, 'with surprising skill and alacrity', pretended to his servants to be ill in his house while he travelled rapidly to Jorhat during the night with a few armed men. The young raja, a tool in the hands of his dewan, Maniram Dutta Baruah, was placed under arrest and, after treasonable letters were discovered from Maniram (a loyal ally of the East India Company when young) he also was arrested in Calcutta where he was tried, convicted and executed.²

In November 1857 the 34th Native Infantry, stationed at Chittagong, mutinied. After burning their lines, breaking open the jail and plundering the treasury, they subsequently emerged in the southeast of the Sylhet district with the intention of pushing through the south of Cachar into Manipur. Major Byng, the commandant of the Sylhet Light Infantry, routed the 200 rebels but was killed, and a few days later a further detachment of the Sylhet Light Infantry again attacked the mutineers. The remaining rebels continued to head for Manipur and were joined by some Manipuri princes (pretenders to the Manipur throne) with a few followers. These men were repeatedly attacked both by regular British troops and Kuki scouts, who received a reward for each mutineer whom they killed. Finally, of the whole number that had left Chittagong only three or four escaped death or capture.

In 1860 the General Codes of Civil and Criminal Procedure were extended to the Brahmaputra Valley and in 1862 the Indian Penal Code came into force. These enactments superseded the Assam Code, but there was still great uncertainty as to the operation of other laws in force in Bengal and the general opinion of Assam officers was that these needed only to be followed in the spirit 'as far as applicable'. This ambiguity was solved by the passing of the Scheduled Districts Act in 1874, empowering the Government of India to declare by notification which laws were in force in particular districts and to place the plains of Assam in much the same legal position as other parts of India. However, it was deemed that the inhabitants of the hill tracts were not suited for the elaborate legal rules laid down in the procedure codes and that there was a requirement for them to be governed in a simpler and more personal manner than the occupants of the more civilized and longer-settled districts. The Frontier Tracts Regulation of 1880 provided for the operation of unsuitable laws to be barred in all the hill districts, the north Cachar subdivision, the Mikir Hills tract in Nowgong and the Dibrugarh frontier tract in Lakhimpur. By orders issued under this regulation the tracts in question were excluded from the operation of enactments relating to criminal procedure, stamps, court fees, registration and transfer of property and a simpler system of administering justice in civil and criminal matters was prescribed by rules framed under the Scheduled Districts Act.[3]

The British Takeover of Assam

For some time, the inconvenience of governing Assam as an appendage of the unwieldy province of Bengal had become obvious. The Assamese territory was remote and inaccessible, and few lieutenant-governors visited the area. The local conditions were quite unknown to the British officers of the government of Bengal, who had neither the time nor the inclination to make themselves acquainted with the challenges of Assam. But the territory had value and proposals for its severance were always vigorously opposed until Sir George Campbell became the lieutenant-governor of Bengal in 1871. Sir George felt strongly that the position of the Bengal government should either be enhanced by the incorporation of the Board of Revenue or lessened by lopping off some of Bengal's more remote territories. The Government of India preferred the latter alternative and in February 1874 the districts which subsequently formed the province of Assam were separated from Bengal and formed into a chief commissionership under Lieutenant-Colonel Richard Keatinge, practically vesting in the chief commissioner the powers of a local government in respect of all legislative enactments in force in the province. The new commissionership included the five districts of central Assam (Kamrup, Nagaon, Darrang, Sibsagar and Lakhimpur), together with the Khasi-Jaintia Hills, the Garo Hills, the Naga Hills, Goalpara and Sylhet/Cachar, comprising about 54,100 square miles.[4]

The earlier British administrators of Assam had included several men of great ability and energy, and the preliminary arrangements for the government of the territory were sound, but after some time the administration had been allowed to deteriorate. The district officers were in almost all cases military officers transferred from local regiments to civil employment and if their orders were not openly flouted and revenue was collected punctually, they left most matters in the hands of their subordinates and maintained little involvement with the details of district work.[5] However, the formation of the chief commissionership led to a marked improvement in the government of the region. The commission was strengthened by the addition of trained civilians from Bengal and the business of the local officers was more closely and efficiently supervised.[6] Every branch of the administration was overhauled, and many necessary reforms introduced. Special enactments were drafted to provide for local needs and the requirements of the new industries of the province, and the maze of incomplete and conflicting executive instruction was replaced by clear and precise rules. The British administration was conducted from headquarters at Shillong in the Khasi Hills by the following personnel: the chief commissioner, reporting directly to the Government of India, assisted by a secretary with two assistants; two judges, one for the Surma Valley in East Bengal and one for the Brahmaputra Valley; a conservator of forests; a deputy surgeon-general; an inspector of schools; an inspector-general of police; and a director of agriculture. During the cool winter months, these officers travelled through the province on inspection work and in the hot, wet summer returned to headquarters and issued the annual reports of their several departments. In addition to these officers, there were deputy commissioners, one for each of the districts into which the province was divided.[7]

At the start of British rule, the protection of the frontier was wholly in the hands of military authorities, but as greater precautions were taken to prevent raids, the outposts to be garrisoned became too numerous for the limited number of troops available and some were entrusted to the district police. By 1879 there were four regiments in the region, who held fourteen outposts, and about 2,200 armed police, distributed over ten districts and entrusted with the defence of thirty-five outposts. The chief commissioner, Sir Steuart Bayley, proposed an increase in the armed police to 3,000 men, entrusting them with all frontier outpost duty. The men were mainly Gurkhas and Meches (members of the Bodo tribe, belonging to the Cachari tribal grouping) and were placed on a footing very similar to that of the native army, giving excellent service not only on outpost duty but also in various expeditions against the hill tribes for which, as they were able to travel lighter, they were often employed in preference to regular troops.[8]

During this time, the British government actively supported immigration into Assam as a local policy. When tea cultivation gained momentum and the local people of Assam proved unwilling to work in the tea gardens, the planters were driven to import indentured labourers from the densely populated areas of Bihar, Orissa, Bengal, Central Provinces, United Provinces and Madras. In 1867–68 the total population of the labour force in the gardens of Assam was 34,433, of whom 22,800 were immigrants. The discovery of coal and petroleum in upper Assam in the latter part of the nineteenth century brought further commercial opportunities. In addition, the colonial administration needed a skilled, educated labour force to maintain various departments and to construct roads and railways, resulting in inducted immigration of professionals mainly from Bengal, Bihar, Uttar Pradesh, Rajasthan and Nepal.

More significantly, following its detachment from the administrative control of the Bengal presidency in 1874, Assam absorbed the most populous Sylhet district of East Bengal. Sir Henry Cotton, chief commissioner of Assam, promoted food grain production in the large tracts of fertile arable land lying unused in the province, accelerating the immigration of land hungry peasants into the Brahmaputra Valley from the Sylhet, Mymensingh and Rangpur districts. Nepalis were employed as dairy herders, porters and agricultural labourers and similarly encouraged to colonise new territory. The subsequent immigration of traders, merchants and small-scale industrialists from other parts of India, such as Marwaris and Sikhs, stimulated capital development in Assam and strengthened the ties of the province with India. The Marwaris acted as the moneychangers, bankers and agents of tea garden managers and, although a small community, the Punjabis were the principal contractors, carpenters and skilled mechanics operating on the railways and in tea gardens in upper Assam. Due to this huge influx of migrants, Assam was to become the fastest-growing region of the Indian subcontinent throughout the twentieth century. The ethnic composition of the state was transformed, and the political and economic prerogatives of the native Assamese were gradually diminished. As a result, ethnicity and migration became prominent issues in Assamese politics.

Twentieth Century

Adding to the ethnic complications, as early as 1868 the Government of India had seen the need for an independent administration in the eastern part of the Bengal presidency. By 1903 the division of the presidency was seen as inevitable, not only to relieve the pressure on Calcutta, the capital of British India, but also to provide prospects for Assam's commercial expansion. The British promised increased investment and jobs in the new province, to be called Eastern Bengal and Assam. The partition of Bengal, proposed by the viceroy, Lord Curzon, was put into effect on 16 October 1905, stoking controversy among hard-line Hindu nationalists, who described the move as an attempt to divide and rule the Bengali homeland. Moreover, to add to Bengali discontent, it was evident that Eastern Bengal and Assam possessed some of the most fertile territory in the British empire. The Eastern Bengal delta was the rice basket of the Indian subcontinent and produced 80 per cent of the world's jute. Assam was not only home to the largest tea plantations in the world, but also a centre of the petroleum industry due to crude oil production in the province. In addition, the international trade of the port of Chittagong began to flourish with a connection to the interior via the Assam Bengal Railway. The failure to address Hindu fears resulted in a period of violent and non-violent political agitation and on 1 April 1912 the two parts of Bengal were reunited. A new partition based on language resulted in the administrative units of Bihar and Orissa province to the west and Assam province to the east again under a British chief commissioner, a post which was upgraded to governor in 1921.

The Montagu Chelmsford reforms, enacted through the Government of India Act 1919, expanded the Assam Legislative Council and introduced the principle of dyarchy, whereby certain responsibilities such as agriculture, health, education and local government were transferred to elected ministers. The Government of India Act 1935 provided provincial autonomy and further enlarged the elected legislature to 108 elected members. In 1937 elections were held for the newly created Assam Legislative Assembly, established in Shillong. The Indian National Congress had the maximum number of seats with thirty-three, making it the largest single party but not in a position to form a ministry, and the governor of Assam, Sir Robert Reid, called upon Sir Syed Muhammad Sadulla (leader of the Assam Valley Muslim Party) to head the assembly. Sadulla's government resigned in September 1938 and the governor invited in his place Gopinath Bordoloi of the Indian National Congress, whose cabinet involved a future president of India in Fakhruddin Ali Ahmed. In 1939 all the Congress ministries in British Indian provinces resigned and a new government under Sadulla was formed. Sadulla remained as chief minister of Assam until 1946, barring a brief period. During the Japanese invasion of India in 1944 some areas of the province, including the Naga Hills district and part of the state of Manipur, were occupied by Japanese forces between mid-March and July. After the war, when fresh elections to the provincial legislatures were called in 1946, the Congress won a majority in Assam and Bordoloi was again selected as chief minister. Prior to the independence of India, on 1 April 1946 Assam was granted self-rule, and on 15 August 1947 it became part of the Indian Union.

2

Geography

The region of Assam which was formally annexed into the British empire in 1838 consisted of a long, narrow valley with an alluvial plain roughly 450 miles long with an average breadth of 50 miles, bounded to the north by Bhutan and to the south by the Khasi-Jaintia and Garo Hills, which extended in a western and southeastern direction. The hills skirted the British districts of Sylhet and Cachar, to the south of which lay the Lushai Hills. Towards the east and north the Lushai range evolved into the Naga Hills and the Mishmis, which extended into Burma and China with substantial peaks frequently covered by snow. The large number of ranges and plateaux varied in altitude from 12,000 feet in the Naga Hills, gradually sloping down to 6,449 in the Khasi district and 4,700 in the Garo Hills. The province was intersected by the mighty Brahmaputra River which, as it descended from the Himalayas, took a westerly course and finally fell into the Bay of Bengal. Thirty-four tributaries flowed from the northern and twenty-four from the southern mountain ranges and as a result Assam was spectacularly well watered.[1] There was scarcely a portion of the valley through which the river had not at some time or other flowed. Having left a great number of deserted channels, it at last settled down about halfway between the two ranges which provided insurmountable barriers to its erratic course. In the nineteenth century where the river had once flowed and receded vast beds remained which became swamps covered with tangled and high grass, much of which was quite impassable for laden elephants. Vast herds of elephant, rhinoceros and buffalo lived in these almost impregnable areas, unmolested save for the occasional European hunter who, ignoring warnings of the prevalent deadly malaria, had penetrated the wilds. To the educationalist William Robinson,[2] writing in 1841, Assam was

> a naturally beautiful tract of country, and ... occasionally presents a scenery comparable perhaps to the richest in the world. Its plains decked with a rich verdant robe, and abounding with numerous crystal streams, which winding along the base of a group of beautifully wooded hills, covered to their very summits with trees, interspersed with dark and deep glens, and heaving their swelling ridges into a bright blue sky, constitute altogether a scene of extraordinary magnificence ... till their blue conical summits are relieved by the proud pinnacles of the Himalaya.[3]

Assam was usually approached through India's great metropolis, Calcutta, where from Sealdah station an Eastern Bengal train with 'considerable shaking' took the traveller 150 miles to Goalundo, the terminus of the Eastern Bengal Railway and according to the tea planter George Barker, writing in the 1880s, 'the confines of the whole civilised world'. The town appeared as

> an unpretentious enough place, made up of a collection of small huts stuck up on the banks at the point of junction between the rivers Ganges and Brahmaputra ... The inhabitants are frequently flooded out ... and twice in the course of the year they are obliged to shift their residences, according as it is the dry or rainy season, when the river rises tremendously.[4]

The advantage of Goalundo was that at this stage it was possible to embark on a double-decker steamer for any part of Assam. After four or five days of highly monotonous landscape of low-lying banks of sand, Dhubri, the first station, was reached at the point

Geography

of the map where the Brahmaputra turned northeast. From there the valley of Assam lay on each side of the river, following a northeasterly course for about 800 miles until the town of Sadiya, where the river bent directly north to the Himalayas.

On leaving Dhubri with its government offices, post office and telegraph office, a few hours' steaming brought one to Goalpara, a picturesque place with its wooded hill dotted here and there with bungalows. However, by the end of the nineteenth century the area was mostly deserted. As a result of Goalpara's notoriously unhealthy reputation due to the swamps lying back from the river, most of the officials had moved to Dhubri and the American Baptist missionaries to the town of Tura on the Garo Hills. A climb to the large, flat top of Goalpara hill (which made a 'capital lawn tennis ground, big enough for a cricket match'[5]) was well rewarded with an extensive view of the great Bhutan and Himalaya ranges to the north and the Garo Hills to the south. The native town of Goalpara clustered around the base of this rocky hill. Less tea was grown here than in any other district but there was a large amount of other cargo transported by boat and steamers coming from the interior, principally mustard seed, dry chillies and lac.[6] A larger number of boats were seen here than at any other station on the Brahmaputra, employed in running up small streams to bring down produce in bulk which was then bagged and shipped in larger vessels to Calcutta.[7]

In the line of country between Goalpara and the station of Gauhati (one day's steaming) the scenery began to improve on both sides of the river, with lush areas of foliage lining the shores down to the water's edge. There were many betel nut trees in the district and the large trade formerly carried on in the area gave the place its name, *goa* being the Assamese for betel nut and *hati* (*haat*) a market. To Robinson, the betel nut palm was a fine plant 'and scarcely anything can be more graceful than its slender high pillars, when backed by the dark shade of bamboos and other similar foliage'.[8] Gauhati was the most attractive station on the river, with surrounding hills studded with bright green tea bushes and a bank protected from the encroachment of the river current by the rocky spurs of the Khasi range jutting out into the stream. It was at one stage the seat of native royalty before becoming capital of the province and, for some years after British possession, the residence of the highest officials. When Assam became a chief commissionership the government headquarters were established at Shillong and the number of European residents dwindled, although the native town remained large and busy.⁹ In the 1880s the native population was said to be about 11,500, a large proportion of which was Muslim, and the boys' schools were noted for their excellence. However, despite its location on the river, Gauhati like Goalpara was deemed a most unhealthy place probably due to undrained swamps at the back of the town, and in 1852 cholera killed one-third of the population.

The district, possessing a large bazaar, was noted for its numerous temples and sacred resorts for pilgrims and before British occupation human sacrifices were not uncommon. The monasteries were said to have housed a great number of priests and nuns, and no less than five hundred women

> were consecrated to the temple service, whose filthy songs and more obscene dances attracted crowds of people to the midnight orgies; a song was not tolerated which did not contain the most marked allusions to unchastity, while those that were so abominable, that no person could repeat them, received the loudest applause.¹⁰

Several large temples on the western side of the town were said to have been built on the site of an ancient Ahom citadel of huge proportions. There was evidence of this in the quantity of granite blocks scattered over the hill, cut into pillars, plinths and cornices of great size which were beautifully carved in relief with figures, flowers and scrolls, and numerous spacious tanks 'choked up with weeds and jungle'.¹¹ In passing Gauhati a small, rocky island in the middle of the river, formerly housing many peacocks, was considered a sacred spot by Hindus who believed it was formed by the god Sib from the dust which marked his forehead. On the island the temple shrine of Hanuman, the monkey god, was a favourite of immigrant Marwaris. Immediately below the town, the perils of river navigation were apparent, where

> hills confine the Brahmaputra to a breadth of one thousand two hundred yards. There in the rainy season boats are necessitated to be moored till a westerly breeze springs up of force sufficient to carry them through the narrow strait, but there is often great difficulty even when the river flows in an open bed.[12]

Shillong, the residence of the chief commissioner and other local officers of the Government of India, was situated due south of Gauhati in the pine-covered Khasi Hills, with a climate so salubrious and with such spectacular scenery that it was termed 'the paradise of Assam'. The carpets of violets, buttercups and daisies and the birds and fruits were a comforting reminder of home and the town possessed an attractive artificial lake conceived by the chief commissioner, Sir William Ward, and known locally as Pollok's Lake after the engineer Fitzwilliam Thomas Pollok, who played a significant role in planning and designing it.[13] The elevation of Shillong Peak, the highest hill in the district, was 6,450 feet above sea level and the surrounding plateaux consisted of a succession of undulating downs, broken here and there by the valleys of the larger hill streams. In the higher ranges, where the Khasi tribes had denuded the hills of forest for fuel for iron smelting, the land was covered by short grass, becoming longer in the lower elevations. A remarkable feature was the presence of numerous sacred groves situated just below the brows of the hills in oak and rhododendron woods. The fir tree (*Pinus Khasia*) first appeared at an elevation of about 2,500 feet on the road from Gauhati to Shillong[14] and, although the road was said to be a model of engineering skill, it was a tedious journey. The distance of 67 miles was made by riding or by *tonga* (a two-seater cart drawn by ponies), taking ten or twelve hours, or by bullock train, taking two days. Bizarrely, the location was hardly an ideal one for government officers to become acquainted with the Assamese race or their language since the Khasi language was quite unique and allied to the Indo-Chinese.[15]

Above Gauhati, the following station on the Brahmaputra was Tezpur on the north bank which appeared from the river as three hills each topped with a bungalow, behind which were lakes and tanks and a tidy green lawn where the church and government buildings were situated. Gigantic carved granite blocks – the remains of former temples and altars – were piled up on the grass, many in an unfinished state, suggesting that the buildings were destroyed 'by some hostile power opposed to the propagation of Hinduism, assisted perhaps subsequently by a convulsion of nature'.[16] On the north boundary of the district stretched the mountain ranges which were home to the Bhutia, Aka and Daphla tribes. The town of Nowgong lay directly opposite Tezpur, 32 miles inland from the river steamer landing stage of Koliabar. It was situated on a cleanly kept level plain scattered with handsome government buildings, offices and mission bungalows, with a native population skirting the area. Due to its low and level situation, the climate in the hot season was extremely sultry. Numerous rivers and lakes afforded a plentiful supply of fish, and large quantities of betel nut, pan leaf, sugarcane, opium and silk were produced. The rice crop exceeded that of any other district. Nowgong was said to possess 'as pretty a circle of carriage roads as any *zillah* [administrative district] in Assam ... passing beautiful gardens, cultivated fields and innumerable hamlets, which evince the comfort and prosperity of the inhabitants'.[17]

From Tezpur to the terminal steamer station, Dibrugarh, there were no villages directly on the river. On each side was a monotonous low-level bank covered with grass jungle with the occasional dark blue hill in the distance and no sign of life except flocks of water birds and wild buffalo coming to drink, or alligators sunning themselves on the sand. According to the missionary Susan Ward,

> This lifeless scene is due mainly to the river which, instead of being called a son of Brahma (the Creator), more properly might

Geography

be termed the son of Shiva (the Destroyer); for destruction is its constant work, breaking away embankments and piling up sand bars that obstruct navigation.[18]

In the cool season a dense fog descended over the river and hid the course of the channel until it lifted (often as late as ten or eleven o'clock) and a steamer could proceed. The shifting current accounted for the absence of human habitation on the banks, moreover during the rains the river could reach a height of 30–40 feet above its usual level. Villages that were miles inland could be inundated and it was possible to see gardens of plantain trees and betel nut drifting into the swift current. The recorded annual rainfall varied in different parts of the Brahmaputra Valley from 60 to 111 inches, falling mainly from June to September. Cherra Punji in the Khasi Hills district was said to have the greatest rainfall in the world, with an average of 489 inches. Apparently 805 inches fell in the area in 1861, of which 366 were in the single month of July.[19]

The next two landing stages of the steamers above Koliabar were Nigriting and Dhansiri, each of which connected with Kohima, the government station in the Angami Naga Hills. The former was linked to the nearest direct road for travel, the latter to the Dhansiri River, a subsidiary of the Brahmaputra, for the conveyance of luggage and commissariat stores to Golaghat, a subdivisional station of the Sibsagar district. Both of these places saw much action during the Naga campaign of 1879–80, being the landing place of officers, regiments of soldiers, scores of bullocks, ponies, mules and elephants with all the paraphernalia of war.[20] The government buildings were on the spur of a hill, 300 feet below the Naga village of Kohima, where a deputy commissioner, surgeon and half a regiment were stationed, and the climate and scenery much resembled that of Shillong with 'precipitous crags and forest-clad slopes', its views extending over the valley of the Brahmaputra and 'beyond it the Bhootan hills and the snow-clad peaks of the Himalayas'.[21]

On the route from Nigriting to Kohima in dense forest were the ruins of the deserted city of Dimapur, first recorded by the officiating collector of Nowgong, Lieutenant Henry Bigge, in 1841 when on tour to the Naga Hills. In the vicinity were several huge tanks of clear water, the largest of which was at least half a mile long and a quarter of a mile wide. According to legend, a past ruler of Dimapur had ordered that upon his death his body and jewels should be enclosed in a golden boat and sunk in the largest lake. The boat was secured by a strong chain to the bank, which proved too great a temptation for some of the inhabitants, who procured half a dozen elephants and a crowd of men to try to pull it out. The boat emerged a little and then suddenly slipped back, drowning both men and elephants. Rumour had it that Dimapur was wiped out by invading hordes in the middle of the sixteenth century, and it is quite possible that treasure was indeed hidden in the lake as it was a favourite way of hiding valuables in India. One of the old gateways of the city was still standing, although greatly damaged by trees growing out of it, and inside the perimeter were rows of curious collapsed pillars, both round and square and intricately carved with lotus flowers, peacocks, tigers and elephants.[22] It was said that each pillar was the appointed seat of a grandee according to his rank and that every year on a fixed day all the nobles assembled in the audience hall, where a human being was decapitated between two square pillars in the centre of the hall as a sacrifice.[23]

Sibsagar, the head of the district, was connected by road to the steamer landing of the Brahmaputra by 17 miles in the rainy season and 22 miles in the dry season when the river was low. The road was for many years only a path through the jungle in the dry season and impassable in the rains, but the government eventually procured the resources to make it viable throughout the year. Sibsagar in the 1880s had an urban population of about 5,000 in an area of 7 square miles and was considered one of the most attractive and healthy stations in Assam. It possessed a beautiful artificial pond, 2 miles square, constructed in terraces with a deep square in the centre. The rainfall and evaporation kept the tank full and the water fresh. It was excavated with forced labour during the Ahom dynasty and three solid brick temples dedicated to the Hindu deity Sib were built on one side.²⁴ The people held many superstitious notions about the tank, believing that there were golden turtles in it. Ordinary turtles were in fact often seen, and fine large fish could be caught with hook and line or spears. In the cold season large flocks of wild geese settled on the tank in the morning and in the late afternoon, 'with a loud rush of their wings', swooped off to the Brahmaputra. No bathing or washing was allowed, to ensure that the water remained pure for drinking purposes, and the embankment of the tank provided a high, airy situation for government buildings and for the bungalows of the European residents. The bazaar lay along the bank of the river Dikho, half a mile from the tank, and on the opposite bank were the ruins of the ancient capital, Rungpore. The *ronghor*, or theatre of the Assam king, was a two-storey massive brick building and not far from it were the ruins of a palace with high gateways and huge stone blocks scattered around, with representations of the actions of gods cut in relief upon them. Numerous dungeon-like underground rooms suggested that this accommodation was intended for political prisoners.²⁵

Nazerah, the packing and forwarding station of the all-powerful tea-producing Assam Company, was situated about 10 miles south of Sibsagar on the bank of the Dikho River, upon which traffic could flow to the river steamers on the Brahmaputra at the mouth of the river. Jorhat, 35 miles southwest of Sibsagar, connected with the steamers at Kokilamukh, 10 miles away. At the time of British occupation Jorhat was the home of native royalty and thereafter the place of residence of the deposed royal family. The Lakhimpur district, over which Britain assumed control in 1839, comprised the whole of the northeastern extremity of the province of Assam on both banks of the Brahmaputra. It was separated from the Sibsagar district by the Lohit River and extended to the territory of the hill tribes abutting Burma and China, where the boundary was not well defined. Lakhimpur, where the Subansiri River joined the Brahmaputra, of which it was the largest tributary, was the most sparsely populated part of Assam in the nineteenth century and an area rich in minerals. Lecturer in clinical medicine John McCosh, writing in 1837, described how

> this beautiful tract of country, though thinly populated by struggling hordes of barbarians and allowed to lie profitless in impenetrable jungle, enjoys all the qualities requisite for rendering it one of the finest in the world. Its climate is cold, healthy, and congenial to European constitutions; its numerous crystal streams abound in gold dust, and masses of the solid metal; its mountains are pregnant with precious stones and silver; its atmosphere is perfumed with tea growing wild and luxuriantly; and its soil is so well adapted to all kinds of agricultural purposes, that it might be converted into one continued garden of silk, and cotton, and coffee, and sugar, and tea, over an extent of many hundred miles.[26]

The work of gold washing was popular under the Assam kings, but in the latter part of the nineteenth century the inhabitants were more attracted by employment in the numerous tea gardens in the district.

Describing the vegetation of the territory surrounding the Subansiri River in 1845, Lt Edward Tuite Dalton, the junior assistant commissioner of Assam, declared,

> The verdure of the valley is very beautiful; the rocks themselves are frequently covered with moss and ferns of the brightest emerald green; whilst springing from the soil above them bamboos of a peculiarly light and feathery appearance, the shafts not thicker than the most delicate trout rod, curve and wave in the slightest breeze. The pine-apple tree, ... the Toka palm, varieties of cane and the mountain plantain, are all characteristic of this scenery and blend together in luxuriant mass.[27]

There were two famous places of pilgrimage in the region: the 'Brahmacund', a circular basin in a narrow gorge of the Himalayas near where the Brahmaputra turned from its southerly course to a southwesterly direction, and the 'Deo Dubi', a dark pool of great depth through which the Desang River left the Naga Hills. Journeys to both places were difficult and dangerous but the sites were supposed to create such an aura of sanctity that many people endured the hardship.[28]

At the end of twelve or fourteen days on the river, which 'a stick on the sand' or a break of machinery might prolong to twenty, one would gladly reach the end of the steamer route at Dibrugarh, the civil station of the Lakhimpur district, which was founded in 1838 by Captain Hamilton Vetch, political agent in upper Assam. Dibrugarh became the largest station of its kind in Assam due to a railway development scheme to reach the extensive coalfields in the Naga Hills and eventually extend the line to Burma to reopen the old trade route between Assam, Burma and China. In the rainy season the town could lie on the riverbank but, due to the 'capricious flow', was about 5 miles inland during the cold months. In the rains the river was navigable to Sadiya, a subdivisional station of the district 62 miles north, and by observing the amount of cargo that the river steamers brought and removed it was possible to gain some idea of the sheer volume of industry that existed on the Brahmaputra. Tea manufacture, chiefly carried out by Europeans, supported two lines of steamers running weekly from Calcutta. In addition to its commercial activities, Dibrugarh boasted the prettiest church in Assam. It was built according to a design by the English architect Augustus Pugin, from a fund collected as a memorial to Colonel Adam White who was killed at Sadiya in a night attack by Khamti tribesmen and whose remains were interred under the tower of the building.[29] A Church of England chaplain was stationed in Dibrugarh and also a regiment of soldiers. The principal buildings were the *cutcherry* (court/public office), the jail, the fort, the church and the 'Planters' Stores', while there were numerous bungalows occupied by the officials of the district, planters and others whose business brought them there. The population of the town was estimated at about 10,000, of whom more than 100 were European, and following the first stage of the railway construction it was estimated that the population had almost doubled. Tea planting was a growing industry in the district, 'converting a vast extent of waste land and desolation into fragrant gardens'.[30]

For the European not faced with the necessity of having to eke out a debilitating daily living from the soil or in the teahouse, it was possible to paint an idyllic picture of all that Assam had to offer. Comparatively speaking, Assam enjoyed a greater equality of temperature than was general throughout India. The river was much frequented as a health resort where the air tended to be bracing with an occasional breeze after sundown. To Susan Ward, a traveller arriving after the rainy season could enjoy about five months of the healthiest season of the year in a refreshingly dry, cool and unchangeable climate. It was not considered safe to travel until the early part of November, but from this date until March the climate was excellent with the sky cloudless for weeks and the burning sun of the rainy season now mild and quite harmless. The temperature throughout the year ranged from about 45 to 100°F, seldom rising above the latter in the hot season or falling below the former in the cold season, when it was possible to make a comfortable tour of the province riding, driving or going by elephant. Much had been done to improve the means of communication between the stations and tea estates yet, in a country where rivers and streams were so numerous and the annual rainfall so high, much remained to be done in the elevation of roads and bridging rivers and ditches to make travel safe and comfortable. However, in Ward's opinion little stood in the way of an enjoyable tour through

> wild virgin forests, richly decked with ferns and flowers, now and then broken by the low level rice fields of the villagers ... and here and there a tea plantation with its bungalow, tea-house, and cooly[31] lines, and all around rows of the dark green fragrant bush stretch away over plain, slope and hill.[32]

On any high ground, looking northward, when the air was clear, a fine view might be had of the snow-capped pinnacles of the Himalayas where 'glistening snow, covering successive undulations of valley and height, are so clearly distinct, that we can scarcely believe they are at a great distance'.[33]

Other Europeans were not as euphoric in relating their experiences and it was said that

> Delicate subjects seldom continue for any length of time in the province without complaining of a sensation of langor [sic] and debility, such as they never experienced in Upper India ... probably owing more to the extreme dampness of the climate and the prevalence of the cold northeasterly winds, than to any other cause.[34]

Oscar Flex was one of the rare non-British Europeans whose adventurous spirit had brought him to Assam. For three years from May 1864, he worked as a tea planter with the East India Company, before giving up the career and returning to Germany to live in Berlin for the rest of his life. To Flex conditions in the northeast were hardly ideal:

> The climate of this region is humid, the abundance of jungles hampers wind from blowing across and induces enormous heat. The area experiences the heaviest rainfall in India. The rains, which commence in March, continue till November, and the rivers are filled with water eight months of the year. The enormous quantity of water induces an insalubrious atmosphere causing innumerable ailments, such as fever, dysentery, malaria etc. There are huge storms during the monsoons which wreak havoc in tea gardens. The region also experiences frequent earthquakes.[35]

For Flex, even the least aggressive time of year had its downside: 'Winter sets in from end of the November till beginning of February, which is the season of relaxation for Europeans. During winter fog sets in around every midnight and lasts till at least 11 am the next morning. Nothing is visible through the dense fog.'[36]

The robust Captain Fitzwilliam Thomas Pollok, responsible for road construction in the latter part of the century, was more positive about the climate of the region, declaring that he suffered little from malarial fever in the northeast,

> but there is one thing a man in Assam must avoid and that is (if he encamps near the foot of a range of high hills) sleeping within the influence of the wind, which nightly rushes down from the elevated plateau to take the place of the exhausted air of the plains, through one of the numerous gorges abutting into the plains, through which almost invariably a river flows.[37]

The close of the rains was said to be the unhealthiest season of the year, when the water which had spread over fields and marshes was subsiding. Yet many British had managed to live for many years in Assam without experiencing fever by observing a few simple precautions:

> viz., always wear flannel next to the skin, take some refreshment before going out in the morning, and never remain in wet garments except when in active exercise; when exposed to the sun wear a large sola hat, and if necessarily long exposed, place a wet handkerchief or piece of a plantain leaf on the head; be temperate, and do not hope to ward off disease with 'pegs', the slang term for a mixture of brandy or whisky and water; – it has been proved beyond question, that total abstinence is as conducive to health in India, as in any other country, and there are strong reasons for the opinion that liquors are far more injurious to the European in India than in a European climate.[38]

However, even with care the humid atmosphere of the rainy season and the northeasterly winds were not suited to people of an unsound constitution. The Assamese were seen by the British as weak and sickly and many died from fever and dysentery. Goitre was especially prevalent around Nowgong, elephantiasis and leprosy were common throughout the region, and smallpox and cholera appeared annually, becoming epidemic roughly every five years. At such times 'the poorer classes and opium eaters are carried off; the disease finds easy victims in those who live on damp ground and drink from stagnant water and tanks, eat unripe fruit and decayed fish and have only a thin cloth to cover them in the coldest nights'.[39]

During the rains there were sudden squalls called northwesters, which were of extreme violence, usually in the evening twilight. The approach of one of these storms was frequently combined with

> circumstances of considerable grandeur. The low sharply-defined black cloud, which occupied nearly one-half of the horizon, is towards the centre gradually raised into a gloomy arch ... when the storm is about a mile distant, a deadly calm prevails ... and the temperature of the atmosphere rapidly sinks. The storm continues to approach with a slow and solemn motion, till it has attained a certain altitude, when a most tremendous gush of wind bursts forth at one with sudden fury, frequently tearing up trees by the roots and carrying before it every light substance it can take up.[40]

As Flex observed, Assam was also well known to be subject to earthquakes. A particularly dramatic one in 1663 was said to have lasted for half an hour and, centuries later, earthquakes in 1869 and 1875 caused much local damage in Cachar, Shillong and Gauhati. However, the earlier seismic activity of the nineteenth century was eclipsed by the earthquake of 12 June 1897 (8.7 on the Richter scale) when the epicentre was not far from Shillong. It was said that 'the surface of the ground moved in waves like those of the sea; large trees were swayed backwards and forwards, bending almost to the ground; and huge blocks of stone were tossed up and down like peas in a drum'.[41] In the course of a few minutes all masonry buildings were destroyed. The destruction was almost as severe in Gauhati and Sylhet where huge cracks were made in the alluvial soil, extensive tracts of land subsided and became impossible to cultivate, and in many places roads and railway embankments were completely destroyed. More than 1,500 people lost their lives, chiefly owing to landslides in the hills and the collapse of riverbanks in Sylhet. However, had the catastrophe occurred at night instead of in the afternoon the loss of life would have been far greater. Tom La Touche, an officer from the Geological Survey of India, toured the Goalpara District to evaluate the extent of the damage. In some places he had noted to his horror that 'nearly all the houses ... are half buried, up to the eaves in sand and mud which was thrown out from cracks in the ground, and it is a wonder that most of the people were not buried'.[42]

On a day-to-day basis the most extreme climatic conditions were experienced by the various hill tribes on the northeast frontier, whose habitat was described by the colonial officer Sir George Dunbar as

> a close succession of thickly wooded mountains, their sides as steep as the roof or the walls of a house, [which] rise higher and higher northwards to the main Snowy Range. Up to the furthest limits of the Indian monsoon these highlands are drenched under very nearly the most torrential rainfall in the world ... One of the greatest rivers in Asia thunders in its deepest gorges on the long journey from Tibet, through a labyrinth of mountains echoing with streams, down to the wide expanse of the Assam Valley and out into the Bay of Bengal. The razor-edged foot-hills [sic] are covered with sub-tropical forest, where orchids grow on the branches above and the thick undergrowth is infested with leeches ... Midway between the foot-hills and the main Snowy Range there is a narrow zone of open valleys, where flourishing villages are set amidst their fields. This is the heart of the tribal country. It is beyond the influence of Assam with its Indian and western forms of Civilisation, and it is too far south to be affected by the religious ideas and customs of Tibet.[43]

The British had significant dealings with the occupants of this remote territory.

3

Hill Tribes

The English historian Edward Gait arrogantly declared that the history of the Ahoms revealed how 'a brave and vigorous race may decay in the sleepy hollow of the Brahmaputra Valley ... [where] it was only the intervention of the British that prevented them from being blotted out by fresh hordes of invaders, first the Burmese, and then the Singphos and Khamtis, and also, possibly, the Daflas, Abors and Bhutias'.[1] However, this was not strictly true. Although the Burmese did indeed invade the country, prior to the arrival of the British the Ahoms were never in danger of being overrun by the hill tribes. Although raids and retaliations occurred with notable frequency, there was more to early valley–hill interactions than hostilities. Where acts of warfare did exist, hill people tended to raid the plains out of sheer necessity because the uplands were less productive than the more fertile lower territory. The booty from a successful raid on the plains invariably consisted of grain, goods, weapons, agricultural tools and people, who were subsequently enslaved in agriculture and animal husbandry in the hills or used as tribute to neighbouring tribes. After a hill polity launched a successful raid on the plains, the Ahom king tended to retaliate by directing his military forces into the hills. Violent battles could ensue, killing or capturing a large number of hill people. However, more frequently, the Ahom army would find the hostile village completely deserted as its inhabitants took refuge in the jungle or moved to higher altitudes. Ahom forces were usually able to recapture some of the stolen goods and take revenge by burning the abandoned village, but hill peoples regrouped speedily and their thatched houses were quickly rebuilt. It was only a matter of time before they gained sufficient strength to pillage the plains again.[2]

When in the long term military intervention against hill communities proved inconclusive, time-consuming and expensive, the Ahom government replaced coercion by a policy of seduction in the form of the so-called *posa* system, a government scheme that offered conditional long-term coexistence to hill tribes as an alternative to Ahom rule. Peace was bought by allowing those hill chiefs who were traditionally aggressive to levy an annual tribute of a percentage of the crop yields from nearby villages in the adjoining plains. The Ahom rulers remained overlords of the hills and plains but, in the more immediate domains of the hill tribes, the chiefs were allowed a certain degree of local suzerainty over some local communities with the promise of sparing such villages violent raids, looting and slave-taking. For instance, during Pratap Singh's reign (1603–41) the Akas, the Daflas, the Miris and the Abors were granted the right of levying *posa* which, apart from the annual collection of goods in specified areas, included labour service of the Assamese *paiks* who were given corresponding remission from the state's revenue demand. In return for these privileges, the hill tribes were to refrain from making inroads into Ahom territory. Commercial relationships were also created or sustained, such as that with the Noctes (ethnically related to the Konyak Nagas) who controlled the salt wells located in the foothills. Although previously routed by Ahom forces, the Noctes had over the years regained strength and driven back the rulers' incursions with notable success. The Ahom, eager to ensure regular supplies of salt, resorted to a policy of seduction. In return for negotiated access to the salt wells, the government recognised the political ascendancy of the Nocte chief, bestowed an honorary post upon him and offered the Noctes an annual supply of foodstuffs from the plains.[3]

Prior to British colonisation, the northeast region was a diverse trading and migratory route between the Indian subcontinent and its neighbouring countries in southeast Asia and, even before the First Anglo-Burmese War, the East India Company had occasionally come into contact with various semi-independent chiefs and tribes of the northeastern frontier areas. Infrequent communication with the tribal people continued after the war as the British concentrated on administering the plains, which were commercially viable in ways that the 'barren' hills were not. Lord Dalhousie, governor-general of India from 1848 to 1856, expressed the general determination to remain detached from the tribal areas when he declared,

> I dissent entirely from the policy which is recommended of what is called obtaining a control, that is to say, of taking possession of those hills, and of establishing our sovereignty over their savage inhabitants. Our possession could bring no profit to us, and would be as costly as it would be unproductive.[4]

It was accepted that the complicated procedure adopted for the administration of the Brahmaputra Valley area was not suitable for the hills, where rural policy and maintenance of law and order was better left to the local chiefs. Punitive expeditions were sent only against those tribes who violated agreements, committed raids and disturbed the peace of the borders.[5] However, when persuasion failed to reduce the constant raids perpetrated upon the occupants of the plains, the British were forced to bring nearly all the hill areas under direct administration, including the territories of the Nagas, the Garos and the Lushais. At the same time, no less important than the protection of the plains from tribal incursions was the question of the defence of the Indian northeastern frontier, requiring a greater knowledge of the border territory and its occupants.

The British administrators, soldiers, missionaries and explorers who during the nineteenth century made contact with the hill tribes were not anthropologists. Their information was not always correct, and some of their material was obviously guesswork and heavily marked by personal bias. Nevertheless, they were fresh to the country and their observations became a source of invaluable information about each area and a tool for colonial administration. Attempts were made during the nineteenth century to provide a comprehensive account of the tribes, covering physiological traits, village economy, village administration, social organisation, customary laws and practices, religious beliefs, rites of passage, folklore, domestic life, food habits, dress, ornamentation and housing. Unsurprisingly, the documentation carried out by the men and women of Victorian Britain reflects a Eurocentric valuation of people and society. For the most part the Victorian opinion of the tribes was a low one and their attitude was all too often patronising or scornful, displaying an undeniable air of cultural supremacy in their identification of tribes as backward, uncivilised and barbarous in varying degrees.[6]

Factors such as geographical isolation, simple technology and living conditions, adherence to animism, tribal language, and physical features all contributed to the classification of a primitive population which lacked the positive traits of a modern society. Moreover, in many cases methods of data collection were based on non-participant observation, since colonial ethnographers were unable to speak or understand the local language. In no field were records more imperfect than in that of religion, as most European officers in the nineteenth century failed to take seriously any religion other than their own. The outlook of the colonial administrator Sir James Johnstone, in his account of his term in the Naga Hills, was typical in urging

> the advisability of establishing for the Naga people a regular system of education, including religious instruction, under a competent clergyman of the Church of England ... they would want a religion and we might as well give them our own, and make them in this way a source of strength, by thus mutually attaching them to us.[7]

The conviction that the tribal people of Assam had no belief or, alternatively, that what religion they had was 'a mixture of all the various idolatries and superstitions of the natives with whom they have intercourse ... with no fixed principles',[8] did not encourage unbiased and scientific enquiry.

The Bhutanese

In locating the lands of the hill tribes of Assam, it is possible to follow the course of the Brahmaputra up towards its source in Sadiya and, turning south, to traverse the eastern hill tracts before moving westwards along the southern ranges of the Assam Valley. Due north of the point where the river turned to the northeast were the Bhutanese, one of the first tribes who provoked close scrutiny from the British due to their consistently aggressive behaviour. Covering the southern base of the Bhutan Hills, a tract of fertile land ranging from 10 to 20 miles in breadth extended from the Dhansiri River in Assam on the east to the frontier of the Darjeeling district of Bengal on the west, sloping downwards to the plains. The tract was linked with the hills above by a number of hill passes called *duars*. The possession of these passes was always a bone of contention between the rulers of Bhutan and those of Assam, and the inhabitants of the 'unhealthy, malarious' tracts were mostly Bhutanese.

The Bhutanese were racially of Tibetan stock. The most eastern members of the Bhutanese tribe were the Thebengea, who traded with the British in the annual fairs held during the winter months in the border areas. They sold ponies, dogs, bulls, handloom products of cotton and wool, precious stones and herbs to Indian traders and purchased cheap industrial commodities. Their own garments consisted of a long, loose robe wrapped around the body and secured by a leather belt with 'a legging of broad cloth attached to a shoe, made generally of buffalo hide', topped by a cap of fur or coarse woollen cloth.[1] According to the historian Leslie Shakespear, the people were 'professed Buddhists, though still propitiating evil spirits; polyandry is the prevailing domestic custom … The men are strongly built, with athletic figures, of dark complexions, and unpleasantly heavy and cunning faces.'[2] Captain Robert Pemberton, on a mission to Bhutan in 1838, considered the people to possess 'an equanimity of temper almost bordering on apathy and are indolent to an extreme degree. They are also illiterate, immoral, and victims of the most unqualified superstition [despite] the extensive prevalence of monastic institutions.' In describing his encounters with senior officials, he declared,

> The highest officers of state in Bhootan are shameless beggars and liars of the first magnitude, whose most solemn pledged words are violated without the slightest hesitation. They play bully and sycophant with equal readiness, exhibiting in their conduct a rare compound of official pride and presumption, together with the low cunning of needy mediocrity.[3]

However, within four years of Pemberton's damning report Dr Archibald Campbell, an ethnologist in the Bengal Medical Service sent to enquire into a frontier dispute in the western *duars*, declared that in most cases the Bhutanese were no more culpable than other troublemakers living under British protection on the Indian side of the frontier. Moreover, in his opinion the Bhutanese were not hostile to the British government, only to those British subjects who invaded their land.[4] Yet, despite Campbell's more measured approach, the Calcutta government in its determination to bring the tribe to heel chose to support the negative opinion of Pemberton.

In the area of the Bhutanese border there were eighteen *duars*, eleven on the frontier of Bengal and Goalpara and seven, with an area of 1,600 square miles, to the north of Kamrup and Darrang. The former had been annexed by the Bhutanese long before the British came into possession of Bengal, but the latter were held by the Ahoms until King Gaurinath's reign when they were surrendered to the Bhutanese for an annual tribute of Rs 4,785. However, the tribute by the Bhutanese gradually fell into arrears and frequent dacoities were committed in British territory. It was therefore decided in 1841 to take over the whole of this section of the *duars* and a yearly payment of Rs 10,000 was paid by the British to the Bhutanese authorities.[5] Although there was peace in the Assam *duars*, those abutting the province of Bengal were frequently a source of surprise attacks. In 1860 Sir Ashley Eden, secretary to the Bengal government, was sent to the Bhutanese capital, Punakh, to deal with the existing situation along the border and to stress the urgent need to stop the raids which, British officials claimed, were inspired, instigated or conducted by the Bhutanese. Sir Ashley aroused considerable displeasure by crossing the Bhutanese frontier and entering the capital uninvited with a huge entourage which included armed soldiers. He was virtually held prisoner and only by signing a treaty under protest was his party guaranteed a safe exit from the country by the Bhutanese durbar.

Unsurprisingly Sir Ashley's subsequent report on the state of Bhutan was high-handed and scornful, declaring that the Bhutanese were 'a cruel and treacherous race' who were indifferent to everything except fighting and killing one another, in which they seemed to take genuine pleasure. For a Bhutanese, crime was 'the only claim to distinction and honour' and their nation 'had no ruling class, no literature, no national pride in the past or aspirations for the future'.[6] Sir Ashley was equally damning of the judiciary, scoffing that 'the Bootanese have no laws, either written or of usage' and in religious practice the people only 'nominally profess the Buddhist religion ... their religious exercises are merely confined to the propitiation of evil spirits and genii, and the mechanical recital of a few sacred sentences'.[7] Of the revenue system, he concluded, 'strictly speaking there is no system. The only limit on the Revenue demand is the natural limit of the power of the official to extort more.'[8]

In the wake of Sir Ashley's humiliation, in November 1864 four British columns advanced into the lower hills: two from Bengal, one from Goalpara and one from Gauhati. The Bhutanese forces were said to number 10,000 men armed with matchlocks, bows and arrows (with which they were particularly proficient) and short, heavy swords.[9] At first no serious resistance was encountered, and orders were issued to annex the *duars* that still remained in the hands of the Bhutanese and to break up the British field force. Simultaneous attacks by the Bhutanese were then made suddenly on different British posts. The attacks were easily repulsed, but at the fort of Diwangiri the defenders suffered some losses and were cut off from their water supply and communication with the plains. Colonel Robert Dallas Campbell, in command, considered that his force was too weak to dislodge the assailants and took the decision to retreat. He evacuated Diwangiri at night, but the main column lost its way in the darkness when the guns and many of the wounded were abandoned and all the baggage lost. Reinforcements were sent up from India and in less than two months Diwangiri was retaken with very few casualties on the British side, but with 'excessive and needless slaughter' of the Bhutanese who were found within the post, effectively concluding the war.[10] Conditioned by years of misunderstanding of the Bhutanese perspective and fuelled by negative reporting from frontier officials and observers such as Pemberton and Eden, Britain appropriated the eighteen *duars*, which would in a short time become revenue-spinning tea plantations.[11]

The Akas

Due east of Bhutan, the part of the Himalayas with Assam to its south and Tibet to its north constituted the habitat of four tribes: Akas, Mijis, Daflas and Abors. The first three of these tribes occupied the hills on the southern side of the backbone of the snow range of the Himalayas; the Abors alone dwelt on both sides of it. Adjacent to the Bhutanese lived the Aka tribe. The Akas were divided into two clans: the Hazari-Khawa Akas, or 'eaters at a thousand hearths', and the Kopaschors, or 'thieves who lurk amid the cotton plants'.[1] These two clans lived apart and at times fought each other. They intermarried, but in all other respects behaved towards each other as separate unities. The Akas asserted that they came originally from the southeast of the Assam Valley, which was possibly true as their language bore a greater resemblance to that of the tribes bordering Manipur than the language of their immediate neighbours, the Daflas and the Bhutanese. They also claimed that they were of noble origin and every free Aka considered himself more or less a raja, wielding a certain control over the inhabitants of the Balipara district of upper Assam, who were forced to provide them with free board and lodging whenever it pleased the Akas to visit the plains, and to pay them an annual tribute in the shape of pigs, fowls and silk cloths.[2]

The Akas were great agriculturists and 'no idlers'. As well as rice, they grew tobacco, chilli and various kinds of vegetables by means of *jhum* cultivation,[3] but avoided terrace cultivation owing to the precipitous nature of the hills. They also hunted wild beasts and birds. They kept large flocks of *mithun* (semi-wild ox) and cows, of which the flesh was eaten but the milk never consumed, and bred pigs, fowls and pigeons in great numbers. However, they prided themselves in only eating 'the food of civilized people', never touching the flesh of dogs or elephants 'or other objectionable animals', while indulging in the use of opium and tobacco and a species of beer called *mod*.[4] The importance of the tribe lay in their geographical position between Assam and the numerous Miji clans over whom they exerted a great influence by acting as middlemen in trade, as the Mijis rarely visited Assam and were able to purchase Assamese silk and cotton from the Akas. The Akas also traded with Bhutan and Assam, buying from the former warm clothes, ornaments and *daos* (broadswords), and selling rubber to the latter. In addition to bows and arrows (often poisoned with aconite obtained from the Mijis) the Akas carried a longsword with a 4-foot blade. Both males and females wore a type of toga made of rough Assamese silk or Bhutanese blanket cloth and the men had a half-trouser which consisted of a piece of cloth tied beneath the knees, allowing its fringes to hang down over the ankles to provide an admirable deterrent for leeches and stinging insects. As a headdress, the Aka men often wore a kind of ring-cap made of cane with tall tail feathers in front, or the felt caps of the Bhutanese, and the women wore round their heads 'a striking and pretty filet of silver chain-work' with 'large vase-shaped silver ear-rings'.[5]

The British saw the Akas not as animists but 'demon worshippers', although at the start of the nineteenth century a priest from Lhasa introduced the Buddhist faith and constructed a monastery in their region. Despite being polygamists, the Aka men showed considerable respect to their women, although this high esteem did not prevent the deployment of females for the hard work in the fields while the husbands stayed at home to tend the children. Aka stockades were strong and well built. All the members of one family or clan, including slaves, lived under the same roof. The house of the most prominent chief could be 200 feet long and 40 feet wide, with a long row of separate compartments running the whole length of the building. The Akas were very hospitable, teaching their children to pay particular respect to their guests. According to the explorer Major C. R. Macgregor, they assumed a 'very bold and dignified air; noblesse oblige is clearly marked in their deportment, if not in their conduct' and they looked upon the occupants of the plains with the greatest contempt.[6]

The Hazari-Khawa Akas were on the whole peaceable and never took up arms unless under provocation, and then only in open warfare, not by secret attack as was the case with most of the hill tribes. However, over many years the Kopaschor leader, the Tagi Raja, committed numerous robberies and murders in the plains and in 1829 he was captured and imprisoned in Gauhati jail. He was released in 1832 and continued his violent attacks until 1842, whereupon he accepted a small pension and agreed to take up residence in the plains. In 1883 later Kopaschor chiefs Mehdi and Chandi carried off and detained several native officials. A punitive expedition occupied Mehdi's village and recovered the captives and some loot but was unable to force the chiefs to submit. A blockade of the frontier followed but it was not until 1888 that the chiefs tendered their submission. In 1894 Captain Henry St Patrick Maxwell, political officer with the Aka Field Force, observed that 'of all the Savage races on the Northern Frontier of the Assam Province, the Akas have been most contumacious and troublesome'.[7] However, in the twentieth century the tribe won the respect of their visitors. In his 1914 ethnological report Colonel R. S. Kennedy observed that they were 'a much more enlightened and civilized people than the other hill tribes further east' and Captain Neuville wrote in 1925 that the Akas were 'an excellent and interesting people ... capable of much improvement'.[8]

The Daflas

To the east of the Akas was the territory of the Dafla tribe. Their boundary to the south was the 'Duphlaghur', an old road running along the frontier from southwest to northeast. They inhabited hills ranging from 2,000 to 7,000 feet and a great portion of land had been cleared for cultivation by cutting and burning the forest. During the winter months, the snowfall was said to be very heavy. The Daflas tattooed their faces in order that they might be recognized in the next world and were described by William Robinson as having a 'somewhat ferocious' appearance.[1] Their features were decidedly Mongolian and their language closely allied to that of the neighbouring mountainous hill Miri tribe. The ordinary dress of the Dafla men consisted of a short, sleeveless shirt of thick cotton, frequently striped cheerfully with blue and red. The women were generally wrapped in a shapeless mantle of striped or plain cotton cloth enveloping the body from the armpits to the centre of the calves and their ears were 'loaded with huge brass or silver rings and the ear-lobes so stretched with the weight of great metal knobs that they not unusually reach down to the shoulders'.[2] A noticeable peculiarity about the Dafla women was the sing-song manner in which they talked, the voice rising and falling half a dozen times and pitched in as many keys during the utterance of a short sentence.[3]

As far as the spiritual life of the Daflas was concerned, sacrifices were considered to be more worthy than offerings. Hogs and fowls were the animals most frequently sacrificed, accompanied by libations of fermented liquor. The office of the priesthood was not hereditary, and was taken up and laid aside at will, so that every man, when occasion demanded it, might fulfil the role. Since diseases were supposed to arise entirely from a preternatural agency, priests were also diviners who consulted auspices of many different kinds, including the entrails of young chickens.[4] The people subscribed to polygamy and polyandry and their villages were large and rich in livestock. The chiefs in general possessed a great many Assamese slaves who had been captured from the plains. As a result there were two classes in the community: free men and serfs, the latter of whom could hold property and have a voice in the government of their village but could never become free men. Their form of government was oligarchical, with sometimes eighty chiefs in one clan, however the Daflas were 'not so much a single homogenous tribe as a horde of petty clans independent of each other and generally incapable of a combined action'.[5]

There were frequent Dafla raids prior to 1852, and later violence in 1870 and 1872 when the cause was tribal dissension rather than the plundering of inhabitants of the plains. As a punishment for the raids a blockade was established which proved ineffectual. A military force was then sent into the hills to which the Daflas gave little opposition and in the end surrendered their captives. The Apa Tanangs or Ankas were an offshoot of the Daflas, a 'timid, good-natured, industrious and loquacious people, far inferior in pluck and physique',[6] occupying the valley of the Kali River behind the hills which formed the northern boundary of the North Lakhimpur subdivision, with 'a magnificent elevated plateau laid out in highly cultivated terraces'.[7] The Ankas used articles of Chinese manufacture, although there was little information on communication between the tribe and Tibet or China. In 1896 they made a raid into British territory, killing two men and carrying off three captives, and a punitive expedition made its way unopposed to their principal village to rescue the captives.

The Miris

The Miris and Abors lived to the northeast of the Daflas. Both tribes belonged to the same tribal stock and originally came from the same habitat. While the Abors, 'being the later wave of immigrants into the border hills of Assam, retained more of their pristine savagery and hardihood', the Miris had been 'polished by their association with the plains and the sedentary habits of civilization' and as a result had lost their ability to forge *daos* and weave coarse cloth. However, they were very much alike in all material respects and the dealings between them were 'constant and intimate'.[1] The Miris inhabited the plains and lower hills along the north banks of Brahmaputra from the area of Lakhimpur to the Dihang (the upper stretch of the Brahmaputra) and numerous members of the tribe lived in the hills west of the Dirjmoo, sacrificing to sylvan spirits and practising divination from the examination of bird entrails. Many of the Miris of the plains were to some extent Hinduised, and joined in Assamese festivals, but never seemed able to subscribe to a pure form of Hinduism as long as they were 'compelled by poverty to eat every sort of food from a rat to a tiger'.[2]

A particularly pejorative account of the tribe in 1897 stated that 'they are in fact poor, helpless ... savages, without religion, without arts, and without laws',[3] and the Scottish army surgeon John McCosh, who included a chapter on the hill tribes in the 1837 *Topography of Assam*, condemned their manners and habits as 'wild and barbarous'.[4] Notwithstanding the free use of tobacco, their teeth were 'very fine and white: their complexion what the natives of India would call fair, but they have rosy cheeks and ruddy lips ... stoutly built, generally short of stature'.[5] The Miri houses were built on piles with pigs and poultry housed beneath the structure. The chiefs of the hill Miris placed in their ears 'a silver ornament, the size and shape of a wine glass', and on their heads 'a cane cap with a peak behind, over which is a huge tiger or leopard skin, including the tail, which gives them a droll appearance'. The women wore a short petticoat secured by a broad leather belt ornamented with brass bosses, with hair 'neatly parted in the centre and allowed to hang in two braids, and on their necks are enormous quantities of turquoise, agate, cornelian and onyx beads'. The Miri women made faithful and obedient wives and 'express astonishment at the unbridled tongues of the Assamese women'.[6] As a tribe, the Miris were considerably less hostile to the British presence than many of their neighbours and it was felt that a better acquaintance with them would be of mutual advantage.

The Abors

The Abors (divided into the Menyong, Panghi, Padam and Shimong clans) lived further east in the hills bordering the Dihang and the Dibang rivers, and the Bor Abors (or 'Great Abors', said to be the original line of the tribe and dreaded for their brutality) occupied the ranges of the interior. Their real habitat was the high mountain ranges, from 8,000 to 12,000 feet, between Assam and Tibet, but their 'super-abundant population, for the want of room and land, overflowed into the valley of Assam through the gorge of the Dihang and spread east and west to the lower ranges of hills on the outskirts of the plains'. The Abors, although speaking the same language, differed greatly from the quiet and inoffensive Miris in character and a British report declared them to be 'in a manner insolent and rude beyond all other tribes of this frontier'.[1] A tall, strong race, with Mongolian features and copper-coloured complexion, they did not practise polygamy and women were treated with great consideration. Despite this sensitivity, they were said to be 'the most ruthless savages on the whole of the northern frontier' and the absence of population on the north bank of the Brahmaputra from opposite Dibrugarh to Sadiya was due chiefly to fear of their raids.[2]

Respected by all the neighbouring tribes for their martial spirit, the Abors were agriculturists who kept *mithun* and other cattle and cultivated rice, cotton, tobacco, maize, ginger, red pepper, roots, pumpkins, and a variety of sugarcane. Although their villages were reported to be open and undefended, the sites were chosen in inaccessible territory of dense tree jungle and undergrowth, with houses containing ten to twenty people in batches of sixty or eighty, one terrace above another. The *moorung*, or meeting house, could reach 200 feet in length with some sixteen or seventeen fireplaces, around which groups of adult males were seated. According to the Miris, whenever a few families of Abors united into a society, fierce feuds over women and summary vengeance soon broke up or scattered the community. They therefore preferred to build apart and depend

Hill Tribes

on their own resources for maintaining themselves in their isolated positions.[3]

The Abors armed themselves with bows and arrows, and prepared for war with a dab of poisoned paste made sometimes of pig's blood and aconite or the juice of the croton plant, which was put on just behind the arrowhead. In most cases if made up too soon the poison lost its deadly efficacy, though it still caused a festering wound. Abors also used crossbows, with which they were said to be highly accurate, and carried spears, heavy shortswords and long knives. They claimed an absolute overlordship over the plain Miris and an inalienable right to all the fish and gold in the Dihang River, however there was little doubt that the Abors, all the Miri clans and the Daflas were one great tribe, quite different to their neighbours on their west and east (respectively the Bhutanese and the Mishmis) but bearing a strong resemblance to the Nagas.[4]

The Abors extended northwards up to the frontier of Tibet where they were involved in commercial activity. A large number of markets were scattered along the Indo-Tibetan border and trade percolated along both north and south routes with a strong tide of commerce coming south from Tibet through Mishmi country and sweeping along the lower Abor Hills to the Subansiri River. As most Abors wore dark red woollen coats with other articles of clothing and ornaments obtained from Tibet, these distinguished them from their neighbours, the Mishmis, whom they otherwise much resembled in appearance, dress, manners and customs.[5] The lower dress of the male Abors consisted principally of a *suria*, or *dhoti*, made of the bark of the udal tree (*sterculia*) which answered the double purpose of a carpet and a covering. Tied round the loins, it hung down in loose strips about 15 inches long and served also as a pillow at night. Their war helmets of cane were of a 'very formidable and picturesque appearance ... adorned with pieces of bearskin, chowry[6] tails dyed red, boars' tusks, and, to crown all, the beak of the buceros' (the great hornbill).[7] All young Abor females wore

> suspended in front from a string around the loins a row of from three to twelve shell-shaped embossed plates of bell-metal, from

three to six inches in diameter ... these plates rattle and clink as they move like prisoners' chains ... and even adult females often have no other covering.[8]

Tattooing was universal. Men had a cross on the forehead and women on the upper lip. On both sides of the cross, above and below the mouth, were stripes.[9] The hair of both males and females was cropped short by lifting it on a knife and chopping it on a stick.

Despite British observations that the Abors were supremely rude, Edward Dalton, the junior assistant commissioner of Assam who, in contrast to other British officials, displayed an attitude of respect, interest and affection towards the tribal people he observed, admired the 'practical utility' of the Abor living arrangements and 'the ready alacrity and good feeling and discipline' of the tribal members.[10] John McCosh also found the Abors to be 'a hospitable and even a social race; and a constant round of festivity is kept up from one end of the year to the next'.[11] Moreover regard for old age was pushed to its extreme limits. Old people were exempt from work and constituted a separate class, gathering in the council house to socialise while the young were out at work. To the French missionary Father Nicholas Michael Krick (from his travel accounts a witty, sympathetic and courageous man) the Padam Abor, subscribing to a purely animistic belief, was 'very active, jolly, a lover of freedom and independence, generous, noble-hearted, plain-spoken, more honest than the average Oriental, not over-moderate in eating and drinking, at least as far as quantity is concerned'.[12]

The Abors appeared to be on friendly terms with the British until 1848 when the political agent Captain Hamilton Vetch led a small force into the hills to rescue some kidnapped Cachari gold washers and burnt a village as punishment for a night attack on his camp which, 'however righteous an act in itself, tended greatly to disturb the generally harmonious relations hitherto subsisting between the Assam officials and the wild tribes in this quarter'.[13] Several other Abor raids followed but not of a serious nature until 1858 when the tribesmen destroyed a gold washers' village only 6 miles from Dibrugarh. Two British punitive expeditions were sent against the tribe with limited success and a third, stronger force entered the hills in 1859 and burnt several of their settlements. Whereas one section of the Abors submitted, another group renewed hostilities in the following years, leading to the construction of a road along the frontier and the establishment of a line of outposts. In 1881 it was noted by British officers that it was 'the openly expressed intention' of the Abors to push across the Dibang and annex much of the territory of the Mishmi tribe to cut them off from the plains, and it seemed wise that aid should be given to the Mishmis, who were particularly friendly with the British government.[14]

During the next few years, a series of undemanding agreements were concluded with the different Abor communities by which they were given an allowance of iron hoes, salt, rum, opium and tobacco so long as they remained on good behaviour. Later this was turned into a monetary stipend of Rs 3,400 annually. In Shakespear's view,

> Small wonder that the Abors after all these futile efforts at punishment on our part and their recent substantial gain should have had an exaggerated notion of their own powers. Their outrages in various petty ways still continued, and still they received their 'posa'![15]

However, there were no further serious occurrences until 1889 when four Miris were decoyed across the frontier and murdered. The final disturbance occurred in 1893 when Abors of all groups attacked several parties of police. An expedition occupied the principal Bor Abor villages after overcoming a great deal of resistance and a blockade followed which lasted until 1900 when there was general submission. Lieutenant Colonel Alban Wilson, serving in the 8th Gurkha Rifles in the punitive action of 1894, described in one village a virtually impregnable stockade 10 or 12 feet high and over a mile long, made of three rows of tree trunks laced together with cane and covered with a frieze of bamboo spikes, upon which British 7-pounder guns fired with little effect. When the Abors were eventually drawn out, they charged through the British line, slashing soldiers with their swords and 'plugging the elephants so full of arrows that they stampeded, throwing their load into the jungle and scattering the coolies who were near them'. Retribution was swift. Any village that provided substantial opposition to the British was

> destroyed in the most systematic manner; first of all, rice was removed from the houses for use by the [British] column if required, the live-stock killed and eaten, the jungle all round thoroughly searched for caches of food-stuffs and other property, and then the village was burnt.[16]

The Mishmis

Beyond the Abors eastward were the various tribes of the Mishmis. Roughly all the hills bordering the northeast corner of Assam were inhabited by these hillmen. In Major Butler's view,

> They are a very wild, roaming race of people, constantly engaged in petty war amongst themselves and their neighbours, the Abors and Singphos, when the most remorseless reprisals and massacres are committed. They have no written language, and appear to belong to the Tartar race ... of diminutive stature, but stout, active and hardy.[1]

Butler added that, on being afflicted by famine, sickness or other misfortunes, they invariably sacrificed fowls and pigs, 'that the evil might be removed, and the wrath of the invisible spirit appeased by their offerings and submission'.[2] All the Mishmis, men and women, were habitual smokers, possessing bamboo pipes very similar to those of the Lhota Nagas. The Mishmi male dress consisted of a cloth bound round the loins, which passed between the legs and fastened in front, and a coat without sleeves down to the knees. The dress of the women consisted of a bodice which 'barely serves to cover the breasts' and a skirt down to the knees. On the head a tiara of silver was worn, with a profusion of beads suspended around the neck. The principal weapons used were the spear and a straight Tibetan sword, 'to which was occasionally added a matchlock or cross-bow, from which are projected poisoned arrows'.[3]

Mishmi dwellings were few in each village, but of great length. The house of a chief could be 130 feet, divided into many apartments, which, in the opinion of Thomas Cooper (described as 'one of the most adventurous of modern English travellers' and a vocal proponent of opening Tibet and China to British trade), 'more resemble cowsheds than human habitations'.[4] The Mishmis were great polygamists, with every man having as many wives as he could afford to buy, the price for a wife varying from a pig to twenty oxen. However, slavery was not practised by them, nor did they exact money or the service of other tribesmen under the system of *posa*. Although Cooper wrote that 'the laxity of morals among the people is conspicuous, and this, coupled with the vice of inordinate use of opium, constitutes one of the greatest drawbacks to industry and progress', the British found little difficulty in overlooking these shortcomings in their amicable dealings with the tribe.[5]

From the Dibang to the Digaru River in the hills to the north of Sadiya were the Chulikata Mishmis, the most dangerous of all the Mishmi clans (who derived their title of Chulikata, meaning 'cropped hair', from the habit of cutting the hair square across the forehead), and to their east were the Bebejiya (outcast) Mishmis. Their features were of a 'Mongolian type' with a skin colour varying from dark brown to the fairness of a European brunette and some of the girls were 'decidedly good-looking'. The Chulikatas were, according to Dalton, 'entirely devoid of religious feeling' and, utterly rejecting 'all notions of a future state or of immortality of any kind', worshipped demons and evil spirits.[6] The tribe had an 'inordinate love of giving feasts' and as soon as a Chulikata acquired any money, he at once spent it on *mithun* and pigs to feed his friends.[7] They were a trading people, with large parties continually on the move to and from Tibet via a route which was

> excessively fatiguing, difficult and dangerous. In many places a false step would be attended with fatal consequences; precipices must be crossed at a height of a hundred feet above the foaming bed of a river, the only support of the traveller being derived

from the roots and stumps of trees and shrubs, and the angular character of the face of the rock.[8]

The Chulikatas were probably the most ingenious of the Mishmi family in their use for clothing of many of the fibrous plants that grew wild in the hills. With a nettle fibre they were able weave a cloth so strong and stiff that, made into jackets, it was used by both Mishmis and Abors as a type of armour.[9] They had neatly made oblong shields of buffalo hide, attached to which was a quiver of finely poisoned *panjis* (bamboo stakes). The Chulikatas were 'greatly detested and mistrusted by their neighbours, the Abors', and much dreaded by the Sadiya population due to their 'prowling operations' to kidnap women and children. The chiefs were hereditary and had considerable influence over their clansmen, but no power over their persons or property, and no authority to punish crime.[10] Chulikata villages contained between ten and thirty narrow houses, each lightly framed and measuring about 60 feet by 12 feet. The most striking feature of the interior was the number of skulls of *mithun*, bullocks, buffaloes, bears, tigers, deer, monkeys and *takins* on display.[11]

From the Digaru River westward and on both sides of the Brahmaputra, reaching the Tibetan frontier to the north and the Nemlang River to the south, lived various other Mishmi tribes: the Tain, the Mezho and the Maro clans. The Tain, or Digaru, tribe to the west of the Du River (a tributary of the Brahmaputra) traded and communicated with the British, whereas the Mezho Mishmis to the northeast of the Du River traded with Tibet. The Maro were found to the south of the Brahmaputra in scattered settlements mixed with Khamti and Singpho villages. They were a pastoral people with large herds of *mithun*. The men of the interior and higher ranges were of good physique and some of them were very fair, with strong Mongolian features. The Digarus, unlike the Chulikatas, wore their hair very long and tied in a knot on the top of their heads, and most of them wore caps made of the skins of martens or hill foxes and a type of waistcoat made from the skin of the *takin*. They were wilder-looking than the Chulikatas and were supposed to inhabit the highest ranges just below the snowline, where

Hill Tribes

the mountainous country they inhabit is described as very grand and beautiful, but most difficult to travel; a path winds round steep precipices with only a narrow ledge for a foothold, and, in some places not even this: only holes in the face of the precipice for the hands or feet.[12]

Under these conditions the members of the tribe who visited Sadiya took a month or more to make the journey. It was evident that the Digarus had direct or indirect intercourse with the Chinese as they possessed Chinese coins, metal tobacco pipes and other Chinese goods. Like the Chulikatas they strongly objected to strangers passing through their territory or attempting to approach the Tibetan frontier. They cultivated *Coptis teeta* (a bitter root much esteemed for its medicinal qualities) and carried it into Tibet where it was said to be in great demand. They likewise took musk-deer pods, dyed cloths and skins of tigers, bears, deer, leopards and otters to barter for *daos*, cattle, guns, pistols, powder and caps.[13]

In 1854 Father Krick reached the confines of Tibet via Mezho Mishmi country but was murdered with a fellow priest the following year by a powerful Digaru chief, Kaisa, when repeating the visit. The crime was punished by an expedition led by Lieutenant Frederick Grey Eden, consisting of a small body of twenty sepoys, forty Khamti volunteers and a few hill porters. After forced marches for eight days in succession 'swinging across dangerous torrents on bridges of single canes, climbing for hours at a time without water and in bitter cold', the offending chief was surprised and captured.[14] He was tried and hanged at Dibrugarh but not before he had killed two of the jail guards, and there were frequent raids in the years that followed. In 1866 the British tried to create a militia by supplying arms to the local Khamtis and giving a monthly payment of one rupee to all members of the tribe who would settle along the section of the frontier. This proved successful, and little trouble was subsequently reported apart from two small raids in 1878 and the murder of three Khamtis in 1899 by a group of Bebejiyas, after which the guilty villages were burnt.[15]

The Khamtis

The Khamtis lived to the north of Sadiya and to the southeast of the Mishmis. The tribe was originally from Bor Khamti, the mountainous region between Assam and the Irrawaddy Valley. Its members were of Shan descent, followed Buddhism and only arrived in the Sadiya district at the end of the eighteenth century, having crossed the Brahmaputra and ousted the Assamese governor of the region.[1] Their territory contained many broad, fertile and well-cultivated valleys. They were an active, intelligent and shrewd people, viewed as 'very far in advance of all the northeastern frontier tribes in knowledge, arts, and civilization'.[2] Prince Henri d'Orleans, in his expedition from southwest China to Assam in 1895, commented that their appearance strongly resembled that of the people of Laos, being paler than the Assamese with Mongolian features, while the Khamti dress was similar to that of the Burmese with a tight-fitting upper garment and a lungi or skirt of cotton or silk plaided in bright colours.[3] Their long hair was drawn up from the back and sides in a large roll which rose 4 or 5 inches above the head and was encircled by an embroidered band, the tasselled end of which hung down behind. Both sexes were great smokers, using a long pipe (often 3 feet) with metal bowl, silver mouthpiece and bamboo stem. The principal amusement of the Khamti chiefs was to 'most ingeniously work up iron and silver into a variety of forms for arms, ornaments, and pipes'.[4] The Khamtis were entirely agricultural, cultivating rice and opium in the valleys. Their villages were 'always strongly stockaded, the houses inside rather crowded and the numbers of temples and pagodas showing up among the surrounding forests give a very picturesque note to the attractive and wild scenery'.[5]

Khamti priests were 'men of great importance' with even greater influence than their chiefs. They were also schoolmasters, and every freeborn youth was compelled to attend school in the temples where he learned to read and write his own language. Khamtis were one of 'the few tribes who have a written character ... evidently derived from the Burmese, while their language more closely resembles that spoken by the Siamese'.⁶ Although professing to be strict followers of Burmese Buddhism, they nevertheless killed and ate all animals and Thomas Cooper was of the opinion that 'their religion is little more than polytheism under a thin veil of Buddhist pantheism ... while many of their customs are altogether opposed to Buddhism'.⁷ Some of their temples were of considerable size; one was described by the entrepreneurial tea planter J. Errol Gray as standing

> in a forest covered island in the Nam Kiu river, and is in regular Burmese style, 95 feet high and 125 feet in circumference at the base; four flights of stone steps lead up to the plinth on which it stands, each flight guarded by gigantic figures of fabulous beings. At each face of the compass on the plinth are four marble images of Buddha of excellent workmanship.⁸

In 1835 there was a fresh immigration of 230 Khamtis into land at the head of the Assam Valley. Their advent was welcomed by the British authorities, who intended to prevent a fresh Burmese invasion by the settlement of friendly warlike tribes along the frontier, with the understanding that the area reserved for tea cultivation was left undisturbed. The Khamtis, although left untaxed and allowed to manage their private affairs under their own chiefs, were deprived of control over the local Assamese whose jurisdiction was maintained by the political officer at Sadiya. Their slaves were also released and they suspected that the government planned to tax them and to lower their status. The discontent culminated in January 1839 in a treacherous night attack on the British garrison at Sadiya. Colonel White, the political agent, was killed and eighty other men were killed or wounded. A punitive force was dispatched and in December 1843 the last of the rebels gave themselves up; some were deported to the western part of the district and others were settled above Sadiya town to form a screen between the Assamese and the Mishmis.⁹

The Singphos

The Singphos who lived intermixed with the Khamtis in the region linked by the Buri Dihing, Noa Dihing and Tengapani rivers were merely an outlying section of their own tribe. Their real home was in the hill country between the Chindwin River and the Patkai range of mountains. Racially identical with the Kachins of Burma, they were divided into twelve principal tribes of which the one named Beesa, whose chieftain lived by the gorge of the Patkai pass, appeared to be the most prominent. During the reign of Gaurinath Singha, the Singphos drove away the Khamtis from the lands below the Patkai and settled east of Sadiya. According to William Robinson, the Singphos were the most powerful and most numerous tribe bordering on the Assam Valley, and Dalton described them as 'a fine athletic race, above the ordinary standard of height and capable of enduring great fatigue; but their energies are greatly impaired by the use of opium and spirits'.[1] To Major Butler, who seldom had a good word to say about the hill tribes in general, the Singphos were 'a rude treacherous people', so indolent that, despite having the most fertile soil in Assam, during several months in the year they were 'reduced to subsist on yams and other roots found in the jungles', and every petty ailment was ascribed to the influence of some evil spirit which had to be propitiated before the sick person could recover.[2] It was the Singpho custom to bury the dead. Those of the poorer classes were interred soon after death, but the bodies of chiefs and important individuals were sometimes not buried for years until decomposed, to allow 'the widely scattered relations of the deceased to have time to attend, who would not fail to take deadly offence at being deprived of an opportunity of paying reverence'.[3]

Their features of the Singphos were 'of a Mongolian type, very oblique eyes, mouths wide, cheekbones high, and heavy square jawbones', with a tawny complexion. Their dress consisted of a piece of coloured cotton cloth, often in broad horizontal bands of red and blue, a jacket and a scarf. The chiefs adopted the Shan or Burmese style of dress and wrapped themselves in plaids of thick cotton 'much in the fashion of Scottish Highlanders'.[4] Their villages contained fifty to sixty large houses ranging from 80 to 100 hundred feet long and 20 feet wide, with a raised floor and open veranda, the timbers of some of the larger buildings being of such enormous size and length that, when one village was surprised by British troops in 1843, it was regretted that it was necessary to burn 'such a magnificent residence' as the chief's house.[5] Although a peaceful people, they were 'addicted' to raiding for slaves and the Duanias, or Singpho-Assamese half-breeds, were the result of the intercourse between Singpho captors and their Assamese captives.[6]

Singpho chiefs, like their Mishmi and Abor counterparts, exchanged presents annually with the British political officer at Sadiya, however they paid no tribute to Britain, Burma or China, thus forming a neutral ground between British India and China. Their territories towards the south and further west of Sadiya were extremely rich in precious metals and the amber mines, only a few days' march from the Indian border, were famous. Serpentine, jade and other valuable minerals, as well as precious stones, were found in the region in considerable quantities and the Chinese travelled close to the Indian frontier to trade in these commodities.[7]

During the Burmese occupation of Assam, the Singphos had proved a constant source of trouble, carrying out persistent raids on the Assamese and removing thousands as slaves.[8] When in June 1825 roughly 600 Burmese linked up with the Singpho rebels, the British in a series of attacks overwhelmed the Burmese and expelled them from the Singpho villages. The defeat severely affected Singpho prosperity and the resulting resentment led to several risings. Beesa Gaum, the principal Singpho chief whose region was seen of strategic importance, was granted a monthly allowance from the British of 50 rupees a month to serve 'as an organ of communication with the other chiefs and a spy upon their action' with the duty of identifying activity which might cause agitation beyond the frontier.[9] The last tribal uprising took place in 1843 and included not only all the Singphos on the Assam border and the territory abutting Burma, but also a number of Shans and Burmese. British troops were called up and the hostilities, after dragging on for several months, ended in the capture of the leaders of the rebellion and the complete submission of the Singphos. It was suggested that their subsequent peaceful attitude was due to their universal habit of eating excessive quantities of opium, which robbed them of their old warlike proclivities.[10]

The Nagas

To the southwest of the Singphos the various Naga tribes were scattered over the hills, extending from the Singpho country of Lakhimpur in the east to Nowgong in the west and to the confines of Manipur and Cachar in the south. The Patkai Nagas inhabited the northern slopes of the Patkai mountains and the Sibsagar Nagas had their habitat in the low hills to the south of Sibsagar district. Across the Doyang River westward was the territory of the Angami Naga tribe. Other important branches of the Nagas were the Kacha Nagas, the Lhota Nagas, the Semas, the Aos, the Hatigorias, the Rengmas and the Lengta Nagas. Further east, as far as the Patkai, there were several Naga tribes who were in subjection to the Singphos and seemed to be harmless. However, there was no evidence of the use of the title 'Naga' by the tribes themselves for self-identification. The term appeared to be a colonial construct. The British Army officer Lieutenant Robert Woodthorpe, mapping frontier regions for the Survey of India in the 1870s, wrote, 'The name is quite foreign and unrecognised by the Nagas themselves ... A Naga when asked who he is, generally replies that he is of such and such a village.'[1] The characteristic feature of the Nagas was their inter-tribal feuding, and the various clans eyed each other with open hostility. Village was pitted against village and sometimes a settlement contained antagonistic parties within itself.[2] Each individual tribe spoke its own language and called itself by a distinctive name, although a noticeable habit common to all Naga tribes was that when a man was carrying a load, at every other pace he expelled his breath with a loud 'How' in a deep musical sound which, when many men were walking together adopting different notes, had 'a very impressive effect'. Hence the Manipuris spoke of all Nagas as 'How'.³

In Major Butler's typically derisory description, the Nagas were 'a very uncivilized race, with dark complexions, athletic sinewy frames ... reckless of human life' and, as far as their diet was concerned, 'the most unprejudiced race [devouring] dogs, rats, elephants, tigers, rhinoceroses, cows, pigs and fowls'. A dead elephant was esteemed 'a great prize as well as a delicacy' and the flesh merely dried by smoking without further cooking. They were extremely fond of rice beer (*azu*) which played a significant role in personal and social life, such as religious rituals and ceremonies, feasts and festivals and rites of passage from birth to death.⁴ According to Robinson, although appearing to acknowledge a divine power to be the maker of the world, Nagas possessed 'no temples erected in honour of their deities, and no ministers peculiarly consecrated to their service'. Instead, they practised ceremonies handed down to them by tradition 'to which they adhered with a childish credulity'.⁵

The toughest and most warlike of all the peoples of the northeast frontier, clad often in a cane crinoline and jacket without arms, the Nagas were widely known as headhunters (according to Shakespear, largely because women would not favour men who had not taken heads or been in raids).⁶ British accounts of Naga headhunting as purely barbaric suggests that European observers were guided by their own value system rather than the cultural importance of such acts, and the depiction of Nagas as the perpetrators of savage practices undoubtedly provided fuel for a European 'civilising mission' to eliminate such barbarity. However, the practice of headhunting was not simply acknowledged by Nagas as a sign of bravery but also intrinsically connected to the religious rites and ceremonies of their tribes, in the belief that a new injection of creative and vital energy would come to the aggressor's village when he arrived home with a head.⁷ Missing the cultural significance, British accounts were suitably dramatic in their descriptions of tribal bestiality. Robert Woodthorpe termed the Nagas, bloodthirsty, treacherous and revengeful ...[with] an article of faith that blood once shed can never be expiated except by the death of the murderer or some of his near relatives and though years may pass away vengeance will assuredly be taken one day.[8]

The missionary Susan Ward expressed her horror at the way men were said to lie in wait on hill paths, 'to spring upon any travellers, cut off their heads and hands, and bear them back off to their village to drink, dance and carouse ... without provocation, simply to gratify a blood thirsty [sic] disposition, and gain honour among their people'.[9]

It was said that to surprise and destroy was the greatest merit of a commander and elicited the highest pride of his followers. On approaching enemy territory, he would collect his troops and advance with the utmost caution. If unobserved, the tribesmen would set fire to the enemy's huts and massacre the inhabitants 'as they fly naked and defenceless from the flames ... and tearing off the scalps of all those who fall victims to their rage, they carry home those strange trophies of their triumph'.[10] At the entrance to their villages was the *moorung*, where a wooden drum called the warriors together and where their trophies of victory were hung. According to Susan Ward, 'in one, over 350 skulls of men, women and children were displayed'.[11] Frequently the inhabitants of defeated villages were, if not killed, taken into slavery. In his report on the province, Andrew John Moffatt Mills wrote that 'the value of slaves and cattle is strangely estimated at the following rate, a male slave is worth one cow and three conch shells, a female slave is worth three cows and four or five conch shells'.[12]

The Angamis were a fine-looking, athletic tribe with the flat noses and high cheekbones of Indo-Chinese stock, described by Captain John Butler (political agent in the Naga Hills from 1869 to 1875 and a man who was infinitely more sympathetic towards the northeastern tribesmen than his father, Major John Butler) as the most 'powerful and warlike' but also the 'most enterprising, intelligent and civilized' of all Nagas, despite their belief in a variety of good and evil spirits to whom they offered animal sacrifices.[13]

Brave 'but vindictive and treacherous', the only article worn by the men was 'a dark cloth kilt, a mere fig leaf, weighted with cowrie shells or brass ornaments' with numerous strings of beads, boars' tusks and shells hung around the neck. The ears had 'several large holes in the lobe for the reception of brass rings, heavy square glass drops, ornaments made of cane and goats' hair, dyed red and yellow', and the warrior wore on his head bunches of feathers intermingled with plates of brass and animal teeth, and 'a badge of honour on his chest, platted [sic] of bamboo, cane and coloured goats' hair, mingled with human hair from the heads he has cut off'. A chief distinguished himself by wearing 'a high cap of cane-work, decked with boars' tusks and toucan feathers, standing erect, and with a scarlet blanket over his shoulders'.[14]

The Angamis, deficient in hair either in beard, whisker or moustache, were much tattooed, which was also a mark of honour for having beheaded an enemy.[15] To Dalton the women were 'short, ugly and waistless; too hard worked perhaps to be beautiful' but notable for the correctness of their behaviour.[16] The Angami men confined themselves to one wife, of whose chastity they appeared very jealous. The love of dancing was a favourite passion, and the war dance the most striking of their performances. Robinson described how

> the women dance in an inner circle, whilst the men holding up their weapons in their hands dance around them, beating time and singing in strains of wild and plaintive melody ... [the women] move in slow and decent movements, but the men, arrayed in their full war dress, enter with enthusiastic ardour into their several parts; they exhaust themselves by perpendicular jumps and side leaps, in which they exhibit considerable agility.[17]

Angami villages were built on the summit of the most inaccessible hills and fortified with stockades, deep ditches and massive stone walls. The hillsides were bristling with bamboo spikes and in some cases the sloping side of the hill was cut away to form a perpendicular wall. Woodthorpe noted how the houses were built on unlevelled ground, the floor being carried out to the rear on bamboo piles, the back veranda being frequently a great height above the ground. These are not railed round at all, and on my asking if the small children never fell off, the reply was 'of course they do, many are killed that way' in a tone conveying the impression that my informant looked upon it as an ingenious method of giving effect to Malthusian theories.[18]

Major John Butler described seats of planks of wood in the houses, arranged around the fire with 'fowls, pigs, children, men and women' having free access.[19] The approaches to the villages were

> tortuous and narrow, only wide enough to admit the passage of one man at a time, and lead to gates closed by strong heavy wooden doors, with look-outs on which a sentry is posted day and night. Often these approaches are steeply scarped and the only means of entry is by a ladder consisting of a single pole fifteen or twenty feet high cut into steps.[20]

The universal weapon of the Nagas was a javelin, usually adorned with coloured hair. The total disuse of the bow seemed 'a very singular circumstance, especially as the weapon is common to all the surrounding hill tribes ... [but] the steadfast retention of their own weapons of offence, may be considered as one strong mark of nationality ... consecrated in their recollection as the weapon of their forefathers'.[21]

The hilly tract inhabited by the various Naga tribes had never been subjugated by the Ahoms and it was no part of British policy to absorb it, as it seemed likely that the opposition of the tribesmen would make it extremely difficult to maintain communications throughout the region. However, the 'more turbulent' Angamis were less amenable than their fellow tribesmen and consistently failed to remain within the bounds of their territory. For some years it was the practice to rely upon the raja of Manipur to exact reparation for raids committed by them, however this somewhat ineffectual policy was abandoned in favour of one of repression by British troops. The

Nagas first experienced western military invasion in 1832, when British troops led by Francis Jenkins and Robert Pemberton entered their territory. Mackenzie wrote that the two 'led 700 Manipuri troops with 800 coolies [porters] from the Manipur Valley' to fight their way through Angami Naga country.[22] Although it was alleged that the initial contact between the Nagas and the British was led by the British desire to create a communication route between Manipur and Assam, Jenkins was also asked by governor-general William Bentinck to explore and assess the northeast region, leading in the long term to extensive tea cultivation in the area.[23]

Between the years 1835 and 1851, ten military expeditions were led into the hills to deal with reported raids by Nagas to the west of the Naga Hills, where British cultivation was heavy and where, it was argued, the expanding tea gardens had encroached upon the traditional *jhum* lands and hunting grounds of the hill people.[24] Moreover, established trade routes and the exchange networks of the hill communities were further disrupted by denying the Nagas access through colonial estates during their travels to the foothill markets. In response to the majority of raids, British troops would attack villages, set fire to houses, kill any Nagas who resisted and force the survivors to flee into the forest. On occasions relatively innocent villages, who had provided little more than food or shelter to their aggressive fellow tribesmen, were burned which, even in Major John Butler's uncompromising view, was 'a harsh, vindictive measure, calculated to exasperate and even to make them implacable enemies'.[25] Still more reprehensible, if a village would not provide provisions for British troops it also would be destroyed and notice sent to other clans that if they withdrew their assistance their settlements would share the same fate. As a result, 'an ample supply of rice' would then appear, proving that the burning of the village 'had the desired effect'.[26]

The size of British expeditions was substantial. Butler reported that for the capture of the Angami fort of Khonoma in December 1850, the party, fortified by two 3-pounder guns and two 4-inch mortars, consisted of one major, one captain, three lieutenants, one assistant surgeon, one sergeant, three subadars, three jemadars, seventeen havildars, twenty *naicks* (corporals), three buglers and 281 sepoys.[27] The historian Birendra Chandra Chakravorty commented that during the years of successive military operations, 'the Nagas suffered much, being reduced to homeless wanderers, and living in impoverished huts in jungles infested with ferocious beasts'.[28] After 1851 it was decided to try a policy of non-interference in internal tribal quarrels. The governor-general, Lord Dalhousie, wrote in a minute of 20 February 1851,

> We should confine ourselves to our own ground; protect it as it can and must be protected; not meddle in feuds or fights of these savages; encourage trade with them as long as they are peaceful towards us; and rigidly exclude them from all communication either to sell what they have got, or to buy what they want if they should become turbulent or troublesome.[29]

However, in the first year after the inauguration of this policy, twenty-two Angami raids took place in which 178 persons were killed, wounded or abducted. In 1854 an officer was posted in the area and a line of frontier outposts was established which proved of little use. Finally, in 1866 the Angami tract of land was formed into a district with headquarters at Samaguting, which in 1873 was moved to the town of Kohima in the Naga Hills.

In October 1878 a serious outbreak occurred when the political officer of the Naga Hills, Guybon Henry Damant, was murdered and some of his escort killed or wounded. The Angamis then rose in a body and attacked the British headquarters at Kohima, occupying the town for eleven days. The garrison experienced great hardship with little food and water until Colonel James Johnstone raised the siege with a force of 2,000 troops supplied by the raja of Manipur. A campaign against the Angamis ensued, during which every one of the thirteen villages which had participated in the attack was either occupied or destroyed. As a result, the tribesmen agreed to pay revenue, to supply labour when required and to appoint a headman for each village to maintain good order and to carry out the wishes of the government. Indirect measures of occupation were adopted, including the gradual establishment of administrative posts in the Naga Hills by annexing the smaller and more amenable Naga villages with the promise of protecting them from larger settlements. The government also introduced a policy of requiring the tribesmen to lay down their spears and *daos* before entering the administered region to trade with the plains people. The British occupation of the Naga Hills marked the presence of an imperial power unseen and unimagined in the life of the Nagas. Major John Butler noted that they 'had hitherto never encountered a foe equal to contend with them, and in utter ignorance of the effect of fire-arms, they vainly imagined that no party could penetrate through their territory'.[30]

Describing the situation in the 1880s, Mackenzie wrote,

> The attitude of the tribes ... was one of partly exhaustion and partly of expectancy. The indirect results of the war were far more grievous to them than the actual hostilities; and those on whom the blow had fallen hoped, by quiet and peaceable demeanour, to earn some relaxation in the stringency of the conditions to which they were bound.[31]

The British prided themselves in the fact that thereafter it appeared that steady progress was made in the establishment of peace and stability and, as they saw it, the quiet submission of the Nagas to British rule. Blood feuds and headhunting were largely erased and all disputes that proved unable for the village elders to settle were brought before local officers for adjudication.[32] The Naga tribes along the eastern frontier, distinguished by the names of the passes through which they descended to the plains, carried on a good trade in cotton and other hill produce, which they exchanged for salt and rice. Individuals guilty of misconduct were refused access to the plains until reparation was made and, although frequent internal quarrels were said to exist, it was made clear that it was not British policy to meddle in domestic feuds.[33] However the naturalist and tea planter Samuel Peal, who visited the Naga Hills in 1865 and 1883, noted sadly that '"progress" is in the air everywhere, and we shall soon lose much of the material out of which their past histories might have been recovered'.[34]

The Mikirs

West of the Angami territories and surrounded by Nowgong district to the north, the Khasi-Jaintia Hills to the west and Cachar to the south stood the North Cachar Hills, inhabited by six different hill tribes: Hill Cacharis, Hozai Cacharis, Mikirs, Aroong Nagas, Old Kukis and New Kukis. Bordering upon the plains of Nowgong district were two hill tracts, one inhabited by the Rengma Nagas and the other by one of the most numerous and homogeneous of the Tibeto-Burman races in Assam, the Mikirs. In 1838 the total number of Mikirs was probably 20,000 and they were considered to be a 'fine athletic and industrious race of people'.[1] During the Burmese war, they deserted their settlements in the submontane tract and fled into the higher hills. Many Assamese were reported to have taken refuge with them during this time and to have been absorbed into the tribe. In the Mikir Hills there were summits which reached 4,000 feet, but the greater part of the terrain was of a much lower elevation, clothed with forest growth, chiefly of bamboo, figs of different species, cinnamon, *artocarpus* (mulberry) and *nahor* (Indian rose chestnut), where the Mikirs practised a primitive method of cultivation by axe, fire and hoe.

Although belonging to the Tibeto-Burman family, the people claimed no kinship with other tribes in Assam and did not possess typical Mongolian features. The girls were often fair. The dress of the Mikir man was a loincloth of cotton, or silk if he was wealthy, and a sleeveless striped jacket with long fringes. The woman wore a petticoat, kept tight around the waist by an ornamental girdle, and they were adorned by large silver ear tubes and many necklaces of gold, silver and coral. Mikir villages stood in clearings in the forest and the communities moved on as soon as the soil was exhausted by cultivation of mainly rice and cotton. Mikirs carried on a small trade with the natives of the plains, bartering their cotton and *eri* silk thread for salt and various small articles of luxury. Their houses were large, often containing the families of married sons as well as the original family. Polygamy was not permitted and adultery rare.[2] Generally considered to be the most peaceful hill tribe in Assam, with little evidence of criminal activity, they sacrificed to the sun, the moon, rivers, waterfalls and large stones in order to avoid sickness and procure good harvests. Such local divinities of the jungle were propitiated chiefly to avoid attacks from the many tigers which patrolled parts of the Mikir Hills. Unusually, the tribesmen neither ate the flesh nor drank the milk of the cow, possibly due to Brahminic influence, although they were much addicted to homemade rice liquor and opium.[3]

The Jaintias and Khasis

West of the North Cachar Hills the Khasis and Jaintias (also known as Pnars or Syntengs), thought to be descendants of the first Mongolian migration to India, formed one matriarchal tribal community and were amiable and sociable. The Jaintia village consisted of a scattered settlement of bamboo houses. Influenced more than other tribal groups of the region by Hindusim and Aryan practice, settled farming was acceptable and some cattle were reared in the Jaintia Hills.[1] However, the main occupation of the Jaintias consisted of the cultivation of rice, maize, jute, cotton, areca nut, ginger and betel leaf, although some members of the community also engaged in hunting and gathering. Jhum cultivation was preferred, and the village council owned and allotted forest land to members of the tribe. Sacred groves, consisting of virgin tracts of forest, were said to be residences of local deities and it was believed that by maintaining them in an undisturbed condition, welfare would be bestowed upon the people. Elsewhere, in clearings and fields *landoo* trees were planted for the rearing of the lac insect for dye and varnish, and the spinning of *eri* silk and cotton thread for weaving into cloth was a sizeable industry in some of the villages of the Jaintia Hills.

The traditional dress for men consisted of a *dhoti*, a sleeveless jacket (*jymphong*) and a turban, while women wore an unstitched striped cloth around their lower body with a full-sleeve blouse and a piece of cloth folded and wrapped around the shoulders and waist.[2] Jaintia festivals were mainly concerned with agricultural seasons, prosperity and entertainment and in the July ceremony after the sowing of rice, the young men of the tribe made a symbolic gesture of driving away evil spirits, plague and pestilence by beating the roof of every house with bamboo poles, while the women offered sacrificial food to the spirits of their ancestors. A popular local liquor known as *kiad* accompanied every religious festival and daily consumption in small amounts was considered a remedy for ailments such as urinary tract infections and dysentery. The Jaintias worshipped gods who required to be appeased by sacrificial offerings and as late as 1832 Edward Gait gave reports of the long-standing practice of sacrificing humans to the Kopili river goddess. Frequently the victims nominated themselves, enjoying the privilege, however sometimes the supply of voluntary victims ran short and strangers were kidnapped from foreign territory. The raja was called upon to deliver up the culprits, but he failed to do so and after further transgressions his dominions were annexed in 1835.[3]

Following the imposition of a house tax in 1860, the Jaintia hillmen broke out in an open rebellion which was stamped out by a large force of troops. Measures were taken to improve the administration and remedy the misconduct of local officials. However, the subsequent government decision to treat the Jaintia Hills as other parts of British India by the levy of a new income tax led to a fresh outbreak of violence in January 1862. The police station at Jowai was burnt to the ground and the garrison of soldiers besieged. To quell the revolt, two regiments of Sikhs and an elephant battery were moved into the hills. The Jaintias, although armed only with bows and arrows, fought bravely to maintain their independence but the operations were 'tedious and harassing' and the rebellion was finally quelled in November 1863 when the last of the insurgents surrendered. A household tax was retained, but in other respects everything possible was done to make the Jaintia people content with British rule. Roads were constructed, schools were opened, the interference of the regular police was reduced to a minimum, and the people were given the right to elect their *dolois* (hill headmen) and to form *panchayats* for the trial of civil and criminal cases. The European officer stationed at Jowai was required to qualify in the Khasi language and to visit each village in his jurisdiction at least once a year.[4]

Although the Jaintias had historically possessed a raja of their own, the Khasis developed a type of confederation of small oligarchical republics. A short and sturdy people, 'decidedly Malay in appearance', the Khasis were seen as 'cheerful in disposition, laborious, and in moral character, above their neighbours', despite the consumption of large quantities of spirit distilled from rice or millet.[5] McCosh, writing in 1837, saw them as

> a powerful, athletic race of men, rather below the middle size, with a manliness of gait and demeanour. They are fond of their mountains and look down with contempt upon the degenerate race of the plains, jealous of their power, brave in action, and have an aversion to falsehood.[6]

Although quite illiterate, they were ready to learn and the few schools in the region were well supported. They were said to have more readily adopted Christianity and ideas of European civilisation than any other tribe in India, although many of the tribesmen maintained animist beliefs and the propitiation of spirits both good and evil, principally in times of trouble. A peculiar feature of the region was the 'curious monoliths' which both the Jaintias and the Khasis erected in memory of their dead.[7]

Much like the clothing of the Jaintias, Khasi male attire was a *jymphong* with a fringe at the bottom and females wore several pieces of cloth wound round the body, giving it a cylindrical shape. The women were especially partial to gold and bead necklaces made of coral imported from Calcutta. The greater proportion of the population subsisted by cultivation of potato, orange, betel nut and *paan*, and the rearing of cattle. Hunting was a favourite sport and a common way of fishing was to poison the streams with a mixture of tree bark and the juice of creepers and cactus to stun the fish. The Khasis were also proficient in the hazardous collection of the honey of the wild bee from the crevices of precipitous rocks, smoking the bees out with a smouldering fire at the foot of the cliff.⁸ Their houses consisted generally of substantial thatched cottages and their villages were not built on the extreme summits of hills but often in small depressions to obtain protection from the strong winds and storms. They showed great ingenuity in constructing bridges by which the roots and branches of a *ficus* tree were brought together and interwoven, creating a strong, living structure.⁹ The Khasi weapon par excellence was the bow, although before the arrival of the British they seemed versed in the art of manufacturing gunpowder from saltpetre, sulphur and charcoal. The tribesmen produced cotton, iron, silk, wax, honey, ivory and other items which they traded for rice, dry fish, salt, and different kinds of garments and fabric which they were unable to weave. The Khasi tribe to the south of Kamrup owned lime quarries which were able to supply the entire province of Bengal.¹⁰

The Garos

To the west of the Khasi Hills stood the Garo Hills. To the south lay Bengal, and to the north stretched the Goalpara district of Assam. The region was described by Robinson as 'one confused assemblage of hills and narrow vales, watered by numerous small streams' with magnificent forests in which was an infinite variety of useful and ornamental plants.¹ The soil tended to be extremely fertile and Garo tribesmen were seen as 'a robust active race', cultivating mainly rice and cotton. Both men and women carried their produce to the plains in long baskets on their backs, held by a strap across the forehead, the baskets weighing from 80 to 100 lbs. Their weapons were a spear and a sword, and in warfare they carried shields with a supply of bamboo spikes. Adultery, robbery and murder were said to be punishable by death. They were inveterate smokers, indulged freely in rice beer and were 'not in the least fastidious about their food; cats, dogs, frogs and snakes are all acceptable'.² The ordinary clothing of both men and women was no more than a narrow piece of cloth around the loins with sometimes a sheet over the shoulders. However, in the dealings between the sexes the Garos were reputedly far more correct than their Bengali neighbours, for whom nakedness was 'abhorred as most indelicate and obscene'.³ The women, the heads of the family, wore a profusion of 'twenty or thirty strings of beads and bell-metal ornaments about their necks; in their ears brass rings of a pound weight'. Their hair was never cut but wound up in knots with a piece of cloth. As with many other tribesmen, their troubles were 'attributed to some evil spirit whom they try to propitiate by sacrifices'. Although the tribe was divided into many clans, they were not independent of each other, and the chiefs of the respective clans assembled in council to come to decisions.⁴

At the time of the British arrival in Assam, the Garos terrorised the people of the plains. The zamindars (landholders) of the marches were expected to restrain Garo incursions but it was soon found that the tyranny and exactions of the zamindars were the chief cause of the violence. Reports of Garo raids occurred in 1847, 1852 and 1856, and continued up to 1859. Henry Hopkinson, appointed agent to the governor-general and commissioner of Assam in February 1861, was not satisfied with the system of sending occasional punitive expeditions from Goalpara, declaring,

> Sometimes we (British) must employ coercion, pure and simple, sometimes blockades; very often a judicious system of subsiding will keep tribes quiet for a long time; but still the surest foundation on which to build our control over them will be their fear of us. It is not coercion that has often failed us but failure to coerce.⁵

In Hopkinson's view the annexation of Assam could not be considered as complete without some form of territorial acquisition in the hills, since the government had assumed the obligation of protecting the life and property of its subjects. The idea of embarking upon a 'forward policy' to contain the turbulent frontier tribes gained momentum and subsequent approval from the Government of India. It was therefore decided to place the whole tract under a special civil commissioner who would supervise the collection of the rents from the Garo villages and abolish the levies exacted by the zamindars on hill produce. The Garo villages were paid compensation, the government recouping itself by means of a special house assessment.

These measures proved quite ineffectual and the Garos failed to pay the promised tribute with any regularity. In 1869 it was decided to appoint an officer in charge of the hills and the area was designated a separate district with headquarters at Tura. The change was immediately successful as far as the villages within the administered area were concerned, but some of the more remote settlements continued to give trouble and in the cold season of 1872–73 it took three detachments of police to cover the region before all resistance was overcome. Responsible headmen were appointed, and peaceful administration established, the justification being as elsewhere that the Garo Hills had been annexed on security grounds, in this case without mention of the access to the coal resources in the area.[6]

The Lushais

In the southeast corner of Assam, sandwiched between the Indian state of Hill Tipperah and Burma and south of the Cachar Valley were the Lushai Hills, where the original inhabitants were Kukis, who lived also in southwestern Manipur and the eastern part of Hill Tipperah. Originally 'of savage nature and marauding spirit' during the early years of the nineteenth century, they emerged from the Lushai Hills and created havoc in the southern part of the region, supported by rumours of headhunting and cannibalism.[1] Villages were plundered and the plains people fled to the northern bank of the Barak River. In turn the Kukis themselves were gradually driven northward into the plains of Cachar by the Lushais, who made their appearance on the frontier in about 1840. They appeared to be a cross between the Kukis and the Burmese and were a sturdy, animistic tribal people living off hunting, fishing, food gathering and *jhum* cultivation, while frequently raiding, plundering, kidnapping and headhunting. Robert Woodthorpe described their 'wonderful aptitude for quickly understanding anything new' and, following a British clampdown on the availability of gunpowder from Cachar and Chittagong for their aged British flintlocks, they obtained as a substitute sulphur from Burma and crystals of saltpetre from drained baskets of manure.[2] Writing in the 1880s, Alexander

Mackenzie described the Lushais as a hardworking and self-reliant race, 'the only hillmen in this quarter who can hold their own against the Angamis' and therefore possible for use as a 'buffer or screen between our more timid subjects and the Angamis'.[3]

Lushai dress consisted of one large homespun sheet of cotton passed around the body, secured on the shoulder, and a large tiger's tooth mounted in silver and hanging around the neck was much prized. Men, women and children smoked almost incessantly and there was a great fondness for the thin local wine of fermented rice and water which somewhat resembled cranberry juice. They appeared to have few diseases and Woodthorpe saw only one man marked with smallpox. As a rule, a Lushai village was situated a long way from a major source of water and in consequence they 'bathe but seldom' and were unable to manage a boat or swim.[4] Lushai houses were all gable-ended, about 18 feet long by 12 feet wide, and raised 3 or 4 feet from the ground. A chief's house was of similar construction but significantly larger, divided into one large hall with two or three sleeping rooms opening on to a passage running the whole length of the building. In addition, in the villages there was a large, barn-like building which served as the assembly house.

As the Lushais were 'great eaters of flesh', they relied heavily upon the success of their hunting excursions and there were various kinds of animal traps near the villages. Some were formed by bending down a strong sapling as a spring (which occasionally caught an unwary British expedition member) and a tiger trap was made with a rough cage of logs, open at both ends and calculated to fall upon and crush any animal passing through it. The tribe cultivated cotton, rice, corn, melons, pumpkins, yams and tobacco and 'in carrying loads or cutting jungle, the Lushais work to the cry of a continuous "haw-haw" uttered in measured time by all'. Besides manufacturing cotton cloth, they worked a little in iron and a 'rough but ingenious' forge was found in each of their villages. In Woodthorpe's view, 'with a few exceptions the Lushais impressed us very favourably. Intelligent, merry and with few wants, they were very far removed from the utterly irreclaimable savages which, prior to the Expedition, our fancy had painted.'[5]

However, despite this positive opinion, the unrestricted association which existed between British subjects in Assam and the tribes living on the frontier frequently led to quarrels and on occasions to serious disturbances, in some cases provoked by the traffic in rubber brought down by the hill populace, and in others by the opening of tea gardens beyond the borderline. The increasingly difficult life of the hills, a growing population and shortage of cultivable land forced the inhabitants of the Lushai Hills to move to the foothills where, using a cunning system of surprise and ambush, they committed regular raids and imposed taxes on terror-stricken villagers.[6] In 1871–72 there was a series of Lushai attacks on the tea gardens of Cachar and Sylhet, in the course of which many workers were wounded or killed and a Scottish girl of seven, Mary Winchester, was carried off by the tribesmen as a hostage. As a result, two columns under generals Charles Henry Brownlow and George Bourchier, accompanied by Robert Woodthorpe, advanced into the hills and succeeded in putting down the violence, crushing the Lushai villages one by one and rescuing Mary. There were few further Lushai breaches of the peace until 1889 when a raid was made on the Chittagong border and a number of captives were taken. Troops again entered the area; the captives were released and the chiefs responsible for the outrage were arrested. Military outposts were established at Aijal and Changsil in the northern part of the hills and at Lungleh in the south.

The Lushais appeared to have accepted the situation when, without warning, the tribal people near Aijal rose in a body and murdered the much-detested political officer, Captain Herbert Browne, who in the eyes of the tribal people used coercive measures to exact taxes and to instate forced labour, while also introducing the highly provocative prohibition of unlimited consumption of local beer. In less than two months the outbreak was suppressed, and the ringleaders arrested and deported. The southern portion of the hills was at first administered by the Bengal government and the northern by the chief commissioner of Assam, but on 1 April 1898 the two tracts were amalgamated under the Assam administration. The whole area was then placed in the charge of a single officer, the superintendent of the Lushai Hills.[7]

The Cacharis

Finally, in the plains rather than the hills, the Cacharis inhabited the lower Assam districts of Kamrup, Lakhimpur, Darrang and Goalpara. First-hand evidence about Cacharis came from Sidney Endle, a missionary for the London-based Society for the Propagation of the Gospel, who headed a Cachari mission in the Goalpara district. He described his flock as a hardy, industrious aboriginal race who were cheery, good-natured and well suited to all forms of outdoor labour that required strength rather than skill, due to their active habits and liberal meat-based diet, 'untrammelled by the prejudices and useless observances of the Hindus'.[1] Said to be physically superior to the Assamese, they were of normal height with 'exceedingly well-proportioned limbs'. The women had a masculine appearance, fair in complexion with broad features and 'countenances somewhat forbidding', dressing in two pieces of coarsely spun *eri* silk, one above and one below the waist. The ordinary male attire was a *dhoti* and turban of white cloth or silk. Unlike high-status, Hinduised groups who shunned alcohol consumption, most Cacharis regarded rice beer as an essential staple, forcing them onto the labour market since they brewed their rice crop rather than saving it for food. However, 'even their Bacchanalian feasts were seldom ruffled by serious quarrels', and it was only 'extreme poverty or severe oppression' which led them to crime. Adultery was regarded as a very serious offence and the adulterer became an outcast unless he was able to pay a heavy fine. Nevertheless, cases of separation were not infrequent and both husband and wife could marry again if they parted with mutual consent.[2]

Besides the Cachar district and the Chatgari division of the Darrang district, Cacharis were found all over the province in small settlements. In the hills they spoke their own language and, although those living on the plains understood Assamese, among themselves they used their own tongue. Their language was said to have no word to express a number above eight. They seldom cultivated the same piece of land for more than three years, regularly irrigated their fields, raised large crops of rice and mustard seed, and the forest provided a large quantity of stick lac. Their religion consisted of a belief in a god and evil spirits who could be appeased with sacrifices, although many Cacharis in the plains had become mildly influenced by Hindu practice. Their houses were raised on piles, built with a timber frame and bamboo floor tied together with rattan or stalks of cardamom. The whole house often consisted of only one room which served all the purposes of the family, with pigs and fowl under the floor. Assamese elites, including the last ruler, Purander Singh, played a key role in encouraging the tea industry to identify Cacharis as potential labourers and many were employed on the tea gardens where they proved to be much stronger than immigrants from Bengal, but 'extremely clanish and frequently gave the planters trouble'.[3]

GOVERNMENT POLICY TOWARDS TRIBAL PEOPLE

As the above cases demonstrate, in the wake of tribal unrest Assam proved to be a colonial testing ground for indirect rule of the hill people. In the early years of British rule, the two opposing systems of non-intervention and annexation continued side by side, but after 1857 the approach towards the hill tribes underwent a fundamental change known as the 'forward policy' advocated by Henry Hopkinson, under which the essential difference between the hill tribes and the 'plains' population was emphasised. As the hill tribes were slowly controlled one by one, the nature of indirect rule also differed from place to place. Sir Cecil Beadon, lieutenant-governor of Bengal from 1862 to 1867, suggested that a special consideration for the tribal people of the northeast was being implemented:

> A main principle to be adopted in the administration of these people when they have been made to understand and feel the power of the Government and have submitted to its authority is not to leave them in their old state, but while adopting a simple plan of Government suitable to their present condition and circumstances and interfering as little as possible with existing institutions, to extend our intercourse with them and endeavour to introduce among them civilization and order.[1]

Beadon was thus aiming to form a dual system of control, by separating the administration of the hills (based on local customs) from that of the plains (based on general law). His view that the hill people would benefit from the British decision to refrain from imposing their civil and political systems beyond the plains was supported by other colonial administrators of the northeast.

Captain T. H. Lewin, superintendent of the Chittagong Hill Tracts in the 1870s, wrote,

> Let us not govern these hills for ourselves but administer the country for the well being [sic] and happiness of the people dwelling therein ... let the people by slow degrees civilise themselves. With education open to them, and yet moving under their own laws and customs, they will turn out, not debased and miniature epitomes of Englishmen, but a new and noble type of God's creatures.[2]

The 'forward' policy was first introduced in June 1866 with the establishment of the Naga Hills district. Homelands or reserved areas for tribal peoples were established and indirect colonialism was secured through legal and administrative changes whereby a political officer or resident was given the responsibility for setting up native courts in every district, utilising what the British defined as native law and customs. By treaties and engagements, the clan representatives of the tribes were encouraged to place themselves under the protection of the imperial authority and to run the administration of their respective areas on behalf of the British. It was evident that the Naga question in particular had to be taken up sooner or later and conclusively settled to avoid the constant trouble in the region. With a sympathy lacking in many of his fellow countrymen, Samuel Peal commented of the Nagas,

> They seem to need a combination of the autocratic and patriarchal, – an essentially personal as distinguished from a Departmental Government, with its cloud of Babus, a race morally detested by the Nagas and such-like tribes (and with reason). This indispensable element of personal regard our Government seems to systematically ignore, the most potent tie which can connect us with these people is frequently and recklessly severed, with results that act disastrously on them. Yet, instead of blaming ourselves, who should know better, we blame the savage, and wonder at the result. In time no doubt these people might be educated and understand us and our institutions, but in the meantime they need

an intelligent Chief over them, rather than a department, and one not changed for every little frivolous pretext, but one who will elect to live and die among them and work for them. From being a set of treacherous and turbulent races, they would become a prolific source from which our Indian army could recruit most valuable and trustworthy material.[3]

In line with Peal's views, the government appointment of a 'personal' political agent and his staff in the Naga Hills district proved largely successful over time. The Nagas appeared to be more responsive than other tribal peoples to attempts to modify those cultural practices that did not conform to British mores. With the termination of headhunting, slavery and inter-village warfare, relations gradually became more peaceful, leading to marriage alliances between different clans, villages and tribes.

As the form of governance of the hill territory of northeast India changed to indirect rule, colonial administrators produced two policies to exert their control over the region more efficiently: one to deal with security issues and the other to preserve the cultural identity of the tribesmen. Firstly, through the Bengal Eastern Frontier Regulation of 1873, as a measure 'for the peace and government of certain districts on the Eastern frontier of Bengal', the Inner Line system was introduced, professedly to protect minority indigenous groups in the hill areas of Assam by restricting the entry, business activities, land transactions and settlement of outsiders. In the Lushai Hills in particular, regulation protected the inhabitants from commercial exploitation of land and forest resources by intruders such as Bengali traders and Assamese farmers. No British subject or member of certain classes of foreign residents was able to pass over the Line without a licence or pass issued by the deputy commissioner, containing such conditions as might seem necessary. Any non-tribal missionary, explorer, traveller, businessman, woodcutter, hunter or honey collector was to seek written permission to enter designated areas. Planters were not allowed to acquire land beyond the Inner Line, either from the government or from any local chief or tribe. As it was not always convenient to define the actual boundary of British possession, the Line did not necessarily indicate the territorial frontier but only the limits of the administered area along the northern, eastern and southeastern borders of the Brahmaputra Valley and did not in any way determine the sovereignty of the territory beyond.[4]

By restricting the entry of their subjects, the government reduced the risk to lives from attacks by tribal members. The legislation undoubtedly served colonial interests in other ways. It restricted the extension of the trade activities of the plainspeople into the areas across the Line, where it was extremely difficult to collect taxes. In addition, by the start of the 1870s the economy of Assam was showing promise in the growth of the tea, petroleum, coal, rubber and timber industries, and its success depended upon the administration's ability to maintain law and order throughout the province. All the districts of the Assam Valley bordered upon hills inhabited by tribes whose unrestricted intercourse with Europeans who knew little about tribal practice led to many disputes, sometimes of a violent nature. The Line was also viewed as a traffic regulation for the native population of the valley. The hill tribes were forced at times to travel to the plains to draw supplies and the interaction between the tribal people and the *ryots* (tenant farmers) and Assamese businessmen of the plains frequently caused problems. The creation of a barrier between the hills and the plains was seen as a way to 'reduce contact and consequently friction between the civilized valley-dwellers and the primitive hill tribes'.[5]

Secondly, allegedly to preserve the cultural identity of its inhabitants, the hill territory of the province was demarcated into Excluded Areas and Partly Excluded Areas under the Government of India Act of 1935. The former areas were to be directly ruled under British jurisdiction and the latter were given a system of limited representation under British administrative control. The Northeast Frontier Tracts, the districts of the Naga Hills and the Lushai Hills, and the North Cachar Hills subdivision of the Cachar district were designated as the Excluded Areas. The Garo Hills district, the Mikir Hills, the British portions of the Khasi and the Jaintia Hills district, and the Shillong Municipality and

Cantonment were classified as the Partially Excluded areas. The Partially Excluded areas had few restrictions. These territories were located on the southern and western boundaries of Assam where the terrain was not as rugged as that of the Excluded Areas. The tribes in the valley had a more intimate economic and political contact with the plainspeople of Assam and were more westernised than those within the Excluded Areas, however they did not entirely benefit from the demarcation of territory. The areas not covered by the Inner Line Regulation saw a change in the demographic ratio between the populations of the local tribal people and the plainspeople. Not only the political administration but also the economy of the area slipped gradually under the control of the latter, who were more educated and had better familiarity and links with markets in other parts of the country.[6]

The differential treatment of the people on the hills and in the plains by British officers was guided by the different perception of the two categories. The hill tribes were described by Sir Robert Reid, governor of Assam from 1937 to 1942, as 'not Indians in any sense of the word, neither in origin, nor in language, nor in appearance, nor in habits, nor in outlook and it is by historical accident that they have been tacked on to an Indian Province'.[7] The British wished to keep the tribes under the Excluded Areas segregated from the influence of the Assam plainspeople by arguing that the latter would exploit the tribesmen to their detriment. Because they were tribal domains, the Excluded Areas were seen as 'protected enclaves' which under British protection would allow tribal peoples to practise clan-based 'customary practices' and prevent the assimilation of tribal culture and tradition by strangers. However, there was a negative side to the operation of the Excluded Areas legislation which, as Chanda Kumar Sharma has observed, 'enabled the administration to control the people in the hills while appearing to show paternalistic concern for their customs and livelihood'.[8] Soon all outsiders in the hills who were considered undesirable by the British were removed and most of the tribal indigenous communities became permanently separated from developments taking place elsewhere. Social mobility and assimilation processes were halted, and tribal and non-tribal differences became ossified. Under the new regime, neither the proprietary rights of excluded local peoples nor the traditional use of land were observed. Rights over land were only recognised when it was privately owned and the owners either through their own labour or by hiring others brought specific enclosures under settled cultivation. Such regulation conflicted with the itinerant lifestyle of *jhum* cultivation used by many hill communities, whereby one plot was often left vacant for several years.

The two policies were widely criticised for sowing the seeds of separation and isolation in the region, treating the northeast separately from other areas of British India and thereby creating a problem for national formation and integration into an independent India after 1947. In the twentieth century, negative views emerged from modernising and assimilationist nationalists who asserted that the exclusionary thrust of British policy in the nineteenth century was part of a colonial design to 'divide and rule'. An example cited was the enlistment of Manipuris, Cacharis, Kukis and Assamese for use as soldiers and porters when subjugating the Nagas[9] and the subsequent relocation of armed non-Nagas such as Kukis on rent-free Naga ancestral land.[10] It was also suggested that the purpose of the Inner Line was not to preserve the tribal way of life in a burst of ethnological responsibility but to preserve the strategic British stranglehold on the newly dominated areas of the plains for commercial purposes, such as the acquisition of land for plantations. At the same time, removing the requirement to invest in the development of the sizeable swathe of tribal territory beyond the Line considerably lessened the financial burden incurred by the government of Assam in its administration of the region. Beyond question is the fact that the lack of progress in the hills soon came to carry a stigma. Under the Government of India Act 1919, it was stated that the governor-general in council reserved the right to declare any territory in British India to be a backward area and almost all the hill districts including the Lushai Hills were renamed the 'backward tracts'. The unequivocally pejorative idea of 'backwardness' thus became inscribed in the official designation of the region.[11]

More positively, the unification of the Naga tribes under a centralised administration and the recognition of a common ethnic origin became the basic framework for the formation and growth of Naga identity and political consciousness. In addition, the contribution of Christian missionaries in the field of education and health aided the creation of tribal leadership which later played a crucial role in the political processes of an independent India. After independence, when the distinct states of Arunachal Pradesh, Nagaland, Mizoram and Meghalaya were formed, tribal leaders sought to continue and even strengthen the exclusionary laws. The Inner Line and its restrictions came to be regarded as the only effective mechanism for the protection of tribal identity and culture, even though both the colonial policy of preservation and the post-colonial policy of culturally defined states created problems. As Sanjib Baruah points out, 'The assumption that there are exclusive, territorially based ethnic groups that can all be given autonomy in their regions does not appear to work in a context such as northeast India', where the states are hardly culturally homogeneous and where signs of significant tension have grown between ethnic groups. Furthermore, the legacy of exclusionary policies was not helpful in those areas that did not historically benefit from such policies and absorbed the bulk of immigration, such as the plains of Assam where nativist movements also demanded exclusionary rules. In Baruah's view, 'cultural survival in these areas would depend on developing inclusive and pluralistic definitions of their cultures, not on exclusionary models'.[12]

4

Trade and Industry

The state of the economy of Assam in the pre-colonial period was on the whole prosperous. The French traveller Jean-Baptiste Tavernier, who came to India in 1640, declared that 'the kingdom of Assam is one of the best countries in Asia, for it produces all things necessary for human subsistence, without any need of foreign supply. There are in it mines of gold, silver, steel, iron and a great store of silk.'[1] During this period agricultural products were sufficient to meet the requirements of the people, industry and crafts were developed and the village was the centre of the economic system. A considerable volume of trade was carried out between the Ahom and neighbouring provinces and commercial relations existed with tribes such as the Garos, Nagas and Miris. A limited trade also existed with Bengal due to the low availability of salt in Assam.[2] However, within a few years of British control, a process of deindustrialisation took place as a conscious policy was pursued by the Raj to extract raw materials from India to feed growing industries in England and to promote a market for English products in India. The task was made easier on one hand by the disappearance of the native courts, which had been the main patrons of local arts and handicrafts, and on the other by the chaos which followed the internal disorders in the kingdom and the occupation of the province by the Burmese.

Trade and Industry

Although it appeared that colonial investment deliberately bypassed the local manufacture of products which would have been in direct competition with British imports, it is unlikely that the Assamese economy as a whole would have progressed at the rate experienced in other parts of India without the specifically targeted use of colonial capital. The reality was that such capital would not have been forthcoming without the promise of returns on investment which were guaranteed by a boost to the home market. In his study of nineteenth-century Indian economic history, Morris D. Morris controversially suggests that the colonial government acted as 'a benevolent night watchman'. In his view, the lack of industrial development prior to British investment resulted from the fact that there was not enough demand for machine goods, the average per capita income was low, there was an availability of cheap labour that hindered mechanisation, and, finally, a scarcity of capital existed.[3] However, Amiya Bagchi, following the observations of the economist and political writer Josiah Tucker in the 1750s, points out that far from remaining a 'night watchman', a richer country would be unlikely to lose the economic advantage over a poorer one, with better implements, better infrastructure, a more extended trading network and more productive agriculture. The larger markets of the richer country would provide scope for greater division of labour and a greater variety of products. Moreover, it would attract the able and more knowledgeable workers due to higher incomes and better opportunities.[4] With the annexation of Assam, political control accelerated the mobilisation of the province's resources and ensured the security of British capital investment.

The history of the formidable rise in colonial activity in Assam during the nineteenth century is inextricably linked with the history of the Marwari business community in the region. Assam's transition to a colonial economy involved the monetization of the revenue system, the extension of a market economy, and limited industrialisation in the extraction of resources based on wage labour. The missing link was a community of traders, and in the absence of a traditional mercantile class it was the

Marwaris (locally known as Keyas) who, having migrated from Rajputana, participated in the vast majority of the commercial activities of Assam and created a chain of markets or *golas* throughout the entire province. Marwari agents mainly acted as intermediaries between domestic producers and consumers, and foreign exporters and importers.[5] By the late nineteenth century they controlled the wholesale trade in Assam's unique *muga* and *eri* silks, cotton, metalware and rubber, and were granted the rights to sell opium. In addition, Marwari merchants enjoyed a lucrative trade with the hill tribes, bartering salt and other necessities for lac, gold dust, ivory and other products from the hills.[6] Links between Assam and Calcutta through important Marwari firms meant that traders also provided credit, not only to the indebted cultivator who could ill afford the extortionate repayments, but also to British owned plantations which had head offices in Calcutta. In this way Marwari business houses actually financed a large proportion of the tea trade, although they did not directly export tea out of Assam.[7]

To colonial officials the dubious usurious practice adopted by the Marwaris contributed substantially to the accumulation of surplus capital among their own kind, which was largely returned to Rajputana and in no way contributed to the prosperity of Assam.[8] However, it could be argued that in many ways the Marwaris were no more culpable than the British in their pursuit of financial gain at the expense of the local economy. In the view of the economic historian Tirthankar Roy, the moneylenders' exploitative power has been exaggerated in that they took considerable risks in lending to impoverished clients engaged in unstable livelihoods.[9]

TEA

The Tea Trade

In the nineteenth century the origin of tea in India was a disputed point. The botanical name *Thea chinensis* evidently pointed to China as the native home of tea. However, tea had never been seen or heard of in a wild state in China, whereas it was known to grow wild in Assam, Cachar, Sylhet and other parts of India. In any case, even if not a native of the country, when eventually successfully cultivated throughout much of India it came to be considered 'a thriving and thoroughly naturalized colonist'.[1] Originally the tribes on the northern border had made use of the indigenous tea plant to trade with the Bhutanese. They manufactured the leaves roughly, simply drying and packing them in large bamboos, and a *seer* of tea (2 lbs) realised from 10 to 12 rupees in Lhasa. In 1823 the Scottish merchant Robert Bruce, with the help of the Singpho chief Beesa Gaum, discovered that tea was growing wild in the north of the Brahmaputra Valley and an arrangement was made whereby plants and seeds would be supplied for scientific examination. Robert Bruce died shortly afterwards, never having seen the plant properly classified. It was not until the early 1830s that his brother, Charles, commanding a division of gunboats and ordered up to Sadiya, could arrange for leaves from the Assam tea bush to be sent to the Botanic Gardens in Calcutta for examination. There the plant, a hardy evergreen with white flowers, was finally identified as a variety of tea, or *Camellia siniensis var assamica*. When Lord William Bentinck became governor-general of India in 1834, the viability of tea production on a large scale was investigated. The subject of the cultivation of tea in various parts of India was brought before his council and a committee was appointed to devise a plan for developing the industry.

Trade in tea was the most profitable ingredient of the East India Company's commerce with Asia and through its tea exports from China the Company supplied a rapidly growing western demand. However, with the British espousal of free trade, the Company's monopoly over the China tea trade was abolished under the 1833 Charter Act. At the same time clashes with the Chinese Qing state over the Company's involvement in opium trading made Chinese commerce increasingly unreliable and within the British mercantile community there was a strong feeling that a better guarantee of significant supplies of tea should be found to satisfy the home market. As tea became increasingly popular, the plant's provenance and propagation were studied in depth, and British administrators and botanists became convinced that Chinese experts and the China plant were essential to start the Indian tea industry. An envoy was sent to China to procure plants and labourers to establish tea operations and Dr Nathaniel Wallich with assistant surgeons John McLelland and William Griffith were consigned to Sadiya in 1835 to carry out research.[2] At the suggestion of Francis Jenkins, Charles Bruce was put in charge of the tea nurseries and 20,000 plants and a small number of Chinese workers were sent up to him. Only 8,000 plants were living when they reached their destination and of these none survived.

Subsequently Bruce discovered large tracts covered by indigenous tea plants in the more remote regions of the province. He established friendly relations with hill tribes and their chiefs, through whom forests and wastelands were placed at the disposal of the government. By 1837 Bruce had a consignment delivered to the tea committee in Delhi consisting of forty-six chests filled with tea from indigenous plants, and eight chests weighing 350 lbs were sent to be auctioned in London in January 1838 at a record price of 21 to 38 shillings per pound (about twenty times the usual price for China tea).[3] The general opinion was that the quality of the tea undeniably confirmed the success of the experiment. It was described as 'tea, good, middling, strong, high burnt, rather smoky, Pekoe kind, and if there was any deficiency in the character, it arose from want of care in the preparation, rather than from the quality of the plant'.

In William Robinson's firmly optimistic opinion, with the certainty of a ready market in Britain investment in Assamese, tea

> almost ceases to deserve the name of a speculation, and becomes rather a prudent investment of capital, which at the same time that it offers to all concerned in it, the certainty of a fair profit, develops the vast resources of a territory hitherto unproductive, and will add another to the many fine examples of British mercantile enterprise, which no less than the brilliant achievements of her Nelson and her Wellington, have placed Great Britain in the eminent position she occupies in the rank of nations.[4]

The result of this success was the formation of two companies, one in England and one in Calcutta, which were subsequently amalgamated under the name of the Assam Company. The company was formed in England in February 1839 with a capital of £500,000 in 10,000 shares of £50 each; 8,000 shares were set apart for allotment in England and 2,000 for allotment in India.[5] The current governor-general, Lord Auckland, authorised the transfer of two-thirds of the government plantations, comprising 70,000 acres, to the company. In 1840 it produced 300 chests of tea and the government factories supplied 200. The first few years of the Assam Company's operations were disappointing, and mismanagement reduced the company to the verge of bankruptcy, however by 1852 it had recovered sufficiently to be able to pay a dividend on a crop of 267,000 lbs. The price of tea rose and applicants for 'wasteland' multiplied. The idea of this category of land was to become highly contentious. Land abundance in pre-colonial Assam had allowed many communities to follow an itinerant lifestyle of *jhum* cultivation, often leaving one plot vacant for several years. This practice permitted colonial rulers to define pockets of shifting cultivation as wasteland, whether or not it was infertile. The 1838 Wasteland Rules barred local people from cultivating idle or fallow ground, resulting in restricted access for hunting, fishing and *jhum* cultivation.[6] With the development of the tea industry, access to land became critical and it became possible for the British to allocate increasingly large areas in this way.

Government grant rules were most liberal: forest lands were rent-free for twenty years, high grass tracts rent-free for ten years and one-fourth of the wasteland area rent-free forever. Moreover, the ceiling of such grants was adjusted from time to time to attract more speculators to take up wasteland.[7] In 1853 the terms of land grants were broadened to give ninety-nine-year leases and the minimum area for grant was raised to 500 acres. Applications were made for 1,000, 1,500 or more acres by parties who had neither the means nor the intention of bringing more than a few hundred under cultivation.[8] In 1862 the Fee Simple rules offered outright sale of land at highly concessional rates with permanent, heritable and transferable rights and in that year 71,218 acres were appropriated for tea cultivation (18,322 actually under tea) with a crop estimated at 1,788,737 lbs. In 1865, according to the official report of Henry Hopkinson, commissioner of Assam, there were 366 tea estates, nineteen of which belonged to limited companies, and the estimated outturn of tea was 3,226,756 lbs. The number of imported men, women and children was 36,258.[9]

Tea planting at this time was in a state of great prosperity. Speculation ran high and unreal prices were paid for even the poorest acreage. The government began to look eagerly for its share of the spoils and new rules were made fixing the lowest rate of wasteland at Rs 2–8 an acre. Soon afterwards it was only permitted to sell land at auction and competition often forced prices up to Rs 20, 30 and even 40 for dense jungle which had never been tamed. Indians also came forward as 'brisk competitors with these interlopers of their native soil', not generally for cultivation but for speculation. The early planters, who got their estates for the asking, frequently displacing indigenous inhabitants, were enriched by these 'halcyon days'. A young man after a few years of successful tea planting could return home permanently with an ample fortune. Others with a small expenditure could open out a few acres with seedlings, forming part of a large tract of wasteland, before becoming a shareholder in a company at immense profit. River steamers had cabins full of young men from England or Scotland either in search of a tea garden for themselves or sent as relatives of tea proprietors to take charge of a garden, eager for the high salaries on offer but 'often with a fitness for nothing except to bring disaster on the proprietors'.[10] From only six registered companies and fifty-one tea gardens in operation by 1860, 'tea mania' – marked by the doubling of tea prices and soaring profits – caused the number of tea-producing companies to rise to eighty-six by the end of the boom in 1865.[11]

However, tea interests could not endure such reckless speculation and a general collapse in the market was the outcome. Factories were closed and young men forced to beg their passage out of India. Thomas Kinney, who wrote contemporary sketches on plantation life, recalled how when he first arrived in Assam as a young man land that was 'hastily cleared, and a lot of seed shoved in anyhow, was called a garden ... a few of these gardens were thrown into the market with a flaming prospectus, and a company formed to work the gold mine'. Speculators poured into tea in

> one heterogeneous mass ... Dividends were paid out of capital to keep the shares up in the market till the originators of these fine schemes could sell out quietly; the hastily cleared gardens relapsed into jungle, or the untrained planters made nothing but red leaf. Finally the inevitable collapse came and shoals of planters were thrown out of employ; many of them dependent on the kindness and charity of the steamer captains for a free passage back to civilisation.[12]

Only those Europeans who had operated prudently were able to survive with difficulty and prosper once more in the 1880s, when tea cultivation in Assam rapidly spread to become the chief industry of the province, encompassing more than 80,000 acres and giving employment to more than 600 managers and assistants, and between 200,000 and 300,000 labourers. The industry was also the main support of two lines of steamers running weekly to and from Calcutta. The India General Steam Navigation Company and the Rivers Steam Navigation Company maintained a rivalry which was of great convenience to the tea planters, ensuring regularity (as far as the river allowed), speedier transit and a fixed price for cargo. In the 1880s Indian tea supplied one-third of the consumption of Great Britain and markets were rapidly opening in Australia, the United States and latterly in Europe. In 1888 the Indian product outstripped China tea for the first time. By the end of the century, plantation owners in Assam had acquired just under half a million acres of land: the area under tea cultivation increased from 26,853 acres in 1872 to 204,285 acres in 1900, and production increased from 6,150,764 lbs in 1872 to 75,125,176 lbs in 1900.[13]

The value of land depended upon the quality of its soil, the amount and type of jungle growing upon it and the distance from the nearest station or accessibility to a high road or river. The timber on the property was the most valuable consideration, being of great importance to the planter in building his bungalow, tea houses, 'lines' for coolie dwellings and making charcoal. Another necessity in choosing a site was good water for distribution to prevent epidemics and general ill health among the workers. Rent at first was merely a nominal sum as the land was valueless until cleared, a costly process requiring much labour. The greatest drawback in the system of acquiring land was the difficulty of obtaining a site, incurring considerable trouble and expense. After much travel and time wasted in finding a favourable location in which to start a garden, the applicant would send in a written application for a lease. Measurements would be taken and due notice advertised of the intended letting. On an appointed day the lease would be put up for sale by auction to the highest bidder, at which time men living in the neighbourhood, if they objected to the new arrival or were 'churlishly disposed', could combine to buy up the plot even if they had no intention of making use of it.[14]

In opening out a new garden, there was considerable outlay in buildings and other expenses. The expenses of the first clearance with the necessary buildings, irrespective of the price of the land, was estimated at an average of 80 rupees an acre; for the second and third year it was 70 rupees.[15] Clearing tree jungle for tea planting was a most difficult task. The more productive tea clearings in upper Assam were often situated at considerable distances from each other and the early planters spent much of their time travelling from one patch of tea to another to supervise the work. The only means of travel was by country boats, by dugout canoe along the numerous tributary rivers, or on the backs of elephants. Life was hazardous for those involved in the early years. Hostile neighbourhood tribal communities, wild animals and poisonous snakes, an unhealthy climate and disease and a lack of medical facilities took a heavy toll of lives among the planting pioneers. The Chinese workers initially recruited to work in the gardens, whose expectations about work and livelihood stemmed from long-standing networks in southeast Asia, resented the employment practices of the Assam Company, and proved unable to perform the more gruelling tasks due to physical debilitation and disease. As a result, manual labour was initially undertaken by upper Assamese indigenous inhabitants, such as the Nagas, and subsequently under contracts with the Assamese to clear the land per acre.[16]

Throughout the latter part of the nineteenth century much resentment existed over government attitude towards the tea industry. The Government of India profited immensely from the growth of tea cultivation in the province yet was painfully slow in helping planters out of their difficulties or taking the necessary steps to help the enterprise. Good roads and bridges (destroyed vigorously by the combination of white ants and rains) were sadly neglected and some planters were completely isolated from the outside world for months during the rainy season, lacking a riding path through the jungle or any means of crossing a deep river.[17] An illustration was given highlighting the difficulties experienced owing to the absence of satisfactory transportation links: a boiler was required for a tea estate situated beyond a riverbank. Shipped from London to Calcutta, it was put aboard one of the steamers on the Brahmaputra. Sealed and thrown overboard, it was floated up a tributary river, and then a stream. Three miles of solid virgin rainforest then barred the way. A road was cut and paved with felled trees. A team of elephants took ten days to bring the boiler to the site of the factory and only then did the teahouse become power driven.[18]

The Tea Garden

The best soil for a tea garden was a yellow, light, sandy loam on rolling ground that readily drained any excess water, and forestland was better than grassland. After the ground was cleared, hoes with an 8-inch-wide blade and a long handle were brought in to turn up the soil and bury what jungle remained on the surface. When the soil had been hoed deeply, transplanting from the nursery began. Holes were prepared at equal distances, into which the young plants were carefully transferred by women and children. The plants were placed in a cleared area and kept carefully hoed and pruned until the third year, when the new shoots were plucked for manufacture. They were able to thrive successfully if the weather was favourable, but a succession of hot days with no rain had a disastrous effect on transplants and only a small percentage could be saved.

In the third year the plant began to yield a crop of 80 lbs to the acre, in the fourth year 160 lbs, in the fifth year 240 lbs and in the sixth year, when in full bearing, from 500 to 800 lbs of manufactured tea per acre. The bushes continue to yield at the same rate for twenty years or more, when the yield began to decrease. The leaf was plucked as often as the bushes 'flushed', or threw out new shoots, which ordinarily occurred every ten to fifteen days from the first of March until the middle of November when the plant was comparatively dormant.[1] According to Robinson, the weather was said to have a great influence on the quality of the leaves:

> If there is too much rain, they will become mildewed and broken, of a yellow colour, thin and sickly; if too little, they will be small in size, and the foliage not at all abundant. But if the rains fall equably, and after the showers a bright sun appears, the leaves will be numerous and flourishing, of a bright green colour and luxuriant texture, and the flavour superior.[2]

A heavy hailstorm was seen as a serious threat, cutting the young shoots and leaves from tea bushes 'as cleanly as if they had been lopped with a pruning-knife', causing damage from which a garden would not recover for a considerable period. Among other enemies of the tea bush were 'blight, red spider, bad drainage, too much sun or too much rain (both equally disastrous)'. Bad blight or red spider had the effect of throwing back the plant and depriving the garden of two or three flushes, a serious consideration at the outset of the fifth year when there were hopes of recouping some of the former financial outlay.[3] During the dormant season the bush was pruned to about 2½ feet and to the shape most conducive to producing a large quantity of leaf. The top was levelled to a tabular shape to present a broad surface of new shoots. To Susan Ward, 'a Tea garden in full bearing, clean and well kept, with its regular rows of bright green stretching off in the distance without interruption over hundreds of acres of waving land, is one of the most beautiful sights in the world'.[4]

Those proprietors who could afford to wait for the returns of the season's crop usually sent their tea direct to England, but by far the largest proportion of Assam tea was sold by agents in Calcutta at auction and some companies were so pressed for funds that they drew advances on the season's crop. It became evident that tea planters who worked chiefly through Calcutta agents were heavily handicapped. A bad season or two, a long spell of low prices, or any other cause which might reduce the value of the produce of the garden threw the planter almost entirely into the agent's hands and he could be 'swallowed up' while his garden was either abandoned or flourished in the hands of its new owners, the men of capital. However, to Thomas Kinney not all Calcutta agents were 'tea-garden devouring monsters, crunching the bones of confiding planters, and assimilating hundreds of acres of smiling cultivation which are the result of the labour and outlay of others'. Agency firms often 'propped up tottering concerns, or tided stranded proprietors over shallows' and it was only natural that, when it was clear that the stranded or shaky proprietor could no longer be kept going, they should step forward to reap the benefits of their previous efforts to keep the concern alive.[5]

The work in the garden was extremely taxing for all concerned. The planter usually rose early and after a *chota hazree* – a small breakfast of tea and toast – spent from three to five hours in a walk or ride over the plantation, inspecting the work and giving general instructions to the *sirdars*, or headmen, of the garden who arranged the order of picking for the following day. Each *sirdar* had a certain number of men or women to oversee and was responsible for their hoeing or plucking. His charges were occasionally 'very wilful, and pluck according to their own inclinations instead of carrying out instructions, bringing coarse leaf when fine only is required and doing anything to fill their baskets'. He paraded up and down between rows of tea bushes, armed with a small stick and, with the dignity that his position of authority gave him, shouted at the top of his voice to the pickers, encouraging or swearing and always inciting them to make haste.[6] A *sirdar* achieved his proud role either through being one of the oldest and most trusted workers on the estate, or by having successfully recruited a party of coolies from his homeland. He was held in respect as he had the ear of the sahib and the power to make matters decidedly uncomfortable for any individual who challenged his authority.[7]

During the rains, the gong was beaten at five o'clock every morning and again at six, allowing an hour for those who wished to eat before starting the daily work on the land. In the cold weather the time for turning out was not so early. After the second gong the women, provided with baskets in which to put the leaf, were marshalled by the sirdars and conducted to the part of the garden that was to be plucked. The process of plucking was a great deal more complicated than it looked. The plant required delicate handling and the shoots were nipped off by catching the leaves between forefinger and thumb and cleanly taken off with a dexterous turn of the wrist. The tip and two leaves were taken, the lowest leaf down the stem being extracted in such a way that its stalk was left attached to the main stem, where the new shoot formed, producing another flush in twelve to fifteen days. A great mistake was made by eager planters plucking heavily at the beginning of a season, producing fine tea which was attractive to look at when manufactured and tasty when infused but limited in quantity; the plant, weakened by the strain put upon it too early in the season, proved unable to fulfil its quota during the period for heavy plucking and remained in a weak condition.

By eleven o'clock, the leaf collected by the women was collected and weighed. If there was a good flush on the bush, it was not unusual for them to bring in ten *seers*[8] of leaf each, which was 'no light weight to carry about on a hot day'. By then most of the men had finished their allotted day's work to retire to their huts to eat the morning meal and 'pass the remainder of the day in a luxury of idleness'. At two o'clock the women were turned out again to pluck and those men who had not finished their hoeing returned to complete their task. At about six o'clock the gong sounded again, the leaf was brought in and weighed, and outdoor work was over for the day.[9]

However, in the teahouse, described by Kinney as 'a fearful place' due to the intense heat, the 'damp exuding from the tea leaf, and the peculiar aroma of the tea in its various stages', work continued steadily and, if there had been much leaf picked the day before, firing could last from daybreak until the small hours of the morning.[10] After the leaf had been brought in, it was thinly spread over bamboo frames, covered with close-meshed wire netting and left on racks in a well-ventilated area where it completed the process of withering in order to make the leaf soft and supple before it was rolled. Withering usually took from ten to twenty hours, although after rain the process was slowed by the amount of moisture which needed to evaporate to allow the work to start. Particularly in August, activity in the teahouse was relentless. The planter's assistant would arrive at four or five in the morning to see if the leaf was sufficiently withered to begin rolling. The tea *sirdars* came in at about the same time, then the *teklas* (labourers) appeared and the leaf was weighed out at around 20 *seers* per man. Squatting on a mat on the floor, the *teklas* took a mass of leaf and rolled it about under their hands and arms until it became perfectly flaccid. Then smaller lumps of leaf were taken up to the rolling tables and manipulated with both hands to put a good 'twist' on the leaf. As the nineteenth century progressed, this process was increasingly undertaken by rolling machines, which were expensive items for a tea garden to purchase although, in the light of the cost of coolie or Assamese labour, a machine paid for itself in a very short time.[11] After all the leaf had been rolled – a process seldom finished before noon and often much later if the leaf was unusually wet – it was spread in thin layers on mats and turned over from time to time. As the leaf fermented when exposed to air, a change of colour resulted. First the bright green disappeared, to be replaced by a greenish yellow, then a dirty yellow, succeeded by a bright copper colour. Great differences of opinion existed as to when the leaf was ready for the next process of firing and much depended on the quality of the leaf. The coarser and harder kinds of China tea required more withering, more rolling and more fermenting to procure the requisite colour, whereas the soft, large-leaved indigenous or hybrid plant was easier to work.[12]

When the process of fermentation reached the required point, fires were lit under big pans, and the fermented leaf thrown into the pans where it was tossed about by a tea *sirdar*, armed with bits of bamboo, to heat it thoroughly yet not allow it to burn. When the sirdar considered that the leaf was 'cooked' he threw it out into a *dholla*, or flat circular basket, held at the side of the furnace. The steaming load was then tossed on to one of the rolling tables, along the side of which stood a row of workers. The mass was rapidly divided among them and rolled by hand in the same manner as the green leaf in the morning, but for a shorter time. Passing from hand to hand, each giving it a harder roll than the last, it went into another *dholla* at the end of the table and was carried off to the pans again, where the process was repeated. After the second rolling it was carried off to be dried, which was done over charcoal fires in small circular holes in the mud floor. Over each hole was a basketwork drum, narrow waisted and broad at the top and bottom, called a *dhol*. On top of each of these drums was a *dholla* of an open texture on which a small amount of tea was placed, thinly spread, and covered over by yet another *dholla*. Great care was taken to ensure that the fire was perfectly free from smoke from half-burnt charcoal or particles of fallen tea. From time to time the *dhol* was carefully removed from the fire, the tea was stirred around and respread and the *dhol* cautiously replaced.

The drying process was 'slow and wearisome'. Touch and smell were the only guides as to when the tea was thoroughly dried and not burnt. The tea *sirdar* had the onerous task of seeing that the firing was as perfect as possible before the dry tea was placed in a temporary bin, where it had to be weighed into a permanent container and recorded as manufactured tea the next morning.[13] The fired result now assumed the appearance that it presented on breakfast tables in England: a blue-black colour mixed with a small quantity of silvery-white thread. Women were set to work to sort out the rough leaf from the fine and remove from both the red leaf, of which there was always a small proportion however careful the manufacture. The tea was then passed through different-sized wire sieves and quality and quantity were noted. Boxes, lined with sheet lead and made in Burma, were placed in the teahouse and all the tea about to be packed was refired over fiercely hot *dhols* to remove any remaining moisture which could make the entire chest musty on the voyage. While still hot the tea was put into the chests, shaken down and weighed, then the lead lining was soldered down as quickly as possible, and the weight stamped on the outside with the garden's private mark.

The Tea Planter

The situation of a tea planter was by no means an easy one, despite the fact that he avoided most of the hard labour on a garden. Not only would such work have been physically highly challenging in the climate of India, but it would also have compromised his dignity in the eyes of the natives. The descriptions of the planter, and his ways, habits and tastes, were many and various. Kinney noted,

> The "brutal planter"; *Messieurs les "planters" du the, les sauvages*; the wild European tribes on the Northeast frontier – are just a few of the derogatory names which have been bestowed, half in jest, and half in earnest, on the men who are rapidly transforming by their capital and energy what was a wild, almost unknown

tract of jungle, into one of the most flourishing and promising provinces of the Indian empire.¹

However, as the idea that all mankind outside the European 'magic circle' of officialdom and the services was of a lower order became less acceptable, it was gradually recognised that 'education and refinement are not entirely lost and forgotten as a result of engaging in the management of a tea garden'. In Kinney's view, the planter whose chief enjoyment was torturing his coolies tended to exist only in 'some of the lower vernacular papers', but if not all planters used bestial techniques to coerce their employees into action, the financial pressure to maximise the outlay of a garden was nevertheless relentless.² Planters were constantly under pressure from tea companies to increase output. Monetary incentives, such as bonuses and commissions on profits, as well as the fear of being rendered unemployed, fuelled the drive for the intensification of the labour process, the expansion of acreage by jungle clearings and the push to keep up with higher production targets.

The Assam planter could be divided into four classes: the young man with a little capital who came out to learn tea planting with a view to investing or making a garden of his own; the 'tea expert', or Mincing Lane young man, who came out to show old hands how to make tea and found he had a great deal to learn and unlearn in the process; the youth who had sisters, cousins or aunts on the board of some flourishing company and who came out to a sort of 'covenanted' birth, and sailed serenely on to shares and success unless he turned out to be a 'particularly bad egg'; and, finally, the 'practical engineer' who came in with the development of tea machinery to look after the engine and its adjuncts and who often developed into a thoroughly practical tea planter. Although a view was held in Calcutta that the planter's life was spent chiefly at polo, race meetings and training garden ponies, there was little evidence that his was an existence of undiluted pleasure. On the contrary, he was beset by 'clod-hopping' over clearances, deep hoeing over which to tramp, daily soakings during the rains as he went about his plucking, days of parboiling in the tea house in a temperature of about 120° and, above all, unwelcome correspondence from agents or directors which required a response. In addition, many restrictions and heavy expenses were heaped upon the planter by numerous laws pertaining to land tenure and the employment of labourers. It was generally recognised that statistical figures were 'an abomination' to him, yet the government bombarded him with form after form, 'each having a more bewildering array of columns than the last', and promptly fined him if such forms were not punctually filled in and returned at the due date.[3]

To add to a planter's challenges, on many plantations it was a constant trial to keep his numerous workers supplied with food and, with an insufficient local market, hundreds of *maunds*[4] of rice were constantly being brought up on the steamers for the gardens, with dhal, salt and oil. Government regulation required the planter to supply rice at a fixed rate whatever the market price and, in addition to the high prices for steamer freight, the grain often had to be taken on a long journey on bullock carts from the landing to the garden. In 1879 prices rose due to the general failure of the rice crop and by the end of the season all the gardens faced heavy losses. In addition, despite the undeniable ability of the planters to impose starvation wages and a draconian work regime upon their migrant workers, there were constant complaints about the price of labour. From the 1860s onwards wages doubled, and in some places quadrupled, and in the rainy season coolies were virtually impossible to hire.[5] Moreover, other planters did their best to entice workers away with higher bonuses, higher rates of pay and promises of employment on work which offered double pay, and by the importation of batches of young women 'whose attractions often prove irresistible in seducing the gay and well-to-do time-expired Bengali Don Juans from neighbouring gardens'. The introduction of rules binding members of planters' associations to refrain from luring away each other's coolies resulted in the withdrawal of a significant number of planters from their respective organisations.[6]

By the end of the nineteenth century, approximately 1,000 European planters (comprising individual proprietors and managers of tea companies) were living among a population of over half a million labourers. Terms like 'coolie', primitive', 'jungly', 'slothful', 'scoundrel' and 'absconder' regularly emerged in planters' vocabulary when referring to their workers and such negative perceptions often evolved among planters at an early stage of taking up their post in Assam plantations. In George Barker's account the coolie was seen as possessing 'powers of torture' over and above the troubles inflicted by climate and insects:

> Scarcely a day passes but there is some row in the lines, whereupon the jemadar (head man in the lines) brings up the delinquents on the following morning to the bungalow, with a view to getting at the true cause of the disturbance and the punishment of the evil-doer.[7]

The sahib had to act as judge and jury, listening to the evidence brought forward or endeavouring to listen, 'as the prisoner, plaintiff, and the witnesses on both sides talk their loudest; and all at the same time'. Very complicated cases frequently arose in which a hasty decision could cause great dissatisfaction among the coolies and diplomacy was much needed to arrive at a verdict which was agreeable to all. Between *chelans* (a name given to batches of coolies who arrived together and acted in solidarity during the time that they were on the same garden) feuds constantly broke out and a decision that went against the views of a particular party would often result in a refusal to renew its agreement. As a *chelan* could number thirty or forty men, the loss to the garden would be serious.[8] To add to the woes of the planter, with the progression of the century the local source of labour increasingly dried up as Assamese peasants felt that their precarious hold on respectability might be endangered by association with 'coolie status'. For a long time, the only locals who sustained face-to-face interactions with the migrant workers were the caste Hindu Assamese and Bengali *mohurirs* (clerks/overseers), the supervisory staff on the plantations whose discipline of the labourers on behalf of the plantation's white sahib caused intense resentment. These *mohurirs* were often 'knavish and exacting' and coolies were often cheated out of a portion of their wages.[9]

In Barker's jaundiced view, 'superstition and love of drink are the two curses of the native'. Rarely a night passed in the lines without some form of festivity (no doubt to numb the unfortunate worker to his joyless circumstances) to celebrate either a marriage or a birth and during the season of native holidays and on Sundays the noise was deafening. On Monday the effects were all too apparent with many coolies down with sickness following 'a too ardent admiration for strong waters'. The situation was not helped by the desire of the government to raise money through additional liquor licences, resulting in the establishment of liquor shops outside many of the large tea gardens. This was patently unfair to the planter, who had already paid the government well for supplying the labourers on whose physical condition and powers of work his prosperity depended; and to the coolies, who 'unable to resist the temptation put in their way, spend their hardly-earned rupees in reducing themselves to the state of utter incapacity for to-morrow's work'.[10]

In addition, the tea planter's domestic and social life was hardly enviable, particularly if he was a bachelor. All the lesser stations or villages in the provinces provided a 'desultory, unenterprising race of native merchants, whose stores contained everything that is not wanted, and but few things that are'.[11] Planters generally were good sportsmen and were able to entertain with the luxuries of game pigeon, snipe and wild fowl with an occasional dish of venison. However, the vast majority of foodstuffs had to be brought up from Calcutta by river and, as steamer visits were few and far between, a planter could be reduced to 'a monotonous diet of fowls and rice washed down by river water' until the next boat came up.[12] George Barker bemoaned the fact that the only changes of food that could be depended upon were tinned provisions of all sorts, but 'American meat, jams, whole fruit preserved in bottles, sardines and such things are luxuries even to the wealthy members of the planting fraternity'.[13] The Naga expedition of 1879–80 had a particularly unpleasant effect on the supply of such goods from

Calcutta to Assam when both of the steamboat companies were requisitioned for government service and every steamer that came up the Brahmaputra was loaded with commissariat or military stores. Moreover, elephants which were in many ways indispensable for plantation work were withdrawn for use in the campaign.

The planter's bungalow was often 'a rough affair, built of the product of the jungle' if he was far away from a station, although many planters in the Assam Company had large brick houses by the 1880s. There were two main styles of bungalow. The first was simple and unimposing. It comprised a central room or hall with two other rooms, one on either side, opening out from it. A veranda ran the length of the three rooms in front and a similar veranda at the back, the two ends of which were generally enclosed as bathrooms or godowns. The central room usually had four huge posts, one at each corner, the main supports of the whole building, upon which were laid the cross beams supporting the king posts for the ridge. The walls were simply double rows of reed and were made by tying light bamboo slats horizontally from post to post, vertically laying the reeds perpendicularly on each side of the slats and tying them on with long strips of cane. The openings and frameworks for windows and doors were made by leaving a hole in the reeds and the windows were 'glazed' with a mesh of finely split bamboo with mat shutters. The floor consisted of a mud pile, raised a foot or so above the level of the ground and covered with a coarse matting of split bamboo.

The second style of bungalow was a far more pretentious building. The framework of posts and beams, and the walls and roof, were much the same but the plan was more elaborate. The rooms were all raised on a platform of short posts to a height varying from 3 to 7 or 8 feet. The lower or ground floor was generally left open but sometimes a part was enclosed to serve as an office or storeroom for factory tools and garden implements. The planked floor was reached by wooden steps, more or less grand according to circumstances. But, although the walls were usually made of reed as in the simpler bungalow, the general appearance was very different. There was a drawing room and a dining room, with perhaps a small sitting room or office, and two or three bedrooms with dressing rooms and a fine open veranda. The walls were plastered with mud and whitewashed (earthquakes could make considerable cracks in the plaster) and the smooth plank floor was covered with a superior Calcutta mat. The doors and windows were panelled and glazed. A white ceiling cloth was stretched tightly overhead, there were purdahs to the bedroom doors, curtains, a carpet, a few pictures and probably a piano in the drawing room.[14] As it was no uncommon occurrence to have 2 to 3 inches of rain in a night, bungalow roofs were frequently put to a severe test and necessitated 'an enormous thickness of thatch'.[15]

For the reasonably established planter, the number of servants required was 'at first sight appalling'. Each man had his *kitmutgar*, or waiter, to attend to his wants at dinner, 'a species of butler in fact'. But there were many more:

> a bearer to look after the bedroom and act as valet, then the khansama (cook) and his assistant, two or three pani-wallahs (water-carriers), the mater (sweeper), two chowkeydars (watchmen) one for day and one for night, punkah-wallahs (two or three for pulling the punkah during the hot weather), syces (one for each horse), malis (gardeners, according to the size of garden), moorgie-wallah (to look after the chickens), gorukhiya (cow-herd), and a few others ... There is no bell in a bungalow so servants are summoned by a call; the chowkeydar on duty being at hand, takes up the sahib's summons for the servant in question; the other servants, hearing the shouting, lend their inharmonious voices to the disturbed state of things, and the whole air echoes back the name of the man in request.[16]

Servants were either Hindus or Muslims, the latter secured in Calcutta with difficulty as it was 'no easy matter to persuade Muslim servants to leave the delights of Calcutta life to dare the wilds of Assam', and the former recruited from the better class of coolies on the garden and promoted to bungalow work. Religious prejudices emerged as soon as the native was brought into contact with the European; the Muslim's particular line of service was 'waiting at table and cooking, at which he excels, while the Hindu takes the place of house and parlour-maid, making the beds and doing the dirty work'.[17]

It was not unusual for the Bengal tiger to prowl about the planter's dwelling at night. Venomous snakes might 'ensconce themselves in a corner of his bungalow or stretch their length from the thatch roof above him'.[18] He was unable to escape from ants and was forced to have up to half a dozen cats to deal with rats and mice. During the rainy season,

> everything is damp, moist and unpleasant; clothes get spotted and musty, boots get covered with mildew; insects of marvellous forms and intensely aggravating and smelling powers, swarm round the light of an evening, and, aided by the ever voracious mosquito, make life almost unbearable in the bungalow. Outside it is worse. The roads are simply beds of slush; the high grass on either side wets you as you go through, even though it is not raining. Leeches crawl up your legs from the roots of the jungle and drop down your back from the tops of it. The soft soil of the tea garden clogs round the boots, till one can hardly lift one's feet; and over and above all, the damp, steamy, muggy heat.[19]

Comforts that the planter might have enjoyed were ignored in the haste to get rich and proprietors especially had no wish to remain longer than was necessary to make a tea garden that would sell at a large profit or yield a comfortable income.[20]

When struck by sickness, the planter tended to be dependent on 'ignorant and careless servants' and there might not be a physician within many miles other than his coolie doctor 'with whom he fears to trust his case'.[21] Exposure to sun, an everyday evil that could not be avoided, was seen as 'the foundation on which all diseases were based'. Sunstroke was said to be responsible for 'loss of memory, either temporarily or lastingly, periodical attacks of mental aberration, diverse forms of eccentricity' and, in extreme cases, death. Attacks of 'cold on the liver – a frequently fatal complaint' required the adoption of 'the native fashion of tying round the waist two or three coils of a fine silk scarf, to be worn day and night' and few Europeans during their first year escaped prickly heat, in which the sensation of 'innumerable fine needle points being thrust into the skin' resulted in the appearance of 'a boiled lobster's brilliant hues'. Fever was the most prevalent disease and newly opened gardens were especially malarious. Although comparatively few planters died, some were forced to leave while others, by taking a trip on the river, returned to many years of good health. However, in Barker's opinion, 'With quinine, chlorodyne, and a bottle of brandy, a man can do a great deal towards holding in check the various diseases that were constantly besetting him'.[22]

As every garden included a large tract of country, planters were necessarily in an isolated situation which involved great loneliness for weeks and in some cases in the rainy season for months, with no person to speak to in their own language. In the cold season the roads and bridges allowed a planter to ride a pony to neighbouring planters or to the station. It was observed that the one thing a planter needed most was a wife and family since 'rarely does the married man fall into the excesses which are common with bachelors'. In the opinion of the American missionaries in the province,

> A Planter's greatest danger lies in the influence of his surroundings ... the high moral tone of the home circle is far away, and the sacred influence of the Sabbath; he finds himself as free as the monkeys chattering among the trees to do as he pleases.[23]

The first danger was deemed to be the habit of taking 'pegs', then the gaming table and 'kindred vices follow'. The prevailing custom of offering a caller a 'peg' and the idea that it would not be polite to do otherwise was deemed the worst offence. In the view of the American Baptists, it was highly regrettable that 'the sons of Great Britain, who mostly compose the Europeans of Assam, as yet have scarcely felt the tide of temperance which has flowed over the republic of America, and converted thousands of homes to the total abstinence principle'.[24]

However, by the 1880s there were signs that there had been a marked improvement in planter society. There was more sobriety and application to work, more 'general observance of the Sabbath' and a yearly increase in the number of married planters. Married ladies frequently brought an unmarried sister or friend with them for company in their isolated home, a practice which often resulted in another marriage. Welcoming the curb that marriage gave to overindulgence, the missionary Susan Ward declared,

> We do not intend to leave the impression that the Tea Planter is more given to an erratic course than most young men under similar circumstances, but that the circumstances are especially a severe test of moral character. Among them are fine musicians, artists and scientists; few ever go beyond the bounds of moderate drinking, and it is to be hoped when temperance principles are more generally adopted, and married planters are the rule not the exception, as at present, that Assam will be truly styled 'The happy valley'.[25]

Tea Workers

There was little local labour available for the Assam tea industry. In a few well-located gardens, Mikir tribesmen, Assamese and occasionally even Nagas could be induced to work, but only spasmodically and not reliably. The Cacharis were more dependable but not very numerous. As a rule, the Assamese labourer would only work after several bad harvests when local stocks of food grains were very low and in the uncharitable view of George Barker was naturally indolent: 'While there was a sufficiency of rice, salt and vegetable to eat and a bit of hubble-bubble in the house, he was happy and cared not for the future.'[1] Moreover all local workers tended to come and go as they pleased, irrespective of whether they were Cachari seasonal migrants from lower Assam or upper Assam peasants from villages near the plantations. In 1854 the industry heaped opprobrium upon Cachari workers when the entire workforce, 'thousands in number, and all Cacharees, struck work for an increase in pay'.[2] The dispute was eventually resolved, but the employer–labour relationship had undoubtedly soured and there was an evident need for a new breed of tea worker.

Following the 1863 Transport of Native Labourers Act, the colonial state passed numerous laws to facilitate recruitment and control of Assam's migrant force. The emigrant tea workers, to whom the increasingly pejorative term of 'coolies' was applied, came from Bengal, Sontal, Chota Nagpur and other thickly settled districts. In 1884–85, 44.7 per cent were from Chota Nagpur, 27.2 per cent from Bengal, 21.6 per cent from United Provinces and Bihar, 0.2 per cent from Bombay, 0.7 per cent from Madras and 5.5 per cent from within Assam.[3] In more remote districts the 'jungly', as the Chota Nagpur coolie was called, appeared to do best in his resilience, labouring ability and resistance to disease. Coolies from the northwest and Madras were less handy at improvising and obtaining comforts for themselves under difficulties and required to be close to large bazaars. Those from the northwest had more caste prejudices and, knowing how to assert themselves, gave more trouble than the Madras coolie. It was noticeable that in general imported labour was less efficient than that of the local workforce. In Barker's view, even at their best Bengalis would not compare as tea makers to the Assamese, who 'understand what is required, work well, and seem to stand the heat better'.[4] However, with the excuse that the Assamese were 'enfeebled', the economic opportunities that existed in the valley were farmed out to cheaper imported labour for menial industrial work and a more educated layer of migrant administrative personnel in an effort to improve efficiency. Dismissed as idle and apathetic, little consideration was given to the fact that the general population of the Brahmaputra Valley had undergone great suffering under the warring remnants of the Ahom nobility and the Burmese occupation.

As Rana Behal maintains,

Tea gardens created and sustained a plantation hierarchical structure in which labour was acquired through an indenture system, characterized by 'mobilisation of a large unskilled labour force through non-market mechanism, low wages, extra-legal methods of control and large scale production through labour-intensive, low-skill methods.[5]

Plantation workers could be obtained either through existing employees who returned to their own district to recruit others, or through government agents in Calcutta. During seasons of great drought resulting in famine and disease, recruiters had no difficulty in securing as many labourers as required but with good harvests and an abundance of rice, 'nothing would beguile the Bengali from his native land'. It was then necessary to resort to government agents who procured men through a regular system of recruiting established throughout heavily populated districts (remarkably similar to kidnapping) in order that the supply of labour would rarely run short. In 1884 the price for an individual coolie, duly landed by government agents at the nearest point of disembarkation on the river, was about 90 rupees a head. When it was necessary to procure eighty or one hundred men at a time, the initial expense was deemed 'considerable and unsatisfactory', and such high costs needed to be amortised over a period long enough to make economic sense for employers. In Barker's view, if freedom of movement were granted to emigrant workers, encouraging willing labourers to be independent in seeking a livelihood, 'the authorities would benefit the whole Indian race, and prevent those disastrous famines that are for ever recurring, besides assisting an industry in which voluntary labour was badly needed'.[6]

The method of conveying coolies up country was undeniably brutal. During the cold season a party of 200 to 500 emigrants would at certain intervals leave Calcutta, under the charge of a doctor whose duty it was to accompany them throughout their voyage. They were sent overland to Goalundo by rail where they joined a steamer and journeyed upcountry. The after part of the upper deck was reserved for their so-called accommodation and 'here they are huddled together in a shameful fashion when there happens, as is of too frequent occurrence, to be an excessive number on board'. Fortunately, they travelled with little, 'a blanket, a lotah (brass pot), a hubble-bubble, and a small parcel done up in a handkerchief, containing chunam (lime) and betel-nut, a comb, and one or two other trifles dear to the Bengali's heart'. Each family, or party, took up their quarters by laying blankets stretched out one over the other, occupying a space of about 5 feet square, and when the vessel stopped, a few were given leave to go ashore to cook their food or to buy vegetables, fruit, betel nut or anything else they might need.[7] There was little compassion among their European fellow travellers. Thomas Kinney expressed great sympathy for steamer captains, with the 'multifarious papers' required for each member of his human cargo, 'the water tanks they must provide for him, and the proper scale of diet to keep him between the Scylla of starvation and Charybdis of overfeeding'.[8] Even more despicable in his description of the woes of steamer travel through Assam, the young British arrival John Carnegie bitterly complained of '500 coolies on board the dirtiest brutes in creation swarming with lice and one had cholera last night, what with coolies, mosquitoes and lice I shan't be sorry when this is at an end'.[9]

Despite inspections by doctors along the route, it was evident that the government had failed to address the inhumane conditions involved in transporting 'these poor wretches' up the river in such crowded conditions 'that all idea of a healthy atmosphere is out of the question'.[10] In the early days of tea planting the steamer decks were densely packed with men, women and children with no proper attention given to the sick and no railing to prevent those sleeping near the edge from rolling off into the river. Frequently cholera broke out with a high death rate. The missionary Anna Kay Scott, travelling on board a government steamer to which two flat boats were attached, loaded with labourers for the tea gardens, described how there were 'about five hundred of these Coolies crowded together in filth and wretchedness. The cholera is raging fearfully among them, and victim after victim is pushed off into the Ganges as soon as life is extinct. Bloated, putrid corpses are floating on the water, or are lodged among the brakes and tall jungle grass which line the low banks.'[11]

The attendant doctor could in no way alleviate the suffering of his passengers, for although the ship might be excessively overcrowded, the next steamer would not be due for another week and 'if some fearful epidemic were to break out on the coolie boat during its passage, how many would be landed alive?'[12] Of a total of 2,569 recruits who were sent down the Brahmaputra in two batches during the period from April 1861 to February 1862, as many as 135 died or drowned and 103 absconded, and of 84,915 recruits making the same journey between May 1863 and May 1866, 35,000 had died or deserted by the end of June 1866.[13] Oscar Flex, writing of his experiences as a tea planter between 1864 to 1867, described his arrival at Kokilamukh from Calcutta to discover that the elephant sent to meet him at the jetty had failed to arrive. The stranded newcomer, who had to spend a couple of nights on the riverbank, sleeping upon a bed of sacks and eating boiled rice, described how his steamer 'had also brought in a group of tea garden labourers and I was moved to pity at their plight. They were preparing to spend the night under the open sky because their manager had not come to pick them up ... I considered them to be as unfortunate victims of circumstances as I ... they were as much strangers to this land.'[14]

In 1861, an enquiry commission was formed by the government of Bengal to investigate the recruitment of emigrant labour. However, while the colonial state sought to 'protect' the interests of the labour force it also legitimised the exercise of extra-legal authority by the planters. A penal contract system, introduced in Act VI of the Bengal Council in 1865 and modified in 1882, although failing to remove any of the abuses in the recruitment system (such as the inducement to emigrate by misrepresentation, and the prevention of mortality in transit), provided for minimum monthly wages of 5 rupees for men, 4 rupees for women and 3 rupees for children, a nine-hour working day and six-day week, and a government inspector of labour empowered to cancel the contract of labourers on complaints of ill treatment.[15] But the main provision of the Act lay in the sanctions for breach of contract by labourers: planters were given powers to arrest, without warrant, labourers who absconded, and imprisonment in the plantation-erected private 'prison', or *phatak*, was the penalty for refusal to work. Labour was too precious to be sent out of a tea garden to police and jail custody.[16] Contracts between coolies and garden proprietors were initially restricted to three years' service, but in the interests of the employer this term was later extended to five years to prevent the loss of a man who at the end of three years had become inured to the climate and was skilled in garden work. Barker recounted the difficulty of persuading his workers to renew their contracts due to 'long separation from their relations' sweet society, a longing to return to their own country, illness or perverseness and a thousand and one things'.[17] However, often labourers were coerced or tricked into renewing by ruses such as employing a husband on a different length of contract to that of his wife. The justification for such blatant malpractice was well articulated by Barker who declared of his coolies,

> Lengthy personal acquaintance with their idiosyncrasies is the only means of getting to understand their management, and it is simply ridiculous to hear the remarks made by people in England, as to how they would alter the existing arrangements ... There is no similarity on any one point in the two modes of looking after European and Eastern labour, nor will any amount of theorising be able to break through the intensely practical manner in which natives have had to be dealt with for the last one hundred and fifty years.[18]

The viceroy, Lord Lansdowne, to the disgust of British liberals heartened by the improvement in the standard of employment at home, also protested strongly against the tendency to apply 'British standards to such questions as the employment of labour in mines, in factories, and in the tea gardens'.[19] Moreover a special correspondent of *The Times* reported on the benefits accrued by the 700,000 to 750,000 recruits for the Assam tea industry between 1870 and 1900, announcing enthusiastically,

> The labourer has been withdrawn from the fierce battle of millions amid the storm and stress of varying seasons into the constant shadow of prosperity and peace. He is protected from famine, from fraud, from violence, from usury, from all manner of external ills. For him and for his like alone among the poor of India the problem of life is solved.[20]

However, over and above the basic legal requirement for all employees to be provided with housing and medical treatment, there was little evidence that coolies had migrated to a life of dignity and well-being. There was usually a comfortable bungalow for the manager and, by the 1880s, a fireproof building for the teahouse. Nearby would be squalid rows of huts, the 'coolie lines', forming villages containing a maximum of 1,000 or 1,200 labourers. Housing was segregated between the different ethnic and religious groups (such as Bengalis and Cacharis) who, it was alleged, had been deliberately recruited for their diversity so that workers' struggles could not 'crystallise into a unified and organised labour movement in the Assam Valley'.[21] Although critics identified this practice as an example of British divide and rule, it seems unlikely that in any case the disparate communities would have wished a particularly close association.[22]

It was undoubtedly in the interest of planters to prevent as much loss of labour as possible and in large companies a European doctor was employed, but usually a Bengali educated in a Calcutta college attended to the sick among the workers with medicines supplied by the proprietor. The health of his workforce was not always in the hands of the planter. There was very little surplus food produced in the tea districts and the poor means of communication did not help his provisioning. One official report declared that during the years of high tea speculation 'tens of thousands of imported labourers died from disease by want of proper food, while the others were so enfeebled that their labour quite failed to repay the employer the cost of importing them'.[23] Fever and bowel complaints prevailed during all seasons and cases of cholera among new arrivals were frequent. As the century progressed, most of the larger gardens and collieries began to build hospitals and dispensaries on their premises. The government was also pressurised to establish charitable medical facilities. Nevertheless, epidemics like Kala-azar (or Assam fever)[24] continued to claim a very large number of lives. In 1893 a scheme already active in Bengal was set up to sell government-manufactured quinine as an anti-malarial drug at post offices, to be distributed through the agency of vaccinators, respectable shopkeepers, tea gardens, collieries and railway companies. Although the results were not particularly striking, the general instruction in sanitation, hygiene and medical care imparted by the state and private dispensaries did eventually filter through to the general population.[25]

Even with the best care, loss of coolies by death or desertion often occurred, despite a *chowkidari* system whereby the British employed watchmen and guard dogs to prevent the latter. Tea workers, both native and foreign to the Assam Valley, were not permitted to venture outside the estates and chowkidars prevented them from contacting nearby villages. Hill men were specially employed to track down 'absconders' with the promise of a reward of 5 rupees per head and often 'runaways enfeebled by their sufferings in the jungles, died under or from the effect of the floggings they received when caught'.[26] Harsh treatment of labourers and prevalence of extra-legal practices on the plantations were justified on the grounds that the existing penal laws were wholly inadequate for maintaining 'order' and 'contentment' among the workforce.[27] The young planter Alexander Carnegie did not take long to assume the attributes of authority and power, writing soon after becoming assistant manager of a tea garden in Tezpur in the 1860s,

> I am now in a jungle, a sort of small king among the niggers. Counting women and children I have charge of about 450 people, an awful queer lot the most of them are. They are always getting ill and I am doctor ... two of them are dead but they die here very easily so they don't think much of that ... They not only died, they absconded in a tiresome way.[28]

Flogging was common practice on tea estates. George Barker recalled his recipe for dealing with 'shirking' labourers in his garden during the 1880s, admitting that 'various forms of punishment – from a good thrashing to making him do two or three time the amount [of work] over again – are inflicted'.[29] In his memoirs Sir Joseph Bampfylde Fuller, the first lieutenant-governor of the short-lived province of Eastern Bengal and Assam, referred to the case of a coolie being flogged to death with a stirrup leather by a European.[30] Often there were cases of the tying up and flogging of labourers who were simply physically unfit to work. Many other anecdotal accounts testified to the ways in which female coolies were sexually exploited by their white masters and the mixed-race illegitimate children which resulted.[31] The social reformer Dwarkanath Ganguli underwent considerable risk to his life when he travelled from one tea garden to another to procure first-hand information on the working conditions of tea garden labourers, published in the form of thirteen articles in *The Bengalee* from September 1866 to April 1867.[32] Despite this evidence, the government failed to castigate the management of the tea industry even when labour abuses became widely known and produced protests from officials, missionaries and the general public in the recruiting districts.[33]

The official attitude to the brutalities and ill treatment of labour was summed up in 1888 by the chief commissioner of Assam, Sir Dennis Fitzpatrick:

> With about nine hundred gardens employing upwards of 323,000 hands, there must, of course, be a certain proportion of bad men, perhaps even of thoroughly depraved men, among planters and coolies. There must be a certain amount of harshness and oppression, at time even downright cruelty, on the one side, and of turbulence, conspiracies and maliciously concocted charges on the other; this, unfortunately, is human nature as displayed among all classes of men, and happily we have criminal courts strong enough to deal with it.[34]

As Behal suggests, 'it became standard practice in official reportage to mention cases of violence, physical coercion, and blatant use of extra-legal authority by planters and at the same time to rationalise it as aberrations or deny it altogether when confronted with non-official criticism'.[35]

The arbitrary nature of the planters' power was so extensive that even contemporary British administrators admitted its omnipotence. Henry John Stedman Cotton, a later chief commissioner of Assam, recognised the challenges of persuading the state judicial and civil officers to enforce compliance of labour laws:

> I was never oblivious of the peculiar difficulty which besets a Magistrate, a member of a small European community in a distant land, who may be playing polo or bridge or billiards with a planter one month, or may be serving under him as a trooper in the Light Horse, and who in the next month may be called upon to try and punish him for cruelty to a contract labourer.[36]

As a faint-hearted attempt to deal with the undeniable evidence of plantation abuse, at the end of the century 'coolie protectors' were appointed to enquire into the treatment of the tea labourer in Assam, to the fury of Barker who considered it 'ridiculous to suppose that owners would wilfully maltreat their servants, knowing that everything depends upon their being in a good state of health', and that the sanitary condition of coolie dwellings, the purity of their drinking water and rate of their mortality 'are surely things that must much more closely concern the owner than any Government official'.[37] However, the Reverend Charles Dowding, a great advocate of a more humane treatment of tea workers, contested this view of the benevolent planter. Dowding estimated that in 1892, '57,000 people, or more than one-eighth of the whole garden population of Assam, were dying at the rate of 7 per cent per annum' whereas at the same time the figure for the population of a comparable group unconnected to the tea industry was only 2.7 per cent. To Dowding, the indenture labour system in Assam's tea plantations was little more than 'thinly disguised slavery'.[38]

In 1899 Cotton noted,

> There is a growing tendency in the Coolie class to resent a blow by striking a blow in return and this soon leads to serious results as the Coolies act in combination among themselves and armed with formidable weapons – the implements of their industry. But this exercises a healthy influence in restraining the hot-headed impetuous European assistant from raising his hand against them.[39]

Proving his point, cases of assaults, rioting and unlawful assembly were reported in the annual immigration reports for the years 1884–93.[40] At the same time, leading newspapers in Bengal and Assam came forward to mobilise public opinion by highlighting the dire situation of the workers, supplemented by regular discussion in *The Hindu Patriot* and *Amrita Bazar Patrika*. The continuous reports in the press succeeded to such an extent that the labour problem of Assam featured prominently in several sessions of the Indian National Congress. By the end of the century it appeared possible for some migrants to escape colonial exploitation, as plantation management began to rent out surplus land to time-expired indentured workers.[41] In 1888, out of the 4,464 labourers whose contracts expired in the district of Lakhimpur 788 settled down as cultivators, while in Nowgong the total acreage of land cultivated by ex-garden labourers was 1,224.[42] The Assam government also began to lease wasteland to former plantation coolies, and hamlets emerged where caste Hindus, tribal groups, coolies and newer peasant migrants lived side by side.

In 1900 Cotton earned the lasting enmity of the planters' lobby by his exposure in the *Annual Report on Labour Immigration into Assam* of the 'tale of misery and wrong' that he had encountered when examining the inspections carried out by local officials. It showed that the mortality rate among Assamese tea garden labourers in that year had been considerably higher than the previous two years, due to the low wages of immigrants which had led to vulnerability to disease. Cotton proposed a moderate increase of statutory wages for labourers, pointing out that 'while an indentured labourer was expected to serve for Rs 5 a month ... in the remote wilds of Assam, the same man was in a position to earn in the vicinity of his own home a wage of from Rs 6 to Rs 10 a month' and 'the present low rate of wage had never been sufficient to procure suitable labour for the Assam tea districts'. As a result, frequently the recruiters resorted to unlawful means, as illustrated by the records of the criminal courts which 'teemed with instances of fraud, abduction of married women and young persons, wrongful confinement, intimidation, and actual violence – in fact, a tale of crime and outrage which would arouse a storm of public indignation in any civilised country'.

Cotton declared that he had also 'seen with my own eyes a Government hospital full of sick and dying coolies whose contracts had been cancelled and ... dead and dying coolies lying in the ditch by the roadside and in the bazaar'.[43] He stressed the fact that the Assam tea industry stood alone in its failure to employ free men who emigrated voluntarily and were paid liberally:

> When Ceylon is able to recruit its labour supply from India under a healthy system, when the Dooars and Chittagong tea gardens, the coal mines at Ranigunge, the Jute mills in Calcutta, and the Railways and Public Works Department in Assam are able to do the same, there is no longer any reason why the tea gardens in Assam should continue to be bolstered up by a system of indentured labour which experience and moral sense alike condemn.[44]

In an inevitable response the Indian Tea Association, wielding much political clout in the province, organised protest meetings in defence of tea employment practices and mounted pressure on the colonial and home governments through deputations to the secretary of state for India and the viceroy. In addition, the Anglo-Indian press in India[45] and *The Times* in London launched blistering attacks on Cotton's 'malignity, inveracity, and dishonesty'.[46] A further degree of confrontation was reached when the Indian nationalist press came out in favour of the chief commissioner. Cotton was given much encouragement by the early official and private pronouncements of the viceroy, Lord Curzon, who expressed grave concern on several aspects of the indenture regime in tea gardens, including in some cases 'a most scandalous shortage of wages'.[47] However, in the face of the increasing weight given to the tea lobby, supported by the colonial bureaucracy, Curzon changed his stance. While participating in the 1901 debate on the Assam Labour and Emigration Bill in the Central Legislative Council, the viceroy maintained that, although the tea labour system was 'arbitrary' and 'abnormal', spawning miscarriages of justice in the courts when Europeans and coolies were 'in collision', the Government of India was bound to support 'the effort to open up by capital and industry the resources of a distant and backward province'.[48] Lord George Hamilton, the secretary of state for India, in a letter to Curzon of August 1903, was frank in his agreement that although the present system was 'a modified version of slavery', it was justifiable in that 'without it the tea plantations could not be worked, as outside the half savage tribes from whom the coolies now come, it would be difficult to induce the ordinary Hindu to volunteer'.[49] Flung 'to the wolves' by Curzon when the Anglo-Indian press opened 'floodgates of abuse' against him, Cotton was forced to resign.[50] His crime was joining forces with the nationalists against the planting community at large, and 'the interests of the industry and its trade were of such importance to the state that the brutalities of the indenture labour regime were completely overlooked'.[51]

MINING

The European study of geology played a crucial role in establishing the colonial and post-colonial technological superiority in extracting untapped mineral resources. David Arnold makes the point that, at an early stage of exploration, East India Company officials were unsure of the effectiveness of geological surveys in India. Some British copper and coal concerns did not want their commercial interests jeopardised by a potential discovery of Indian minerals, and a number of Company employees believed that India should remain primarily an agricultural country.[1] Nevertheless, during Company rule, many individual geological studies were conducted under the patronage of the Asiatic Society of Bengal, founded in 1784 by the civil servant Sir William Jones.[2] The early surveyors were mainly amateur geologists drawn from the Company's surgeon-naturalists, officials of the Trigonometrical Survey of India and various members of other government departments. Conducting lonely and isolated field surveys in unfamiliar territory, they frequently depended upon native informants to provide local knowledge and local guides routinely assisted geological explorers.[3] Following the formation of the Geological Survey of India (GSI) in 1856, which fostered a professional growth of interest in metallurgy, the study of rocks, fossils and other mineral resources began to acquire more status than a provincial pastime. However, often exposed to unhealthy conditions and areas affected by malaria, there was a significant death rate among geologists and the GSI had constantly to employ new officers, hindered by the need to find men with an elaborate and comprehensive training.

By the start of the twentieth century there was an increased impetus to maximise the potential of India's great mineral wealth. Under Thomas Holland, appointed as director of the GSI in 1903 and a strong believer in the benefits of applied rather than pure science, the organisation moved from conducting various surveys and publishing reports in periodicals into a scientific body that advised the government not only on the issue of granting mineral concessions, but also on prospecting and exploiting minerals for the development of new industries. As far as Holland was concerned,

> The great end of life is not knowledge but action, and the government has not maintained a Geological Survey for the last 55 years merely to know that Jurassic fossils occur in the Central Himalayas. The objective in view is the development of the mineral resources of the country, and whatever my scientific friends may say, it is the duty of the government and the duty of their scientific officers to make this the paramount object of scientific work in India.[4]

Gold

The region's mineral resources did not go unnoticed before the British arrival and gold was a key element in political negotiations in the Ahom–Mughal conflict. The Ahom rulers dealt with Naga tribesmen, who adopted a simple yet effective method of spreading the fleece of a sheep across a narrow portion of stream in which they caught small particles of gold. The fleece was afterwards burnt and the gold picked out from the ashes.[1] In the 1750s the governor of the French settlements in Bengal, Jean-Baptiste Chevalier, found both the working of gold sands in riverbeds in Assam and an impressive display of gold in Ahom royal palaces despite the poverty of the people.[2] However, it was only with the discovery of tea and the realisation of the plant's ability to create wealth for the British that a parallel investigation of coal and other mineral resources began.

Maniram Dutta Baruah, the pre-colonial noble associated with the tea industry, had foreseen the opportunities of combining forces with the British, but soon explored for his own purposes. He prepared a systematic account of local methods of gold collection from the riverbeds and the East India Company undertook additional exploration to confirm the viability of his research.[3] Despite disappointing results, following the discovery of gold in California in 1849 and later in

Australia, further investigations into the gold-retaining capacities of the upper Assam rivers were made and in 1855 Edward Dalton, junior assistant commissioner of Assam, and geologist Captain Samuel Hannay made a fresh attempt to estimate the auriferous deposits of these rivers. Travelling up the Brahmaputra to locate 'original rock containing the gold in situ', they found that 'the deposits became less and less rich as they penetrated further into the hills' and the two men were forced to return.[4] Moreover it was clear that gold washing was not carried out by the local populace living close to the river. The British first adopted the policy of leasing out the river *mehals* (revenue districts) of Lakhimpur for gold collection, but gradually the auction price of the *mehals* fell to such an extent that in 1865–66 no bidder came forward. In 1882 a ten-year lease was granted to A. Scott Campbell with the right to wash gold in the Subansiri and its tributaries. However, in 1884 only 52 ounces of gold was procured by washing 52 tons of sand. With such an unsuccessful performance his application for the renewal of the lease was rejected.[5] In 1894 a syndicate was formed, and a considerable amount of money invested in the exploration of the rivers of Lakhimpur. Further surveys revealed that although many rivers in Assam were auriferous, the extent and depth of the mineral could not be gauged, and operations could be carried out only in the dry season. It was also unclear whether the supply of gold deposited each year when the river rose would equal the amount removed during the previous season's operations.[6] With these uncertainties, it appeared that gold washing was unlikely to be an economic proposition.

Oil

The failure of gold prospecting in the region did not discourage colonial explorers from expanding their search for geological resources such as coal, lime and other minerals. The possible existence of petroleum in eastern Assam was first noticed in the early nineteenth century, preceding the significant finding of tea plants. In April 1825, a year before the British concluded the Treaty of Yandabo with the Burmese, the army lieutenant and geologist

Richard Wilcox was the earliest observer of oil in an upper Assam village. His survey noted both the geological formations and mineral resources of the region and, while surveying the Burhi Dihing River, he observed a seepage of oil and bubbling gas. Wilcox later wrote,

> the jungles are full of an odor [sic] of petroleum ... There were two beds, one at a little higher level than the other, but both on the plains, filled with liquid mud of various degrees of consistence. One was twenty or thirty feet across, and the other larger. In the middle, where bubbles of air are seen constantly rising to the surface, the mud is nearly white, and is there in a more liquid state. On the edges green petroleum is seen floating, but is not put to any use by the Singphos – neither is the coal.[1]

This piece of information was of some relief to European prospectors who wished to avoid local hostility and others followed Wilcox's chance encounter with oil. Botanical surveyors, military personnel and commissioned travellers noted the richness of mineral resources in the region and logged their findings in *The Journal of the Asiatic Society of Bengal*. In 1828 Charles Bruce reported that he had encountered several oil seepages upstream of the small town of Makum in upper Assam. In 1837, the botanist and explorer William Griffith reported oil in the plains close to the Naga Hills beyond the Noa Dihing River, noting that the colour of the liquid was green to bluish white, which indicated the presence of naphtha.[2] In the same year Adam White, an army major, also noticed 'several springs of petroleum' close to the Namrup River, observing that there also local communities had no use for the resource.[3] White's survey was followed by one of Samuel Hannay, who found 'petroleum rising from some of the coal outcrops'[4] and his observations of 1838–39 were confirmed by Francis Jenkins who reported that 'oil flowed into the pools in the water-course, and four or five *seers* were collected in a few minutes'.[5] Another round of exploration was made by Hannay in 1845 when he investigated an area close to Jaipur, near Silchar, and collected 'earthy and indurated sandy asphalt' containing oil from Nahar Pung, reporting that 'this is indeed a strange looking place and I am told by the Singphos that at times there is an internal noise as of distant thunder, when it bursts forth suddenly with a loud report, and then for a time subsides'.[6]

Such amateur encounters continued: Captain Dalton reported oil finds at Namchik and Makum in 1854 and the tea planter Samuel Peal mentioned oil springs in the Makum area in 1879. The first attempt at drilling for oil in Assam was made in 1854 by a European speculator named John H. Wagentreiber, who, with the provision that he did not interfere with government elephant-trapping operations, retained a ten-year lease over a tract of land between Bappapoong and Namchik. The venture proved unsuccessful.

Mineral exploration acquired a more professional nature in 1865 when Henry Benedict Medlicott of the Geological Survey of India studied the mud from the region of eastern Assam, suggesting that as yet only thin layers of petroleum had been 'skimmed off' by the Assamese and 'everything was in a state of nature'.[7] The two promising indications of a 'copious' discharge of gas and absence of 'water-discharge' favoured the commercial possibilities of the petroleum deposits.[8] Based on Medlicott's findings, James Goodenough of the Calcutta-based firm McKillop, Stewart & Company was awarded a right to explore a larger tract of land in eastern Assam in November 1866. Goodenough initially drilled three bores which yielded 650 gallons of oil per day and, as the yield increased to 2,000 gallons per day, the prospect for commercial exploitation seemed much brighter. However, he failed to establish a petroleum industry in Assam due to transportation difficulties which raised the freight cost, resulting in a price in Calcutta which could not compete with oil from Rangoon or America.[9] The next twenty years saw little activity on the oil front, although by the 1870s extensive explorations had been made in the coal-bearing localities of Assam and a later enquiry into Burma's coal deposits convinced the GSI of the connection between coal and petroleum in the region. While undertaking a survey to find a possible Assam–Burma railway route, the chief engineer of the Assam–Bengal Railway, R. A. Way, commented that 'with oil wells in the vicinity of coal workings, the manufacture of a very high class of compressed coal briquettes should become practicable'.[10]

The commercial initiative to extract petroleum was undertaken by the Assam Railways and Trading Company (ARTC) from 1881. The company was granted a lease over 30 square miles for exploration and formally acquired the rights of an exploration agency in 1884. In the light of opposition from the Assam government, to whom the revenue from forestry appeared brighter than that of the future prospects of petroleum, the ARTC put pressure on the viceroy, Lord Dufferin, and in 1888 a licence was granted to exploit oil in the area of the Digboi field where, some years earlier, elephants used for pulling timber had emerged from the dense forest with oil on their feet. Involved with the ARTC was another speculator, the Assam Oil Syndicate. Until the end of the century oil was sent for refining to Makum[11] in the immediate vicinity and the chief commissioner of Assam recorded in his tour diary of 1898 that the Makum refinery could turn out 1,200 first-rate paraffin wax candles a day.[12]

However, while ARTC drilling continued to be successful, it was both expensive and time consuming. Better results could be expected only with improved methods and the injection of more capital, and after long deliberations the directors of the company decided that profitable developments of the oilfields could be best handled by a separate organisation. Accordingly, all the rights and privileges of the Digboi and Makum oil concessions were transferred in 1899 to the new Assam Oil Company (AOC), the initial capital outlay of which was £450,000, an insignificant amount compared to investment in the tea industry. In addition, in 1899 the Government of India issued further rules to govern licences and mining leases in several parts of the region. The new rules allowed the government to retain rights over minerals and to grant concessions for exploration, and annual licences were given to prospective speculators without any exclusive or preferential rights. Exploration in unoccupied and reserved land was, however, not prohibited and, with the liberal licence regime, the grants in this territory increased rapidly. A number of syndicates were formed by merchants, planters and agency houses to prospect for oil, in spite of the fact that petroleum was a capital-intensive industry requiring large-scale investment in drilling pipelines and substantial technical competence. As a result of these demands, although many stakeholders were convinced of their ability to market their product commercially, syndicates were often forced either to withdraw from the petroleum business or were absorbed by the oil affiliates.[13]

While the Assam administration remained unsure about the advantages of further oil investigation vis-a-vis that of coal, the beginning of the twentieth century saw the oil industry in Assam on a firm footing. However, it had taken over a century to overcome the initial difficulties. The main impediment had been the need to tackle thick jungle with such dense undergrowth that sunlight could barely penetrate to the ground. In such areas human habitation was almost unknown. In reviewing the operations of the ARTC, a member of the board wrote,

> The serious nature of these difficulties will be realised, when we state that it took us six days of hard travelling involving exposure at night in the jungles and on the sand banks in the Dihing river to reach Makum. A few sepoys maintained, at the time, a post of observation over the Naga savages who were the only inhabitants on the south bank of the Dihing ... The Nagas were a terror to the adjacent British territory and punitive expeditions against them were a frequently occurrence.[14]

Added to its impenetrability were the unhealthy working conditions of the jungle. Diseases like malaria and cholera were rampant and sickness and mortality rates high. Like the coal and tea industries, the oil industry was largely dependent upon immigrant labour as the local Assamese and Bengali workers were prone to disappear during the harvesting season with little certainty of return. Migrants were recruited directly or through contractors. In both cases the procurement of labour was expensive when the high mortality rates were taken into account.

Another serious handicap faced by the entrepreneur was the absence of appropriate technological skills to extract the oil on a commercial basis. In the early years the method of oil extraction was very crude. The first wells consisted of a 'planklined' shaft 5 feet square. Once the shaft was completed, the oil diggers were lowered down the walls on a rope over a pulley. In a 250-foot-deep well it took roughly fifteen seconds to reach the bottom. After about half a minute of frantic digging and loading pots in an atmosphere saturated with gas, the diggers were hauled up, requiring half an hour's rest before recovering sufficiently to go down again. The light by which the diggers worked was provided by a mirror at the mouth of the shaft.[15] Mercifully, towards the end of the century more sophisticated technology was introduced and most of the oil was extracted mechanically. Over each well a derrick about 60 feet high was constructed and lengths of steel casing were inserted into the wells. From the tops of the wells, long metal pipes led to huge storage tanks where crude oil was stored. From there the oil was transferred to boilers where it was subjected to various processes of distillation. The kerosene produced was sold in bulk transported by railway tank wagons, or in smaller quantities in steel barrels, iron drums or tins. Country boats on the Dihing River were used to collect the products at Makum for distribution downriver.

Despite the challenges to oil exploration, the GSI was able to satisfy the hopes of speculators in reporting that 'the belt of tertiary rocks, stretching from the northeast corner of Assam for about 180 miles south and west, shows frequent signs of oil nearly always in association with coal and sometimes associated with brine springs and gas jets'.[16] In 1901 the Digboi refinery was commissioned with a production capacity of 20,000 gallons a day and in 1907 the annual output of crude oil in Assam had increased to 3,156,665 gallons. Yet the establishment of the oil industry failed to have any visible impact on the local economy. The entire capital invested had been European and, as the industry was highly technical, all the skilled labour was initially imported from the west with the machinery and tools required for the operation of the plants. The oil industry by nature was more capital intensive than labour intensive and the scope for employment of local people was minimal. Moreover, there was practically no local demand for the products of the refineries. Even as late as 1904 there was only one motorcar in Assam when Newton Gill, a planter, brought his Darracq to the province.[17] Almost all the petrol that was produced was sent to Calcutta while the total amount of the wax by-product was exported to the west. In two decades Digboi was transformed into a European oil town, giving restricted entry to Indians. With a healthy disregard for the less salubrious and segregated labourers' lines beyond the refinery area, Henry B. Buchanan, general manager of the AOC, in his farewell speech of 1927, declared,

> This place [that] was no better than a hamlet in the jungle only a couple of decades ago, can now be called a town with its magnificent bungalows, pucca staff quarters, well equipped hospital, well designed sanitary drainage and the excellent European club.[18]

Coal

As with oil, the first sighting of coal in Assam was chronicled by Richard Wilcox. At Supkiong, on the Buri Dihing, the lieutenant found 'a bed of coal in the middle of the river' and further east on the Dihing River he observed 'thin strata of coal alternating with blue clay in the sandstone rock'.[1] Wilcox's identification of both coal and oil was to have a significant effect upon the economy of Assam. David Scott in his capacity as agent to the governor-general on the northeast frontier had devised a number of schemes for the development of the province before it had been formally annexed by the British. Encouraged by the prospect of having local coal which would make the introduction of steam navigation of the Brahmaputra an easier proposition, he despatched Charles Bruce in 1828 to the valley of the Saffrai, a tributary of the Disang. Bruce, with a party of 100 men, ascended the river in canoes during the rains and started operations on a coal seam which he described as being 36 feet thick with a thin parting of shale, later abandoned due to the difficulties of navigation.[2] A committee was formed in 1836 to investigate the coal and mineral resources of India, to which Francis Jenkins made a series of recommendations for a scientific survey of the southern hills of the Assam Valley, writing of the value of 'the intimate connection of our coal beds with other minerals of the highest value ... to draw European capital and skill to a province, which appears only to want these stimuli to be as valuable to the state as any of the same extent'.[3]

Mineral exploration in the region remained on an amateur footing. In 1837 Lieutenant Henry Bigge and the botanist William Griffith, while on the banks of the Namrup River in Singpho territory, discovered a further valuable seam of coal, noting that the Singphos 'were ignorant about the nature and use of the valuable mineral' and appeared greatly surprised to see large lumps burst into a brilliant flame as soon as they were ignited.[4] In the same year Samuel Hannay examined the Jaipur region and undertook the clearing of a large seam 1½ miles southwest of the town where the quality of the coal was criticised for containing a large amount of sulphur.[5] Although several promising seams were subsequently discovered in the Disang River, at that stage the appropriate department in Calcutta gave little or no encouragement to the exploitation of coal resources on the northeastern frontier. The meagre demand for the mineral, shortage of labour, transportation difficulties and the insecure political conditions dissuaded private as well as state enterprise from undertaking coal operations. But after the foundation of the Assam Company in 1838 and the consequent growth of the tea industry the demand for coal became considerable and, although between 1848 and 1865 no important discoveries were made, small quantities were mined in Jaipur and Makum.

In 1865 Henry Medlicott of the GSI, a fierce critic of the government's all-absorbing interest in tea cultivation to the neglect of the coal industry in the province, was instructed to visit the Assam coalfields and after due examination identified the superiority of the coal from the Makum region.[6] The problem of transportation was solved following the formation of the ARTC in 1881 and the opening of the first line from the Dibrugarh steamer ghat (flight of steps leading down to the river) to Jaipur Road in 1882. Two years later the coalfields of upper Assam were connected by railway line.[7]

Following this development, some speculators attempted to enter the hills for the exploitation of coal on a commercial basis, but without adequate communication facilities it seemed optimistic to expect many private entrepreneurs to risk their capital. Moreover, after the introduction of the Inner Line Regulations in 1873, it became extremely difficult for outsiders to develop the Dikhow coalfields in Naga territory situated beyond the Line. Recognising that more favourable terms would have to be offered to private enterprise, with government sanction agreements were concluded in 1881 between the ARTC and the Nagas, allowing the company to work extensively on the Dikhow coalfields and to cut timber and bamboos on the condition that they paid a yearly rent to the tribesmen;[8] evidence that the line proved to be flexible where necessary to cater to imperial needs.

The construction of a metre-gauge railway line connecting the coalfields on the Dihing with the Brahmaputra in 1882 was an event of far-reaching importance to the coal industry. In the same year the Ledo field adjacent to the town of Makum was taken by the ARTC on lease. As was the case in oil exploration, the supply of labour was fraught with difficulties. The coal reserves were located in extremely desolate areas covered by dense forest and infested with a variety of insects and wild animals. Workers had to be attracted, their houses built, medical services and sanitation provided, foodstuffs and other necessities supplied, and training made available to the majority of employees in their new occupation. The local people were not eager to work as wage labourers and, as in the case of the tea plantations, the coal industry was forced to recruit workers from other parts of India. Management and capital were both European. The work on the Makum field was started by the ARTC's employee George Turner, a mining engineer from South Staffordshire who was a pioneer of coal exploration. In 1882 he set sail from Britain with fifty British workmen of various trades. On his arrival at the Patkai Hills he found Nagas at work on the site of the settlement, and observed that 'the Nagas are renowned for their powers of cutting down timber and clearing jungle; they appear to take kindly to the cutting of coal on the surface of the hill, but are at present afraid of tunnelling or mining ... They are not accustomed to earthwork and it had yet to be seen whether they will undertake this.'[9]

Turner's suspicion proved correct and since nothing could tempt the Nagas to take up underground work, Indian mine workers from the Bengal coalfields were first engaged. They also proved intractable when it came to adopting South Staffordshire methods of obtaining 'thick coal' and it was deemed better to 'train up to the work young Indians, who had never seen a coalmine, under selected thick-coal miners'.[10]

Unlike the usual practice of coal mining where the coal seam was approached from the surface by a deep vertical shaft, in Assam the entry to mines was through a horizontal tunnel which was driven into the hill until a seam was reached. At this point underground roadways were driven horizontally along the seam for up to 2 miles. As the seam itself could be at an inclination varying from 30° to 60°, inclined roadways known as *chauris* were then driven up the seam. At various points in the *chauris*, further roads were driven horizontally. Coal was then brought from the working faces along the horizontal roads and lowered down the *chauris* by means of gravity-operated tramways to the mouth of the pit. Owing to the uncertain nature of the strata, the roofs of the underground roadways were usually supported by steel arches and girders, timber and masonry.[11] From the head of the working down to the branch of the colliery line an inclined plane about a mile long was constructed and laid with a double line of 2-foot-gauge light rails and was worked on the automatic system used in collieries in South Wales and elsewhere. The descending loaded wagons drew up the empty wagons by means of a wire rope connecting them and operating over a revolving drum at the top of the incline. Near this area some very fine sandstone was quarried, which made excellent grindstones equal to the best imports from Europe.[12]

The colliery line from Makum to Ledo was 6¾ miles, running through old Naga clearings on which scrub jungle and small trees had grown. The terrain differed from the virgin forest on the other side of the Dihing, although it could pass for fairly heavy jungle in other parts of India. The line crossed the Namdang River over a bridge of three 50-foot spans and ended in the Ledo colliery. At the opening of the railway on 18 February 1884, Kinney (an invitee) described the bizarre sight of a lengthy file of visitors being led by the 'able and energetic' chief mining engineer, George Turner, through a tunnel which ran through one of the 'curious little hills of coal' for which Ledo was noteworthy. According to Kinney,

> The rain had ceased and an occasional fitful gleam of sunshine was visible. Ladies, a considerable number of whom were present, in all varieties of costume, from the prudent dark-coloured ulster, to the 'reckless of weather' gala dress donned in all its glory; gentlemen in still more varieties of costume, ranging from a regular 'masher' get up, through the graduations of ordinary morning dress, riding suits, planter's kamjhari or 'round the garden in the morning' attire, down to the open shirt, loose, fly away coat, turned up corduroys, and big boots of the British workmen; natives of all sorts; the Rai Bahadur, gorgeous in many-coloured silks and embroidery; the silver bedecked and red or yellow turbaned Kyahs or Marwaris; the sober grey and black chapakan of the court amlah; the shawl, transparent muslin dhoty, long stockings and patent leather shoes of the ubiquitous Bengali Babu, down to the next to nudity of the coolies standing around. Picture a file of pilgrims, nearly 500 strong, in all these varieties of costume, personally conducted ... along a tunnel of coal, right through the base of a hill – a Naga hill too – I am afraid to say how long. It was too dark to think of pacing it, or of anything but scrambling out of the darkness (no lights were taken) into Heaven's blessed daylight on the other side. More coal, more drifts on all sides, till one seemed involved in a labyrinth of coal, and to be suffering from coal on the brain.[13]

Kinney noted that,

> The most interesting feature of this colliery is the number of isolated little hills of coal standing above the surface of the ground. The surface soil has been scraped off one of these curious

coal hills and the quantity of coal estimated at 50,000 tons which can be quarried direct into the wagons. From here a path has been cut through the jungle to the Thikak colliery, ascending some 1,300 feet above Ledo. Here a great coal seam of from 40 to 50 feet thickness has been tunnelled through, the drifts and galleries being nearly a mile in length. The vast quantity of coal which has lain hidden in this hill for ages will be faintly comprehended when it is known that, according to the computations of the mining engineers, one hundred millions of tons are estimated to exist above the galleries; and below them, but above the drainage level, four hundred millions of tons.[14]

The coal, moreover, was said to be the best found in Asia, the analysis giving the quantity of fixed carbon at 66 per cent, the ash ranging from only 1 to 3 per cent. Practical tests in locomotives and steamers proved that the coal, as steam coal, was quite equal to the product of West Hartley or South Wales. The coke prepared from both the Ledo and Thikak collieries was reported to be the finest in India and it was hoped that it would eventually supersede the use of charcoal in the manufacture of tea.[15] The editorial of *The Friends of India and Statesman* of 8 May 1895 reported with enthusiasm that 'Assam coal is soft, but as it readily cakes when put on fire, this characteristic has not interfered with its sale. Indeed, its reputation as a first class steaming and smithy coal stands high. It is fully established in the market, and its demand is increasing due to its use in inland steamers, the railways, jute mills, tea and other factories.'[16]

In the early years, the colliery labour force included not only men from the United Provinces, Central Provinces and Bihar, and Makranis and Peshawaris, but also the Chinese.[17] Recruited for the most part without any previous knowledge of the conditions of the site where they were contracted to labour, they were brought in under long terms of employment, extending to four or five years, and compelled to remain on the estate to serve out the full period of their contract under strict criminal penalties. Obligations which the law imposed on the employer included the requirement to maintain the labourers in good health, however it was pointed out in 1884 by the deputy commissioner of Lakhimpur that the ARTC had failed dismally to protect its employees when it came to working conditions. Impure water and very demanding working hours underground were the principal causes of the extremely high death rate in the mines. A local committee was appointed to deal with the matter, recommending stricter supervision in recruitment under which unsuitable coolies would be returned home, and quarantine arrangements and measures for the prevention of cholera would be improved. Also recommended was a reduction in the hours of labour, an increase in the supply of blankets to labourers, filtration of water supply, proper sanitation facilities and at least one clean hospital and qualified hospital assistants at each colliery.

In justification of its inhumane policy, the Board of Control of the ARTC wrote to the deputy commissioner, stating,

> It is not as if the coolies were taken from districts which enjoy a high standard of health. It should be remembered that the recruiting districts are subject to frequent tornadoes of pestilence reinforced by periodical famines which sweep away the inhabitants in thousands ... the vital statistics of the mines show no grounds for restricting the importation from the congested areas of India into a district in which they can earn good wages and improve their condition.[18]

Despite the company's assumption of the role of coolie saviour, the Assam government continued to stress the urgent necessity to reduce the hours of work of the miners, who were compelled to work at least nine and a half hours a day with no official break during which they could return to their homes to eat a meal. Yet, despite these recommendations, little was done to alleviate their conditions in the nineteenth century. The ARTC records that, apart from mining instruction, labourers were also educated in first aid and care, but in fact divination and incantation were more often applied than genuine medicine in curing diseases.[19]

By 1903 Assam had become self-sufficient in coal. The total output of the province was 293,000 tons (about 5 per cent of the total output of India) with the employment of 1,200 miners under the supervision of nine Europeans.[20] This quantity of coal was sufficient to meet local demand as, until the construction of the Assam Bengal Railway, sales in Assam were limited to the tea gardens (which had formerly relied on wood as fuel) and steamers on the Brahmaputra. A scheme was devised for shipping the excess coal to Calcutta to be sold to various shipping companies for oceangoing vessels, but this proved unprofitable and was discontinued. It is possible that, had the British government so desired, the industrialisation of Assam on a large scale could have been on the agenda as coal was locally available in abundance. However, it appeared that the increasing demand for fuel came from enterprises initiated and run by foreign capitalists who preferred to send the profits home and seldom identified with the local economy.

Iron

In Assam the iron industry was an offshoot of the more developed tea, coal and oil industries, although it made a slow and hesitating start. A geological study of 1876 stated that the principal iron ores found in the province were clay ironstone from coal measures and an impure limonite from the sub-Himalayan strata which gave a lesser yield of iron. The former occurred 'in oblate nodules varying in size from that of a walnut to the bulk of a man's head, but lumps considerably larger than this also exist. When freshly broken, the nodules have a light-grey colour, which changes after time to a brown tint from the peroxidation of the iron.'[1]

Clay ironstone was also found in thin bands, interstratified with shale and sandstone. Both types of ore, but more especially the clay ironstone, had been worked extensively by the Ahoms, often with iron imported from the Khasi Hills. Tirugaon and Hattighar appear to have been two of the most important centres of manufacture with thirty to forty workshops established at one time. But even before the invasion by the Burmese, the industry had greatly decreased due to the internal conflict in the region and according to Hannay the iron workers and smiths, who numbered

3,000 during the most flourishing period in upper Assam, did not exceed 100 after the invasion.² When Charles Bruce visited the Saffrai Valley in 1828, clay ironstone, which was obtained by sinking pits to a depth of 10 to 40 feet, was being smelted at the hill east of Tirugaon. The raw iron was worked into *daos* which were exchanged with the Nagas for hill produce.³ However, according to Robinson, the manufacture of iron in upper Assam was all but extinct by 1841 due to the 'injudicious' taxes levied on the ore by Purander Singh and the underselling of homemade ore by manufacturers from the Khasi Hills, where no duties were levied.⁴ Hannay stated that in 1856 there were 'only from forty to forty five persons in the Sibsagar district who understand the smelting and working of iron ores'.⁵

With the establishment of the tea, coal and oil industries, the importance of local iron grew. As early as 1851, Major Hamilton Vetch, the deputy commissioner of Assam, informed the government at Fort William of the availability of iron in upper Assam and 'the advantages which might arise from the careful investigation into the mineral resources of the valley of the Booree Dehing by qualified persons', and specimens of iron ore sent for examination by the Revenue Department at Fort William received highly favourable comments.⁶ It was hoped that, with improved means of extraction and the setting up of smelting furnaces and rolling mills, Assam's production could be considerably increased to make the northeast of India completely independent of imported iron. However, this did not happen. Shaw Finlayson and Co., when acquiring the concession of the Makum oilfields, also gained the monopoly of the iron of the region but made no attempt to work it.⁷ There was much demand for machinery for tea factories, rails and railway parts and galvanised iron sheets for buildings. Yet the iron industry in the province failed to grow to any great extent beyond the hands of the village blacksmith (generally a Hindu with a knowledge of agriculture) whose manufactured goods were limited to agricultural implements, cooking utensils, tools and other articles used in handicrafts, together with weapons of various kinds.⁸

Although by the end of the nineteenth century there were 600 iron forges in the Brahmaputra Valley, employing around 2,000 people, this indigenous industry survived because it faced little competition from imported goods, which usually consisted of the heavy machinery required for the tea, coal and oil industries. No iron was smelted in the province and there were no large iron and steel factories in Assam comparable to those in Bengal. The railway workshop at Jorhat (set up with European capital and under European management) manufactured cast iron railings, light posts, gates and other items, but heavy machinery was not produced.[9] Most of the large tea gardens had their own workshops where, as the indigenous digging of clay iron gradually disappeared, old broken iron and pig iron ware imported from Calcutta were used for castings. In view of the extensive resources, scope for development and volume of demand, Assam could have become one of the leading iron and steel producers within India, but during the nineteenth century progress was extremely slow and the provincial trade figures for 1892–93 showed a depressing total of almost 22,000 *maunds* of imported iron.[10]

TRANSPORTATION

When the British occupied Assam, most of the areas in the province were covered by thick virgin jungle stretching for hundreds of miles over steep hills and deep valleys through which torrential streams flowed. The majority of its inhabitants settled along the fertile tracts of the Brahmaputra or on the banks of its tributaries. These alluvial plains opened out into a wilderness of tall grass beyond which lay the inhospitable and impenetrable jungle, and the only means of communication available at the time was by boat, elephant or palanquin, the former being preferred whenever possible. Railways were unknown and, since viable roads did not exist, even simple modes of wheeled traffic such as the bullock cart were not available. However, during the nineteenth century the application of steam to transport by land and water, leading to the introduction of the railway and the steamship, enabled the industrial development of Assam to progress at a dramatic rate. The new methods of transport were capable of bridging great distances very rapidly, carrying heavy loads at cheap rates and functioning irrespective of the prevailing climatic conditions.

Railways

The first rail route from Calcutta into Assam was the single line to Paradaha, opened in 1862, and the Eastern Bengal Railway extension to Goalundo was completed in 1870. The journey to Dibrugarh from either of these places took approximately a fortnight. Originally the tea gardens in Jorhat and Dibrugarh were served by the river ports at Kokilamukh and Dibrugarh respectively, but as the tea estates expanded far beyond the river, it became increasingly difficult and expensive to bring materials and labour (skilled and unskilled) to and from the gardens. An alternative means of transport therefore became essential and due to the 'unremitting energy and perseverance' of Dr John Berry White, a retired brigade surgeon in the Bengal Army, the ARTC came into being.[1] During the rainy season of 1878, White while on leave in Shillong received several letters from tea planters on the Sadiya Road, describing the almost impassable state of the highway. Owing to the recent huge increase of traffic on the road and the lack of repairs, the planters pointed out that communications would soon be entirely cut off, preventing them from shipping their produce or bringing in food for their coolies. This information was sufficiently urgent to involve Sir Steuart Bayley, the chief commissioner of Assam, and Colonel Trevor, his chief engineer. White suggested that, as it was impossible to maintain an unmetalled road with the steadily increasing traffic and as the most imperfect form of metalling (with broken brick) would cost roughly Rs 1,000 per mile, it would be almost as cheap and much more advantageous to construct either a tramway or a light railway.

Sir Steuart agreed to request an annual subsidy of Rs 80,000 from the Government of India for a line from the steamer ghat at Dibrugarh to Saikwa on the Brahmaputra (opposite Sadiya). However, further examination indicated that the anticipated traffic would not pay the working expenses even when supplemented by the subsidy. At that stage White suggested a branch line from Dumduma to Makum to further the exploitation of the mineral and timber resources which were known to exist in the area. In this way 'an abundant and remunerative' traffic would be secured for the proposed railway. The chief commissioner agreed that he would recommend an extra subvention of Rs 20,000 per annum for the Makum branch, making a total of a lakh of rupees annually if White could raise the necessary capital to construct the line. White communicated with Shaw Finlayson and Co., the agents of his tea estates in Dibrugarh, and for nearly a year correspondence passed between the governments of India and Assam, resulting in the grant to Shaw Finlayson of three concessions: the construction of a railway in the Dibrugarh district with a conditional subvention of Rs 1,00,000; the working of the entire Makum coal fields, then in the hands of the government; and the exclusive right to fell timber for half a mile on each side of the Makum branch line, on payment of the usual royalties.[2]

On 8 December 1879, under the impression that they had ample support, Shaw Finlayson brought 'The Assam Railway Co. Ltd' to the London market, reserving for themselves the coal and timber concessions. The subscription received from the public was not sufficient for the directors to proceed and the whole scheme remained in abeyance for nearly a year.[3] Indeed many people believed it had totally collapsed and looked upon the Assam railway as 'one of those chimerical and Utopian schemes which would be very beneficial if they could only be brought within the bounds of practicability'. The Sadiya Road planters resigned themselves to the usual rainy season miseries, 'the impassable roads, broken carts, damaged teas, and hungry coolies, mutinous at long delayed rice supplies'.[4] However, before the end of the year the project was taken up by Benjamin Piercy who had successfully financed and constructed the entire railway system of Sardinia, several lines in Wales and various railways in other parts of the world. Piercy's adoption of the scheme was dependent on all the concessions being thrown together into one large company, to include the petroleum concession then in the hands of a private company of which White was the chief shareholder.

Piercy sent his brother, Robert, to investigate the mineral wealth of Makum. He reported back that the coalfields were 'vastly greater in quantity and better in quality, than had ever before been suspected'. Moreover, a railway could be constructed for under Rs 4,000 per mile, promising to provide 'a most remunerative investment'.[5] Following this report a syndicate was formed, composed for the most part of Piercy's personal or business friends. On 30 July 1881 the ARTC was incorporated with a capital of £350,000 in preferred shares of £10 each, and £43,750 in deferred shares of £1 each. On 2 August 1881 the prospectus was advertised in the leading London newspapers and by noon of the same day the company's bankers had received applications for shares to an amount of 28 per cent above the desired capital. A further sum of £250,000 was raised by the issue of debentures, bringing the aggregate share and debenture capital to over £600,000. The government assisted the enterprise by providing a railway concession to facilitate construction and maintenance, a timber concession providing the company with a monopoly over the forest bordering on the Makum branch, and a coal and petroleum concession around the town of Makum at the end of the branch. Thus, following the failure to float a railway company as simply a carrier, the new company was incorporated as both a carrying and trading concern with interests in coal, petroleum and timber.[6]

After securing possession of the land and carrying out surveys, the work was not started until 1 January 1882. At first the difficulties and drawbacks appeared virtually insurmountable. Although no great engineering feats such as constructing the great bridges of other Indian railways were required, the enterprise was still beset by its own peculiar problems and those it created for others. Planters were dismayed by offers to construction workers of more than double the current labour rates of the district and bewailed the 'certain desertion' of all their time-expired coolies and the withdrawal of other members of their scanty local labour force. Officials and local residents feared the rise in the price of provisions, in the wages of domestic servants, in house rent and practically everything else. However, the high wages offered attracted remarkably little labour from the tea gardens. A few coolies left the gardens to 'pick up rupees' as they fondly imagined on the railway, but 'the contrast of camping out and doing task work in all weather was great, when compared with their comfortable lines, little vegetable gardens, small tasks at which they could easily earn "doubles" and general comfort, on the tea estates'.[7]

That the influx of numerous Europeans would raise the prices of food and domestic service was only to be expected, but the labour market was very little disturbed. The railway company imported its own workers, as well as its European staff; it built and purchased bungalows for the superior officers, comfortably hutted mechanics and other specialists and generally interfered with local arrangements as little as could be expected in such a remote place where demand could not naturally and promptly be met by supply. The number of Europeans employed at the works and at the mines during construction was about 100, sixty-nine of whom were

The Khasi Hills in which the chief commissioner of Assam resided at Shillong. (Adobe Stock 321679686)

Kareng Ghar, a major palace of the Ahom kingdom. (Courtesy of Gurpreet Singh, CC-by-SA)

Joysaghar Tank near Sibsagar, an artificial lake built with forced labour during Ahom rule. (Courtesy of Supratim Deka Narakasura, CC-by-SA)

The mighty Brahmaputra, the life force of Assam. (Courtesy of Solarisgirl, CC-by-SA)

Rubber-producing *ficus elastica* trees ingeniously nursed into bridges by the local Khasi people. (Adobe Stock 344142550)

An Assamese village scene captured by Bourne & Shepherd. (PR Archive / Alamy Stock Photo)

A Chang Naga man, photographed at the turn of the nineteenth century. (Courtesy of the Wellcome Collection)

A Konyak Naga boy, photographed in the early 1900s. (Courtesy of the Wellcome Collection)

Assamese tea coolies being paid by a European man, photographed by Bourne & Shepherd. (PR Archive / Alamy Stock Photo)

Assamese women sorting tea, photographed by Bourne & Shepherd. (PR Archive / Alamy Stock Photo)

Work on an Assamese tea plantation, photographed by Bourne & Shepherd. (PR Archive / Alamy Stock Photo)

A captain, pilot and wheelman on a Brahmaputra steamer, *c.* 1895. (Courtesy of the Library of Congress)

Steamers on the Brahmaputra at the Goalundo railway terminus, c. 1895. (Courtesy of the Library of Congress)

Bamboo boats being loaded with tea in Assam, photographed by Bourne & Shepherd. (PR Archive / Alamy Stock Photo)

Above: Neilson and Co. E376, a locomotive working the Assam–Bengal Railway in the late 1800s. (Courtesy of the ETH Library, Zurich)

Right, below right: Two views of the railways in Assam in the wake of the Great Assam Earthquake of 1897. (*Memoirs of the Geological Survey of India*, vol. 29)

Patients at a hospital in Jorhat suffering from Kala-azar (also known as Assam Fever). (Courtesy of the Wellcome Collection)

Above left: Sir Henry Cotton, a member of the Indian Civil Service since 1867 and chief commissioner of Assam from 1896 to 1902. (From Cotton's *Indian and Home Memories*, 1911)

Above right: Lord Curzon, viceroy of India from 1899 to 1905, whose failure to support Cotton's humanitarian reforms forced the commissioner to resign. (Courtesy of the Library of Congress) brought direct from Europe. The number of artisans and coolies imported from other districts from the start of construction to the opening of the line was 5,872 and the amount of money spent locally averaged nearly a lakh of rupees per month, the total local expenditure for the whole period of construction being about Rs 21,80,000.[8]

On 1 May 1882, the first metre-gauge locomotive passed over the section of the line extending from the dry season steamer ghat of Mohana Mukh, some 4 miles below the town of Dibrugarh. From the terminus of Mohana Mukh the line traversed low ground and rice fields for about a mile and a half, then rose on an embankment for about a further mile until it reached the branch for Dibru Mukh, the steamer ghat during the rainy season. In the space between the two branches were the company stores, the workshops, the locomotive and carriage sheds, and the houses of a number of the European mechanics and workmen. Close to where the Dibru River flowed into the Brahmaputra were several bungalows for the senior employees of the company and below these buildings the dry bed of the river was used as a natural but efficient dockyard. The railway proceeded in an easterly direction and, crossing the Sibsagar Road (or the Grand Trunk Road of Assam), the line approached Dibrugarh. It then ran through a tea garden of the British India Company before meeting the Jaipur Road at a place known as Rai Bahadur's, the ancestral homestead of a Mattak family who under Purander Singh conducted negotiations between the Nagas and other hill tribes and the Assam durbar. From here to the next station, Lahoal, the railway followed the Jaipur Road, running past a rum distillery and tea and rice cultivation. At the fifteenth mile from the dry steamer ghat the line crossed the Dinjan River on a 56-foot span bridge constructed entirely of timber, and at the twentieth mile it reached the station of Chabwa, the site of the first tea garden in India. The railway then passed through forest and grassland, with occasional clearings made by time-expired tea coolies, and passed through several substantial tea estates belonging to White, before reaching Tinsukia, the erstwhile residence of the Mattack *gobains* (great councillors of state), where large tanks and the ruins of masonry buildings marked their former dwellings.[9] At 39 miles from the steamer ghat the Makum junction was reached and on 16 July 1883, about eighteen months after the start of the works, the line was opened for passenger traffic.[10]

The branch line running to the Ledo collieries from Makum ran almost entirely through heavy forest composed chiefly of magnificent mature trees, under which was 'matted and tangled undergrowth, dense canebrakes, inextricably confused creepers and parasitical growths'. The principal varieties of timber were *nahor* (*Mesua ferrea*), *sum* (*Artocarpus chaplasha*), and *gunserai* (*Cinnamomem glanduliferum*), surrounded by many other trees indigenous to Assam. The number of imported labourers who were returned to their native land by the ARTC, torn by 'the Assam *baint*, or cane, and prostrated by malarial fever and its resultant organic diseases', testified to the enormous difficulties encountered in opening out the branch. Thomas Kinney described how along the line a few huts and perhaps a 'damp, dripping disconsolate-looking tent' appeared – the temporary home of a gang of workmen and their superior.

> The desolate dreary look of these patches of humanity in the gloom of the primeval forest, particularly on such a dark drizzling day, gave us a vivid idea of the life led by the working pioneers of this great enterprise. One could picture the cheerless return 'home' of these men after a hard day's work, spent with toil, lacerated with thorns, their life blood half drained by leeches and often, notwithstanding the exertions of those concerned to keep the commissariat arrangements in working order, with but short commons and poor fare to look forward to.[11]

After leaving the junction, cultivation either of tea or rice disappeared and every vestige of human habitation disappeared. With no lamps in the carriages a train journey at night in 'an impenetrable jungle haunted by wild and savage beasts, and as wild and savage men' was undertaken in the 'blackness of darkness', lit only by the red gleam from the engine lamps. Kinney reported that,

The scene was occasionally lit up by the reflection on the smoke of the funnel from the open fire-box while stoking, but the momentary glare only served to intensify the blackness of the forest, bringing out tree trunks here and there into startling and ghostly relief against it as we glided past.[12]

The only station on the Makum branch was at Borbhil which, from the fine forests in the neighbourhood, seemed likely to become an important timber depot. After crossing the huge wooden structure of the Dihing bridge, the important trade centre of Makum was reached. The Nagas, Khamtis and Singphos came to the settlement to sell rubber, wax, ebony and other products and to buy goods from Manchester and Birmingham. Several of the large Marwari merchants of Dibrugarh had opened branch stores at Makum and over 300 tons of goods of various sorts changed hands monthly. Near the bridge were the workshops and sawmills, and the bungalow of the chief engineer of this section of the railway.[13]

In 1885, a year after the celebrations of the opening of the Ledo branch line, two small state railways were constructed but their aggregate length was only 35 miles. A more important undertaking was the Dibru–Sadiya Railway, 78 miles long, which brought a large section of the Lakhimpur district into direct communication with the Brahmaputra. This was followed in 1895 by a small private railway from Tezpur to Balipara, a distance of 20 miles. But these lines taken together were insignificant when compared with the Assam–Bengal State Railway, which was incorporated in 1892 and was eventually to run from the port of Chittagong through Tipperah, Sylhet and Cachar, across the North Cachar Hills to Lumding and up the south bank of the Brahmaputra to a point on the Dibru–Sadiya Railway. For some years the government had been pressurised to improve shipping facilities at Chittagong and it was hoped that, while the steamer service on the Brahmaputra maintained the commerce with Calcutta, the Assam administration might by employing rail transport use the port of Chittagong as a further outlet for the tea trade. It was considerably cheaper to send tea chests from Chittagong to London than from Calcutta where the loading and shipping charges were higher and the brokerage rate exorbitant.[14] In addition, there was a consensus on the need to improve railway facilities to carry imported labour. Both officials and non-officials believed that the future of Assam depended on large-scale immigration. Much of the cultivable land remained untouched and it was hoped that immigration would lead to rapid reclamation of the Brahmaputra Valley, resulting in the increased revenue of the province. There was also a suggestion that the railway could cross the southern hills of Assam and connect with the Burma railway system, which had received government sanction for extension into the borders of China, the goal being a great 'Asiatic Continental Highway' from Bombay or Karachi, across India, through Assam, and across China to Shanghai.[15]

The Eastern Bengal State Railway was extended as far as Dhubri in the west of the province in 1902 and a further extension constructed between Dhubri and Gauhati, giving total railway communication from upper Assam to Chittagong on one side of the province and to Calcutta on the other. By the start of the nineteenth century the total length of the Assam–Bengal Railway in Assam was 567 miles and that of the line between Gauhati and Dhubri 152 miles. However, despite the grand schemes for expansion, it remained hard to encourage more private enterprise to finance the construction of a network of small feeder lines connecting the main railway with the commercial centres situated within a reasonable distance of the track. In 1886 it was reported that only two towns in Assam had over 10,000 inhabitants and a few others had over 5,000 each. The great mass of the population lived in small, scattered villages and it was clear that as more importance was given to the tea, coal and oil industries these once flourishing areas would gradually dwindle into insignificance.[16] Unless involved in the operation of trade centres such as weekly markets in the immediate vicinity of new industries, the local people looked at the innovation of the railway with fascination but for them it was little more than an object of curiosity with no practical use.

Waterways

As during the course of the nineteenth century Assam became driven by a plantation economy, extraction of mineral resources, and the timber trade, there was a flood of British officials and military personnel, traders, indentured labourers and peasants into the Brahmaputra Valley. The Brahmaputra served as an essential channel for goods, ideas and people. It was, moreover, the only highway which connected the province with the rest of India and its navigation was exceedingly long and tedious. The members of the commission of enquiry set up by Lord Bentinck in 1834 to investigate the possibilities of growing tea in Assam took four and a half months to reach Sadiya from Calcutta and the entire journey was made by country boat upriver.[1] Three years later, the Scottish army surgeon John McCosh stated that a large boat took between six and seven weeks to reach Gauhati from Calcutta, although the post, which was conveyed in small canoes rowed by two men (relieved every 15 or 20 miles), reached Gauhati in ten days.[2] For government personnel there was no option other than river transport, however challenging. H. A. Antrobus in his history of the Assam Company cites a gruelling account by a government official of a journey with his wife, when 'progress down the Kulling river up to Kopili was slow. After twelve days' tedious travelling, propelling our craft with poles, or dragging it with ropes, on the night of 14th March 1846, we were surprised unexpectedly by the birth of our second son.'[3] In 1853, Captain Hamilton Vetch, the political agent in Upper Assam, also complained of the excessive delay, declaring that 'at present the ordinary time taken by a country boat of 1,000 maunds' burden from Calcutta to Dibrugarh is as great as that of a voyage round the Cape to London by a sailing vessel'. There were no government steamers plying the river and the tea companies had to rely largely on country boats which were scarce and irregular. The acquisition of such boats was not easy and there was reference to small, native boats of 300 *maunds*' capacity costing Rs 250 each. In large stations such as Calcutta and Dacca, the Assam Company built up its own fleet, having to pay about 37 rupees per month as hire charge for a boat of 300 *maunds* and to employ the crew for a year's service at a time.[4]

The first government inland steamer, the *Lord William Bentinck*, started services on the Ganges in 1834 between Calcutta and stations up to Allahabad. By 1836 the government fleet had been increased to four steamers, but they rarely plied the Brahmaputra and, when they did so, it was only up to Gauhati. The inconvenience caused by inadequate transport facilities grew with the expansion of the tea industry which, in addition to the transport of labour, now required essential provisions such as agricultural implements, medicine and most foodstuffs, including large quantities of rice which had to be imported from other provinces. As a result, owing to the delay in supplying vital commodities the management of tea estates at times faced labour unrest. Apart from the difficulties in transporting the packed tea from the factories to the river ghats, there was also the problem of small coin for wage payments. In the early days of Assam's development, there were none of the Mahajan or Kaya moneylending shops where cheques could be exchanged for coin, and the government treasuries at Jorhat and Gauhati seldom had coin to the extent required by the companies. The accountant-general of Bengal was able to send bullion by government steamer if one were available but, in any case, no boat was able to proceed beyond Gauhati.[5]

The Assam Company, as the premier tea company in the province, eventually took the initiative. Urgent requests to the board in London resulted in the purchase of the company steamer *Assam*, which was the first commercially owned steamer to attempt the navigation of the Brahmaputra.[6] However, due to the difficulties of the Assam Company in obtaining labour for the cultivation of tea, the crop was so limited that without support from the Bengal government there was insufficient trade to maintain such an expensive vessel. In 1847, to the great excitement of the readers of the Assamese-language magazine *Orunodoi* (dawn of light), the first government steamer, *Jamuna*, was introduced to ply between Calcutta and Gauhati, and there was an appeal to Marwari traders to opt for steamboats over Bengali boats to transport their goods from Calcutta. The services that were subsequently introduced were far from dependable. The vessels were not only small and ill equipped but also lacked the power to withstand the currents of the huge river. Moreover, since space was extremely limited, they proved inadequate for carrying cargo and tea chests waited for a considerable time at Gauhati for export. Three years later the commissioner, Francis Jenkins, made the proposal that three to four times a year steamers should be allowed to proceed up the valley to Dibrugarh to collect not only tea but sugar produced in two new factories, and merchandise such as rubber, opium, *muga* silks and *munjit* (a creeper used for dying cotton cloth) from Sibsagar and Lakhimpur. This request was turned down by the Marine Department on the grounds of possible financial failure[7] but the proposal was revisited and supported by the judge Andrew Moffatt Mills in his 1853 report on the province. Mills recommended the extension of the steamer service to Dibrugarh on the grounds that the Brahmaputra was navigable by steamers throughout the year and an abundance of local procurable coal existed. He believed that steam communication would not only add to government efficiency but also reduce the expenditure incurred in the transportation of troops.[8]

Instructions were issued in the same year for the despatch of a steamer for the upper Assam route and several subsequent vessels were employed with results that were relatively satisfactory, even from a financial point of view. The journey from Gauhati to Dibrugarh and back took no more than fifteen days, in contrast to the great delay of a country boat. However, the cargo tendered soon exceeded the carrying capacity of the steamers and in 1865 Jenkins complained that the vessels reached Gauhati fully laden with goods shipped from upper Assam with the result that Gauhati and the ports below derived practically no advantage from the downward service.[9]

In 1860 the India General Steam Navigation Company (IGSNC), formed in 1844 by Dwarakanath Tagore (grandfather of Rabindranath) and his European associates, entered into a contract to run two vessels between Dibrugarh and Calcutta every six weeks provided that government boats were taken off the line.[10] Together with the Rivers Steam Navigation Company (RSNC), with whom the IGSNC was loosely associated, a fairly regular service was at last introduced, taking plantation labourers, stores, coal and general goods up the Brahmaputra and bringing back tea. Yet, despite the growing benefits of private enterprise, travelling continued to be a comparatively slow affair and due to the virtual monopoly held by the steamer companies the rates charged at first were high. A ticket from Calcutta to Gauhati cost Rs 150 and freight on ordinary stores was carried at the rate of 1 rupee per cubic foot.[11] Moreover the planters could never rely upon despatching their tea by steamer and were therefore still forced to maintain a fleet of country boats and, having acquired them, to use them. Native merchants faced the same difficulties and, as a result, the greater part of the trade of the province continued to be carried by country boats. In 1861 Colonel Henry Hopkinson, commissioner of Assam, deplored the situation:

> With the furious current of the Brahmaputra, still unconquered by steam, posing a barrier to all access from without, and not a single road fit for wheeled carriage, or even passable at all for a great portion of the year, there is such an absence of the full tide of life running through Assam, such a want of intercourse between man and man, as does and must result in apathy, stagnation and torpidity, and a terrible sense of isolation, by which enterprise is chilled and capital and adventurers scared away. The profits of tea cultivation should attract hundreds where tens now come, but the capitalist is not always to be found who will venture his money in a country to which access is so difficult as it is to Assam, through which his correspondence travels at the rate of a mile and a half an hour, and in which it may take a month to accomplish a journey of two or three hundred miles.[12]

However, the emergence of steamer ghats for anchoring steamers gradually facilitated the speedier movement of river traffic. Godowns were built near the steamer ghat to store goods to be transported by the steamers and the navigation and tea companies appointed agents to supervise the loading and unloading of goods. Oscar Flex, who landed at Kokilamukh ghat in May 1864 after seventeen days' journey from Calcutta, noted the power wielded by one agent named Ramji, 'a big sized Assamese man wearing a golden necklace and jangfai (traditional gold jewellery) earrings' who, as the agent of all the companies who transported their goods through Kokilamukh, controlled the loading and unloading of every item. He knew all the captains of the steamers and, as a result, not a single box of tea would be loaded without his permission.[13]

It was not until Sir George Campbell became lieutenant-governor of Bengal in 1871 that the government investigated river navigation with some urgency. Sir George convinced the Government of India of the necessity of a regular steamer service between Goalundo and Dibrugarh and a government subsidy of the existing steamer companies if a regular schedule were established. The Government of India agreed to pay half the subsidy for a period of five years and tenders were invited from the existing companies. Eventually Macneill and Company, who offered to conduct a weekly service for an annual subsidy of Rs 104,000 or a fortnightly service for Rs 78,000, were recommended. The enterprise was supported by the chief commissioner, Richard Keatinge, who stressed the need to accelerate trade and commerce in the Brahmaputra Valley, declaring,

> The Europeans come from London to Calcutta in twenty five days and it frequently takes them the same time to reach Dibrugarh from the latter city ... The accelerated journeys west of Calcutta have been made possible by Government aid and without it Assam cannot possibly enjoy the same advantage as the rest of India.[14]

Reluctant to endorse financial involvement in the northeast, ten years later the government of the incoming viceroy, Lord Lytton, declared that funds for the project were not available and in a decidedly vague memorandum the hope was expressed that 'means might in future be found to effect such improvements in steam communication in Assam as the growing development of the great natural resources of the province from time to time might require'.[15] Despite this setback, with the increase in the number of steamers of the navigation companies the situation gradually improved. A considerable amount of cargo was carried in these vessels and special cargo steamers with flats were pressed into service to transport bulky freight. In 1883 a daily mail service was introduced between Dibrugarh and Dhubri, seen as a great advance in communications between Assam and the outside world.

The IGSNC and the RSNC were as regular in their services as circumstances permitted, but the latter boasted larger, more powerful and better-appointed vessels for passenger traffic. A general assortment of essential supplies such as cotton and woollen piece goods, liquor, drugs, rice, pulses, and iron and other metals for the use of planters or civilians at the stations were sent up from Calcutta or direct from England and composed the usual cargo upriver. On the journey down the vessels were heavily laden with tea but, if it was not the season for shipping, the complement was made up with seeds and jute. Large round bales of jute were carefully stowed on the flat and taken down to Goalundo where they were placed in specially constructed iron vans. Great precautions had to be taken to prevent jute catching fire as it was highly inflammable, and once alight it became virtually impossible to save a flat from total destruction. It was noted that few captains of flats, 'ardent admirers of the nicotian weed though they may be, indulge in a pipe while there is any jute above hatches, the knowledge of the risk they run being a pretty certain preventive'.[16]

Writing in 1884, the tea planter George M. Barker, described a river steamboat:

> [An] odd ill-shaped looking affair ... A huge black and white mass of floating wood and iron work, she looks all top saloon deck and chimney stacks. The first idea that uncomfortably creeps over one is how easy it would be for her to turn upside down, there is such a vast amount of material above water. All the vessels are

constructed with paddle engines, in order to draw as little water as possible. In consequence of their great length and shallow proportions, the deck is built slightly convex ... for the purposes of cargo carrying. The upper saloon deck (forward) of the vessel, reserved for first class passengers, is comfortably fitted up with cabins and dining-saloon, the after part of the upper deck being set apart for coolies or other native passengers. A thick roof consisting of either corrugated iron, or bamboos thatched over, runs the whole length of the upper deck, for a protection against sun or bad weather. Cargo, coal, stores, cook-house, pens for sheep, fowls etc. to be used on the journey, are accommodated on the lower deck, a part seldom visited by the dwellers above, on account of the general dirt and disorder that prevail. Each steamer tows up one or two flats (the number depending on the amount of cargo expected), lashed to her sides by strong hawsers and wire cables. The flats are built somewhat like the steamer, without chimney stacks, are rather more bluff in the bows, and if possible more ugly and unwieldy. The appearance presented and the amount of room taken up by a river steamer with her accompanying flats is stupendous.[17]

During the cold season dense fog hung close over the surface of the water, adding greatly to the already difficult navigation. Sometimes the fog was so heavy that the steamer could not proceed until twelve or one o'clock when there was 'the rattle of the steam-winch heaving up the anchor, the yells of curious and unfamiliar nautical Hindustani, and the scream of the steam-whistle warning any stragglers on shore'.[18] The chief difficulty in navigating the Brahmaputra arose from the shifting nature of its bed. Huge banks of sand in the centre were submerged and disappeared, only to reappear elsewhere, and a channel that was navigable on one day could in a few days become completely impassable. As a result, the steering of a large steamer and two flats was hardly an easy exercise, particularly when the draft of water was rarely more than 5 feet. The river was divided into various sections or lengths, each of which had to provide a supply of Assamese pilots for the steamer service. According to Barker,

> A pilot's life is not one of unmixed blessing ... Frequently kept waiting on the banks of the river, for two or three days at a time when the steamer is late, exposed to all kinds of weather, uncertain of the date when he may see his home again – the chief excitement in his life is the jump from vessel to shore when his piloting has been concluded.[19]

To avoid delay by stopping the engines, or when the river ran rapidly, the vessel was put in as close to the banks as permitted, and the unlucky individual risked being sucked under by the 'treacherous back currents'. Even with the employment of pilots, river traffic was often delayed for hours and sometimes days on a sand bar, 'frequently tenanted by alligators and turtles, two phlegmatically constituted animals, that repose amicably side by side'.[20]

Boats sent from the steamer to embark cargo were careful not to row too closely to the banks, 'which had a disagreeable knack of tumbling into the river'. The difference in appearance of the banks during the rains and cold weather was so marked that no person travelling during the two seasons would imagine it to be the same river. During the cold season the river settled down into one channel, up which all steamers had to go; during the rains, according to the amount of rain that had fallen, the surrounding country was submerged. The river at some places could stretch to a width of 4 or 5 miles and stations that during the cold weather could not be reached after landing without a 3- or 4-mile drive were suddenly brought to a prominent position on the banks of the river and easy to access. It was understood that the period when the river was falling, just after the rains and before the cold weather set in, was a highly dangerous time for those living near the banks. The jungle and herbage that had been under water for four or five months began to dry out 'throwing off during the process a terrible effluvium that begets the worst form of jungle fever'. Besides the decaying vegetation, fish were left high and dry on the land and

> dead bodies of buffalo and animals that have been drowned during the floods and carried away by the stream are left to rot ... nor is it a pleasing sight, while looking over the side of a steamer, watching the oily surface of the Brahmapootra as it whirls by in large eddying rings, to see a corpse slowly spinning round and round on its way down the stream.[21]

For passengers such as Barker it was an asset when in 1870 the Eastern Bengal Railway was extended to Goalundo. The journey from Goalundo to eastern Assam by commercial steamer was roughly two to three weeks and in most cases plantation workers travelled up to Dibrugarh, the last port of disembarkation on the Brahmaputra. Even as the IGSNC and the RSNC established control of the steamer service on the Brahmaputra, other enterprises made brave attempts to enter the space. One such company was the Assam Railways and Trading Company (ARTC) which bought steamers to carry up materials required for the construction of the railway line from Dibrugarh to Makum and to carry coal and other commodities down to Gauhati.[22] By 1883, with a paid-up capital of £102,415 and a fleet of eight steamers and eighteen barges and flats, the ARTC began irregular steamer services beyond Dibrugarh and ran local steamers mainly to carry the freight of the tea companies from the interior. At this time there were also as many as 275 ferries operated privately or by the Public Works Department for the movement of goods and personnel within the province.[23] The ARTC venture proved unprofitable and came to an end when the RSNC bought up its flotilla. In 1889 the IGSNC and the RSNC ceased their trade rivalries and formed the Joint Steamer Companies, operating joint services but maintaining separate management. By 1910, these two companies jointly owned 208 steamers, 38 harbour tugs and launches, 252 running flats, 72 receiving flats, 194 barges and boats, and 39 dredgers and floating cranes. In the last part of the nineteenth century, railways and steamers began to complement and compete with each other, although between 1896 and 1900 the river-borne commerce still constituted more than 96 per cent of the total transported trade in Assam, despite the high risk posed from the Brahmaputra's unruly channels, unpredictable bank lines, surging floodwaters, cyclones and earthquakes, plus the occasional trade recession.[24]

Roadways

The Assamese had in previous centuries worked highly successfully to produce magnificent buildings and splendid roads. One of the finest remnants was a bund road or military causeway, extending along the whole northern border of the country from Sadiya to Cooch Behar. This road, known as Gossain Kamal Ali after its builder, was about 15 feet broad and raised about 8 feet above the inundation level. The ruins of similar highways were to be found all over the province and the old royal paths through the forest even in decay put to shame the efforts of the British administration to construct modern roads.[1] Captain Henry Rutherford, political agent in central Assam, wrote in 1835 that,

> No country in India had been provided with such a splendid system of highways which were carried uninterruptedly throughout the whole country from Gowalpara from either bank of the river to Sadiya to the great crossroads between the principal towns and the minute ramifications which connected all the villages.[2]

The explanation for the total deterioration of the highways appeared to be the civil warfare in the region, followed by the large-scale devastation of the province by the Burmese. The recurring floods in the Brahmaputra Valley were undoubtedly also a factor. However, for whatever reason the fine roads which figured so largely in the Ahom Buranjis during the period 1650–1750 were virtually non-existent a century later. In 1853, in his addendum to the Moffatt Mills report, the pioneer of Assamese literature and philanthropist Anandaram Dhekial Phukan also deplored the demise of highways and roads connecting the different places of Assam, declaring that, 'owing to this want of means of inland communication, the poor classes can never stir out of their homes during the five rainy months of the year'.[3] When Moffatt Mills visited Assam in 1853 carts and carriages were unknown and, owing to the lack of inland communication, the poor could not come to the courts at the district administrative centres to lodge their appeals. The two great trunk roads which by the end of the nineteenth century ran east and west along both banks of the Brahmaputra had not been started and there were practically no roads at all in Sylhet and Cachar.[4]

However, road development in Assam was always a very slow process, handicapped by the extreme difficulties of the terrain. The ranges of mountains within the province and on its borders made road construction an extremely difficult task and the cost of bridging the many large rivers flowing from these hills placed any but the most basic road system quite beyond the province's unaided resources. In the Brahmaputra Valley another handicap was the heavy rainfall which created a need for embankments at the side of roads in the plains. Owing to the regular floods, rivers were also guarded by embankments, which served as the highways of the country. These were crossed by high, raised pathways which were again joined by smaller embankments. This system, connecting the villages and fields, formed a means of maintaining communication while at the same time retaining or keeping out excess water throughout the region.[5] In 1841 William Robinson wrote that the embankments had been much neglected, leading to the abandonment of large tracts of valuable land.[6] Some years later Susan Ward realised how completely waterlogged the region became while riding along the 'grand trunk road' from Sibsagar to Dibrugarh (raised in some places as much as 10 feet above the surrounding area) where she was informed that long poles erected by the roadside existed 'to enable mahouts to keep their elephants on the road during the rains'. It appeared that the road in question was often submerged under several feet of water and were it not for the poles, the elephants might leave the embankment and swim for it.[7]

The lack of material for road metal (the broken brick or cinders used in the construction or repair of roads and railways)[8] in the valley, combined with the prohibitive cost of transporting it from other areas, made it impossible for most of the roads to be metalled. The most serious handicap to road building in Assam was the unsympathetic attitude of the government of Bengal, which unfailingly cited a lack of funds. Francis Jenkins realised that the development of the province largely depended on the improvement of communications and attempted to set aside a percentage of revenue for the repair and construction of roads. He believed that 'not only would the wastelands be rendered accessible but people would then have the means of clearing them' and the initial outlay would be returned to the government in increased revenue.[9] In support of his appeal for funds, Jenkins quoted contemporary developments in Cooch Behar, a district also under his jurisdiction where, owing to improved roads, the bullock cart had been introduced as a labour-saving device in the transport of commodities. In contrast, in Assam the late arrival of the bullock cart remained a very slow and comparatively expensive means of transport as the use of carts was hindered not only by poor roads but also by the absence of bridges on the rivers crossing the highways. This method of transport did, however, enable some tea planters to access the waterways of the valley. George Barker recorded how 'each bullock cart will take for shipment seven to eight chests (of tea) to the river where they await the first steamer going downstream. Factories situated close to a tributary of the Brahmaputra can ship their products down to the main stream at much less expense than others who have not got the advantage of a waterway.'[10]

The tea companies maintained inter-garden roads to the best of their ability but during the rainy season some planters were still completely isolated from the outside world for months. Without a riding path through the jungle or any means of crossing a deep river, they were unable to see even a neighbouring planter a few miles away. Meanwhile, owing to the extreme reluctance of the government to grant funds for road development, the public roads were sadly neglected. A minute of the Calcutta board of the Assam Company stated that 'since the Government will not assist in repairing such roads, it would be imprudent for the Company to expend money on roads not confined to their own particular grants'.[11] A report of 1844 described the predicament of the newly appointed tea superintendent, J. M. Mackie, with 100 miles of territory to cover from north to south: 'Even a straight journey of such a distance with the means of transport then available, an elephant at three miles an hour, could not be accomplished in under five or six days at the best time of year; but Mackie had twenty tea tracts ... to inspect.'[12]

Forty years later the situation had hardly improved. In 1887 the missionary Mrs P. H. Moore and two others were unable to complete their journey from Shillong to Nowgong in less than one week by travelling in a bullock cart that took their luggage, food, cooking utensils and a man to cook for them. The nights were spent in dak bungalows erected for the convenience of district officials. She also wrote that missionaries had decided to hold their conferences only once every three years due to the difficulties of travel in Assam. Delegates frequently had to be transported across hills in chairs carried by natives or on ponies or in covered bullock carts (where there were roads), moving at about 2 miles per hour.[13]

Apart from forming an important infrastructure for the industrial growth of the province and the general travel requirements of its population, efficient road communication was also important for its security. As early as 1836, an urgent need for a route to facilitate military movements at all seasons of the year was identified. The existing road which connected Gauhati with Sylhet in Bengal was deemed inadequate since Gauhati was situated in lower Assam, whereas the potential danger was on the northeastern frontier, requiring troops stationed in Cachar to move into upper Assam. From time to time correspondence was carried on with the Government of India on the subject but little action was taken due to the usual excuse of paucity of funds. It was not until 1865 that steps were taken to construct a road through the whole length of the Brahmaputra Valley, running along the south bank of the river from Sadiya to Dhubri where it was connected by steam ferry with the road system of Goalpara and northern Bengal.[14] The government granted 40 lakh rupees to further the project, but in many sections it remained 'a myth' and much needed to be done to make travelling on such 'trunk roads' a viable prospect.[15]

British interest in building roads in the hills was undoubtedly driven by the need to control strategic areas, to make territories accessible and to draw recalcitrant hill people and their territories into governable spaces. In 1873 Lieutenant John Butler, political agent in the Naga Hills, identified a pressing need for developing road links in the hill tracts. To bring the Nagas and other hill tribes in the northeast frontier out of their 'isolation', Butler suggested 'good bridle paths which would enable the authorities set over these hill savages to visit them oftener and at all seasons of the year'. Roads, it was argued, would further seduce these wild tribes from 'their present habits of plunder and outrage' towards settled and peaceful pursuits.[16] A flurry of activity involving the construction of a network of bridle paths ensued in the 1870s, of which the Golaghat to Samaguting road was seen as a vital addition for the British in linking the station headquarters of Samaguting with the rest of Assam. Seventy-three miles in length, this road was 'put in cold weather condition' by the middle of November 1873. In 1874, adding to the communication grid in the area, the key 40-mile hill road from Samaguting to Kohima was 'completed and declared open for trade'.[17]

Although promoted primarily on economic grounds with the perceived increase in trading activities with the Nagas, these roads also enabled the government to penetrate the peripheral areas of Assam inhabited by other potentially troublesome subjects. British strategists were aware that the security of the Raj's borderland would eventually hinge on acquiring unfettered access into the interior hill tracts. Plans were set in motion to connect Dimapur with the neighbouring territories of Cachar, Manipur and Burma with the primary objective of funnelling troops more quickly from one garrison to another. However, despite the significance of the frontier tracts in official security calculations, road building continued to take a low priority. District officers such as Major Butler, father of the above lieutenant, complained vociferously that little had been done 'in opening out paths through the hills when we come to consider that we have been in occupation of them since 1867'.[18]

The vital need of a good communications network to firm political control was made abundantly clear during the campaign of 1879–80 in the Naga Hills, one of the largest military mobilisations made on the northeastern frontier. In 1880, with a persistently heavy toll on men and resources, the government deputed Major G. S. Hills to report on local conditions. In his inspection he found the Golaghat to Kohima route 'overgrown with jungle' and the whole route 'utterly neglected'. The bridges 'languished in a deplorable condition', impassable even for ponies, and the transport system was choked between Dimapur and Kohima, with the garrison at Kohima 'living from hand to mouth'. In his 1880 report, Colonel D. Robinson, commanding the Naga Transport Corps, recorded the heavy toll of '100 ponies dead, out of 105 Khasi coolies 40 invalid or died, remaining sick; of 105 Bhutias only 30 or 40 fit for work; of 125 syces, 100 grass cutters and pony attendants, majority are sick and increasing daily'. The losses and expenses incurred on the elephant train from November 1879 to June 1880 reportedly amounted to Rs 4,03,091.[19]

To deal with such severe setbacks the political agent in the Naga Hills, Colonel James Johnstone, recalled how during the Naga Hills campaign, with a detail of sappers and an enlistment of Gurkhas, Khasis and Cachari labourers, he began to open up the Golaghat to Kohima road, easing access in the hills.[20] The immediate result of the 1879–80 Anglo-Naga war was the creation of the district capital at Kohima after which road building in the Naga Hills took on a new 'civilising agenda'. Grand schemes of 'public works' were announced with the aim of consolidating tighter control over the newly acquired territory.[21] Road building projects were largely organised with military priorities in mind by men like Colonel Johnstone, who placed emphasis on keeping important communication lines open throughout the year. Roads, once built, served as rearward routes for communication, reinforcement, troop circulation, and supply and patrol routes. Moreover, rotating district officers and troops were frequent reminders of British power in the hill tracts.

Despite earlier colonial descriptions of the lack of viable roads in the region, as the British set about their own attempts at road construction they expressed much admiration of Naga engineering skills. Robert Woodthorpe, in his study of the hill tracts, declared,

> Their [Naga] roads are constructed with due regard to the easiest gradients, and are not carried up and down over every little hillock. The steeper parts are stepped and paved to prevent the rain-washing channels in them, and in the gentler gradients cuts are made across the road at every change of inclination or direction in the most scientific manner to carry off the water down the hill side.[22]

In laying out a new colonial road, an existing trail was normally preferred and work along Naga paths usually involved levelling out certain sections and filling in holes and ruts. Celebrating the transformation of the Naga path between Golaghat and Kohima, Colonel R. C. Low, deputy commanding transport, remarked that prior to 1881 the road was 'nothing but a goat track' but had been transformed into 'an excellent road for pack animals during the cold season with several sections of it on a gradient fit for wheels' which appeared to be quite acceptable to the local people. However, the local tribesmen would also happily appropriate the road system for their own needs. Robert Brown, the political agent in Manipur, reported 'the damage done to the hill road by travellers squatting on it, digging up the roadway for cooking purposes, and sometimes almost blocking it up by their temporary huts'.[23] The new communication system also attracted itinerant traders who established their role as suppliers of transport animals. In 1887 the Assam Administration Report recorded a large number of Nepalese traders who had camped on an open plain between Langthobal and Manipur and, as well as selling spices, hired out ponies for the carriage of commissariat stores. Marwari traders also moved in to establish control in some markets and, by helping these middlemen to establish *golas* or stores in the hills, colonial officials hoped to secure a reliable supply network for its troops in the case of future frontier contingencies.[24]

To Thomas Kinney the difficulties of finding willing and capable labour was the 'dismal swamp' which before the end of the nineteenth century had stifled every project for developing Assam. In his cynical view, in the past there had been no hindrances such as 'enlightened Government to prohibit forced labour' and the Public Works Department contractor and sub-contractor had not been invented.[25] It was clear that road construction could not take place without the use of coolie labour, however requisitioning such labour was a constant colonial anxiety since concern for crops and families often compelled local workers to return to their homes and villages when needed. Moreover, removing coolies suddenly and marching them off to field service resulted in sickness and much loss of life. As an alternative, officials often drew upon Nepalese coolies engaged by the Assam tea gardens, prompting great opposition from planters. To add to the challenge, with the introduction of the Inner Line Regulation in 1873 mobility between the hills and the plains was placed under stricter restrictions. A large labour force could now only move across the hills under the sanctioned order and supervision of colonial officials. Arguing against the government policy of importing coolies, Colonel Johnstone pressed for more aggressive measures to obtain labour from within the hills and in 1879 a group of 150 Nepalese from the Garo Hills and 50 Mikir tribesmen were employed on the Samaguting to Kohima road. The Anglo-Naga war of 1879–80 proved helpful to Johnstone's cause and, following the pacification of Angami territory, a set of terms and conditions included the requirement for Nagas to work on hill roads for fifteen days a year at the rate of 4 annas a day, as a form of indirect taxation. Recruitment of labour was rotated from village to village and district officials were directed to take the cycle of crops into account and to draw upon the 'contributed labour' only when Nagas were not engaged in agricultural work. However, the impressments were much resented by the local hill populace as it intruded into their everyday life and undermined their long-established choices and freedoms. Frequently drastic strategies were adopted to evade the oppressive colonial labour regime, such as the desertion of homes to take up residence in distant areas, and it was found necessary to introduce the use of registers to prevent undue demands on any one village.[26]

Despite grand colonial claims, the challenges of providing sufficient reliable labour ensured that many of the roads built by the British were often no more than minor improvements over existing local tracks and Naga paths continued to form crucial arteries of connectivity for the colonial official as British political influence expanded in the hills. Heavy rains could turn supposedly 'all weather cart roads' into a quagmire and the much-lauded but unmetalled Golghat to Kohima road in 1899 was said to carry 'heavy soil which when soaked with rain cuts into a morass'.[27] The situation was little better in the early twentieth century and, following the introduction of the Inner Line regulations, some old circulatory routes were blocked off and access to the Naga Hills was sporadically denied or regulated. Even so, a handful of roads slowly worked their way up into the hills. According to the *Imperial Gazetteer* of 1909, the total mileage of roads in the Naga Hills in 1903–04 was 73 miles of cart road and 470 miles of bridle paths.[28] Despite these developments in road construction, and the building of a second trunk road running along the northern bank of the Brahmaputra, the government was not prepared to incur any additional expenditure if it could be avoided. Of the total mileage of 3,173 in Assam in 1903–04, only 42 miles were metalled due to the high rate of wages, the cost of about Rs 1,000 per mile for even the most imperfect form of broken brick metalling, and the difficulties of obtaining material. Thus, ignoring Henry Hopkinson's repeated assertions that an unmetalled road in Assam was a waste of money as it was bound to be destroyed during one or two rainy seasons, the situation remained virtually unchanged. For all practical purposes, most of the roads of Assam could only be used for a few months in the year and their poor condition naturally resulted in the diversion of trade channels to waterways and railways.

FORESTRY

In the early nineteenth century, the entire region of Assam had over 80 per cent of its area under forest cover. Although the Ahom rulers exercised authority over the forests, local people were at liberty to use the forest products and most non-agricultural land was regarded as common property. Forest laws barely existed, and the state's role was restricted to the collection of revenue on some forest products such as aloe wood. However, under British occupation the establishment and growth of the tea, coal and oil industries saw the development of the timber trade in Assam and large tracts of forest lands passed under British protection. The large requirement of wood for tea chests, railway sleepers, bridges, planking, posts, buildings and many other requirements of municipality and local boards made the use of the existing forests of Assam an urgent necessity. Across the upper Brahmaputra the diversified elevation of the land produced a variety of trees. The mixed plane, *sum* and savannah forests were found in the plains, the *sal* forests partly in the plains and partly in the lower hills, the lower hill forests from the foot of the hills to an elevation of about 3,000 feet, the pine forests from 2,500 feet to 6,000 feet and the upper hill forests above 4,500 feet. The timber of the *sal* forests was of considerable value, while the *sum* forests provided the necessary environment for the rearing of silkworms. The mixed and lower hill forests were rich in bamboos, cane, evergreen trees and a number of valuable deciduous trees including *cautchouc*, and the proximity of the lower varieties to streams and rivers provided easy access to the Brahmaputra on which the main trading stations were situated.[1] The boatbuilding industry flourished and there was a considerable trade in canoes hollowed out from large *sal*, *sum* and *ajhar* trees. McCosh commented that 'a boat is as common to every house as a brass *lota* [water vessel of brass or copper] or an earthen pot' and was usually built by its owner, whereas the government employed several thousand craftsmen for the purpose of larger orders.[2]

Forest management was first considered in Assam in 1850 when the collector of Kamrup reported that wood cutters from Bengal, having exhausted the *sal* forests by indiscriminate felling in the districts lower down the Brahmaputra, had found their way to Kamrup in search of timber.[3] Until 1865 the forests of Assam were administered under the Bengal Forest Department but, when in 1874 Assam was reconstituted as a chief commissioner's province, the German plant hunter and botanist Gustav Mann was appointed as the deputy conservator of forests in the region.[4] Although at times during the nineteenth century there were official moves to create and preserve forested territory, those tended to further the political ends of the government rather than to fulfil any ecological agenda. The system of *jhum* cultivation practised by the natives mostly in the hill areas of Assam was perceived by British administrators to be the greatest danger to the forest environment, and harmful for the agricultural sustenance of the plains. The pioneering English forest entomologist Edward Stebbing strongly condemned the local practice, declaring that 'the forests of this region had for centuries been devastated by the cutting and burning of the best timber to form ashes to fertilize ... wretched fields of half wild grains'.[5] This generally held opinion resulted in the imposition of bans on the indigenous rights of forest communities, a move which as a side product freed up more unoccupied land for colonial enterprise. Later in the nineteenth century, to further Government of India policy to secure the border areas of the subcontinent, and officially to protect the people in the plains districts of Assam bordering the hill tracts, the Forest Department was instructed to establish forest reserves to act as buffer or safe zones. In 1877 a huge forested area known as the Inner Line Reserve, consisting of about 509 square miles on the boundary between Cachar and the Lushai Hills, was created and managed by the Cachar forest division. The reserve served the purposes of the Inner Line Regulation by forming a natural barrier between the hills and plains to prevent exploitation in the Lushai areas and to protect the valuable resources of the Cachar plains from Lushai raids.[6]

On a commercial basis, the timber of Assam had not commanded a great deal of attention until the establishment of the Forest Department in 1868. Trees were generally converted into logs in the forest and dragged by elephants to the nearest river from which they were floated down to the required location. They could be felled only with official permits and a royalty, at the rate of 4 annas per cubic foot or 6 rupees for each reserved tree and 1 anna per cubic foot or 2 rupees for each unreserved tree, was charged. In the tea grants, the planters disposed of the timber as they wished. The usual way of clearing jungle trees was to enter into a contract with the local Assamese to clear it at a fixed rate per acre. As the larger trees were cut down, unless the timber was required for building purposes, charcoal pits were constructed in certain places while the felling progressed.[7] The charcoal was then stored in the gardens to be used in the tea house for firing. Major Graham, the deputy commissioner of Darrang in 1873, identified the prodigal waste of timber for charcoal, declaring, 'I lately estimated that on a moderate computation 1,000 [trees] are on average used yearly in this way alone on each garden, while not a single tree is planted to replace them.'[8] The second-class timber was generally converted into crates and large tea containers.

Apart from timber, the forests of Assam produced fairly large quantities of cane. In the beginning there was little trade in this product, but the government earned a considerable amount from payment for the right to cut cane.[9] A related industry was the production of plywood for the tea industry. Initially, planters showed a preference for imported chests. However, as sawmills developed and the quality of their products improved, the demand for local plywood also grew. The first sawmill was run by steam and established in 1882 on the Dihing River just above the junction with the Brahmaputra, and subsequently a sawmill of the Planter's Stores Company was established at Dumduma in the Lakhimpur district. As the demand for railway sleepers grew, several other mills were established. The railway system in Assam increased from 114 miles in 1891 to 715 miles by 1903. Each mile of railway required 860 sleepers and the average effective life of each sleeper was between twelve and fourteen years. To lay 400 miles of railway in the valley would therefore have required approximately 344,000 sleepers, and most of these came from forests such as Nambor near Golaghat.[10] The timber on the banks of the Brahmaputra provided sleepers at a rate of more than 1,000 pieces daily, exerting enormous pressure on the forest resources of the province.[11] By 1901 as many as fourteen sawmills were functioning in Assam.

In the 1880s the entire timber trade was still local in character. With a view to establishing an export trade in first-class wood, the government set up certain experimental plantations for the planting of trees not indigenous to the province. Teak plantations were started at Makum, Jaipur and Kulsi but the results were not promising and seeds of a variety of European trees also failed. It was therefore decided that the extension of the cultivation of valuable indigenous trees such as *sal*, *poma*, *titasappa* and *sum* would prove more profitable than the introduction of new species. It was hoped that with proper management the forests of Assam could provide substantial revenue, but a number of factors contributed towards the sluggish growth of the domestic timber trade at the end of the nineteenth century. When the Forest Department in Assam offered to provide sleepers to railway companies elsewhere in India, most refused to buy this product as they were ignorant of the natural resources existing in the region. No established market for Assamese timber existed in Calcutta or elsewhere outside the province, due to the common assumption of the Government of India and those involved in the Calcutta wood industry that plantation-grown timber such as teak from Assam could never compete with the quality of naturally grown teak from Burma. The situation was not helped by the inaccessibility of timber reserves and lack of substantial roads in the northeast region, making export highly challenging.[12]

The tea chest industry in Assam also suffered great losses when local tea companies chose to import boxes from Norway, Japan, Austria, Russia and England rather than using the local sawmills under the supervision of the Forest Department. Although the royalties on local boxes were reduced in 1897, this measure proved futile. Imported products supplied by Calcutta agents were seen as more durable and less prone to insect attack and rapid decay. In addition, by the last decades of the nineteenth century the plantations of *semul* (preferred by planters) situated in the vicinity of sawmills were to a large extent exhausted by over-felling. Timber to replenish these supplies had to be transported for up to 100 miles to reach the sawmills, resulting in a quadruple increase in costs. The loss of wood through sudden floods in the Brahmaputra was great, camps were at times raided by Abors, and it was difficult to find native contractors to work in remote river areas.[13]

As a result of these considerable setbacks, the Forest Department suffered severe financial losses, not helped by the fact that from its inception it was forced to function in collaboration with other departments like Public Works, Revenue, and Agriculture who exercised parallel authority over many forested tracts of Assam at the time. The loyalties of such departments lay with the flourishing tea industry and the implementation of the government wasteland grant rules, under which the acquisition of wasteland from the government for tea plantations (often considerably in excess of the requirements of the grantee) frequently involved the cutting of trees, reeds and grasslands rather than the preservation of forests. The result of the drastic change from a quasi-feudal economy to a market economy marked an unprecedented and unparalleled ecological degradation in the province. By the mid-nineteenth century the Public Works Department emerged as a major consumer of the forest wealth of Assam for fuel and for the growing construction work in the state. It also had to perform the herculean task of clearing jungle for the building of public roads and for this purpose had large tracts of forest land under its control. Contrary to the objectives cherished by Mann and others in his department, there were instructions that the Nambor forest in particular should be reserved solely to further the growth of valuable timber for the use of the government and for the working of coal beds and limestone quarries.[14] Moreover, to increase revenue through agricultural production, settlement policies were implemented that encouraged peasants from the populous districts of Bengal to colonise and transform forest land into fields. Of these policies, the Assam Land Revenue Settlement of 1886 and the Assam Forest Regulation of 1891 were particularly devastating in their effect on the forest cover of the valley. Despite the efforts of the officers of the Forest Department to prevent deforestation, the need for departmental collaboration to promote the powerful British interests in the province ensured that, for the second half of the nineteenth century, economic success in Assam was seen as a far greater priority than environmental conservation.[15]

AGRICULTURE

Alongside the decline in local economic activity, the British development of new industries in the purely subsistence economy of the Brahmaputra Valley left a deep imprint on the agrarian structure of the region, and the change from the traditional economy to commercialisation was so sudden that by the middle of the nineteenth century land under tea cultivation far outstripped land under other cash crops. Hunter in his 1879 statistical account of the Lakhimpur district wrote that 'rice cultivation is stated to have retrograded instead of advanced during the past twenty years owing to every other description of agriculture having been sacrificed to tea cultivation'.[1] As has been discussed above, tea plantations were associated with the opening up of wasteland at minimal costs, often for speculation. Large tracts, far in excess of the required minimum for viable plantations, were acquired, leading to an under-utilisation of land with important consequences. Although the planters formed the largest landowning class, they contributed least to the revenue of the state and, as a result, the burden of taxation fell heavily upon the *ryots*.

During Ahom rule the revenue of the state had been paid in the form of personal service, whereas under the British a land tax was gradually introduced, and in 1867 the government arbitrarily doubled the rates. The Assamese cultivator held smallholdings devoted to raising food crops such as rice, and cash crops such as jute and oil seeds which were sold to pay the tax. As food crops occupied the major portion of the land, the peasant was often hard pressed to pay the revenue demand and had to resort to borrowing from the Marwari moneylender, especially during times of scarcity. Moreover, the whole province was effectively owned by the Government of India and a *ryot* had no claim on the land he had reclaimed from the jungle, nor on his home. All he held was a *pottah*, a stamped paper which he received annually giving him permission to occupy a tract of land on the condition that he paid a fixed amount. The government held the right to cancel the *pottah* at any time, refusing him the right of occupancy, and many Indian labourers were forced into a position whereby they were tied to plantations. In the latter part of the century tea estates were able to distribute a bulk of surplus land into small plots for workers, often bringing those who bought the land into a cycle of debt and dependence. Coupled with the need to cultivate their own subsistence crops, the price of necessary goods in the market increased while wages remained unfairly low.[2]

In 1889 a further revision of rates resulted in an increase in land revenue tax of 33 per cent on the figures of the previous year, justified in the eyes of the government by the fact that there had been a substantial increase in the price of staples produced by the Assamese and a rise of labour wages since the last settlement. However, little was done to improve the condition of agriculture in the state. Hunter's observation in 1874 that there were no irrigation facilities, that manure was not used and that the system of rotation of crops was practically unknown still held good in 1900.[3] In addition, the agricultural tools used were primitive and, although the tea, coal and oil industries made technological advances, innovation in the agricultural sector remained negligible. Moreover, even though in Assam floods were a common feature and large areas in the vicinity of the rivers were left uncultivated due to the threat of inundation, no new irrigation project was undertaken by the British. In 1874 Hunter reported that with only ten significant embankments in Kamrup as a defence against floods, there was a great need for more of these protective works.[4]

Possibly because of the major challenges facing them, local farmers failed to show any initiative to increase production. As a result of this lack of commitment it was necessary to import rice and prices rose considerably, especially in those areas with a dense population. The annual imports of food grains into the Brahmaputra Valley increased from 0.3 million *maunds* in 1872 to about 0.7 million *maunds* in 1895–96, indicating the extent to which Assamese farmers failed to respond to the growing demand.

By 1875, after nearly fifty years of colonial rule, more than 7 million acres of land remained uncultivated. To fill this void, in the 1890s the British encouraged a slow but steady migration of impoverished Muslim peasants into the uninhabited Assamese tracts from the adjacent overcrowded areas of East Bengal. Nepalis were employed as dairy herders, porters and agricultural labourers and similarly encouraged to colonise new territory. Such migration was seen as beneficial for the sparsely populated valley and essential for economic progress, and it was estimated at the time that at least a million people could be settled with ease on the wide space of the province. The new farmers filled the valley's western frontier as well as the char lands, the low-lying, flood-prone islands in the midstream of the flow of the Brahmaputra, and Muslims led the way in rice cultivation and multiple cropping. For the first time, jute became an important item of export.

AGRO-INDUSTRIES

Rubber

The earliest writer focusing upon Assamese rubber was Dr William Roxburgh of the Calcutta Botanic Gardens, to whom in 1810 Matthew R. Smith of Sylhet sent a container filled with honey, the inside of which was smeared with the juice of a tree growing in the hills. After close examination, Smith had found that the container was perfectly lined with a thin coat of rubber and it appeared that the natives of Assam were familiar with the properties of the product, using it to waterproof baskets and to burn as candles.[1] The nineteenth century saw a rapid increase in the commercial value of rubber. It possessed qualities of elasticity, was a non-conductor of electricity and was impervious to air and water.[2] The huge, noble Indian rubber (*caoutchouc*) tree (known by the Assamese as the Borgach) was 'distinguished from a distance of several miles by its dense, immense and lofty crown'.[3] As described by William Griffith in 1838, although generally a solitary tree, two or three could be grouped together. The trunk differed from other trees in its 'sculptural appearance'; firstly, arising from the propensity of the tree 'to throw out roots both from the main trunk as well as from the branches' and, secondly, from the way in which the roots cohered with the trunk or with each other, ultimately proving self-destructive.[4] The *caoutchouc* forests extended over large areas in the Kamrup, Darrang, Nowgong, Sibsagar and Lakhimpur districts and were generally found in the foot of the hills in low, damp ground within dense evergreen forests. The trees appeared to be far more numerous in the forests beyond the British boundary, causing difficulties in managing the product with frontier tribes.

There were three species of rubber tree found in Assam: *ficus elastica*, *ficus laccifera* and *ficus obstusifolis*. The last two species were found in small numbers and yielded considerably less rubber. The gum or juice was extracted by transverse incisions across the bark down to the wood, with a fully grown tree having many such incisions at the same time. Beneath the incision a hole was scooped out in the earth, sufficiently deep to hold either a large leaf or a plastered clay vessel into which the fresh gum flowed. The early leases for working India rubber were given free of payment, the only condition being that a certain number of trees were to be planted by the lessee. In 1863 new conditions were attached to leases, by which rubber was to be collected only between 1 January and 31 March to prevent excess tapping and a lessee was bound to plant 100 trees within the designated area. Failure to comply with these terms resulted in a forfeiture of the lease, the first of which was made to Charles Bruce in Tezpur at a price of Rs 1,525. In the early stages of rubber production, the Mikirs, who were said to be the best tappers in Assam, were employed on a daily wage of 8 annas a day. Later Nepalese, Assamese or Garo workers were engaged and paid between 20 and 30 rupees per *maund* of rubber collected.[5]

The growing demand for rubber in England encouraged an increasing number of amateurs to enter the field and in their enthusiasm to extract as much as possible they frequently resorted to over-tapping, thereby seriously injuring healthy trees. In 1879 it was decided that artificial propagation of the India rubber tree would not only prevent over-tapping but would also be a sound financial proposition. George Henderson, officiating superintendent of the Royal Botanic Gardens in Calcutta, considered that the establishment of new rubber estates 'must be undertaken' since he considered them to be 'the most lucrative and hopeful of all plantations'. However, in his opinion if such plantations were to pay, they would only do so if established on a large scale and under European supervision. The government planting of the *ficus elastica* should be encouraged along roads and railway lines as 'it grows rapidly, thrives almost anywhere, gives excellent shade and is a very handsome as well as being a very valuable tree'.[6] With the increasing demand, particularly from the expanding rail network, two experimental rubber plantations were set up in 1874, one at Charduar near Tezpur, with an area of 2,754 acres, and the other at Kulsi in the Kamrup district, with 100 acres. However, difficulties were experienced in artificial propagation due to the inability on the part of the colonial botanists to replicate the tree's natural method of growth.[7]

The resistance of the Borgach to domestication stifled the growth of rubber plantations to such an extent that the first systematic rubber-tapping exercise in a plantation only happened in 1897–98, nearly 100 years after rubber was discovered in the northeast. As a result, production depended largely on the raw latex extracted mainly from wild rubber trees, found both within and beyond the assumed political borders of colonial Assam. As early as 1848 the colonial authorities had begun to sell monopolistic rights in the form of leases to purchase rubber from native collectors at auctions conducted in the districts of upper Assam. The indefinitely laid boundaries of these rights, the rubber *mehals*, allowed the state sanctioned *mehaldars* (frequently Marwaris)[8] to increase the area of rubber appropriation by enabling them to venture into regions that did not fall within British jurisdiction. In Darrang district, for instance, the agents of the *mehaldars* made arrangements with tribal groups such as the Bhutias, Akas and Daflas who were seen as the owners of 'the trans-frontier rubber bearing tracts'. In the Lakhimpur district, the Kaya *mehaldars* (referring to a particular group of Marwari shopkeepers owning *mehals*) did not even send their agents to the trans-frontier tracts but conducted a barter system under which tribes bringing down rubber were paid in kind from Kaya shops, often in salt.[9] This system was unquestioned until 1872, when the purchasers of the rubber *mehals* in Lakhimpur petitioned the viceroy, complaining that the rights under their lease had been infringed by the operations of 'speculators' (quite possibly Europeans already involved in tea speculation and unwilling to condone Marwari control of rubber) who were insisting on their right to buy from the frontier tribes direct.[10]

As a result, it was decided to bring the rubber trade under the immediate management of the government to provide a satisfactory solution to the problematic relations with the frontier tribes, to aid the forest conservancy of *caoutchouc*, and to increase revenue.[11] All rubber, foreign and homegrown, was to be brought down to government depots by the tribes who were to be given receipts from the officer in charge. The government would then sell the rubber on to various competitors. It was further decided to impose a uniform rate of royalty and duty on all rubber produced from government trees in Assam and on rubber imported from beyond the frontier. The deputy conservator of forests, Gustav Mann, who predicted that the natural rubber resources in Assam would soon be exhausted, in 1884 requested 'large establishments to watch over forests because rubber is so portable and its removal not just confined to roads or tracts, rivers or so forth'.[12] Rubber differed from tea and timber in that it did not come from a strict plantation environment but was harvested from geographically scattered wild trees. which needed about twenty years at least to mature and provide latex of a good quality. In Assam the juice was either allowed to stand until it began to coagulate, then boiled in water and pressed by the rubber operative firms of the *mehals*, or it was exposed to the air and rolled up in balls. These small rubber balls made it a highly mobile commodity, 'something that could easily walk across borders in the pockets or sacks of the tappers, providing an added fluidity to the already porous ambiguous territorial boundaries'.[13] The distinction between contraband and legal rubber was complicated by the fact that the small balls intimately connected with the contraband trade were also procured by the state-sanctioned rubber operative firms, stamping a mark of legality on the commodity.

Contraband rubber was just one example of the failure of the Inner Line to formalise border operations. With the introduction of the Inner Line Regulation, a person crossing the Line without a pass could be imprisoned for a period of one year, or pay a sum of 1,000 rupees, or both. The regulation further noted that any rubber, wax, ivory or jungle product found in the possession of such a person would be confiscated. However, it was difficult to assess how far the regulation was successful. Seasonal *haats*, or fairs, such as the annual market at Udalguri in Darrang, became well known for their transactions in illicit produce and tribes such as the Akas, Daflas and Miris continued to bring rubber, or *bor attah*, across the Line, and Marwari merchants frequently sent their rubber tappers across the boundary.[14] It appeared that the tribal mode of preparation in small pieces was to be admired in that it achieved a purer result than the more contaminated large blocks pressed by machine. As a result the value of illegal rubber was almost 50 per cent more than the product of the rubber companies, ranging between forty five and eighty rupees per *maund* in Calcutta.[15] The native method of collection also appeared to be superior in its use of a leaf in the 'shape of a rude cap' placed in the ground under the incision rather than a plastered clay vessel which 'contaminated the milk in a very objectionable manner'.[16] Although the native method of tapping, especially root tapping, proved to be the most destructive to the trees, to avoid a large loss of revenue the government did not take action to prevent the damage. It was not until 1906–07 that the duty on root rubber was increased to 50 rupees per *maund* while the duty on tree rubber remained the same at 17 rupees per *maund*. In the meantime, most of the natural trees had been permanently destroyed.

Depressingly, by the end of the nineteenth century, the deterioration of rubber cultivation caused Mann to write,

> On present evidence, it would seem to make investment in Assam rubber a very doubtful speculation in Northeast India. In fact, the only possibility of the *Ficus elastica* culture would seem to be as a by-product to tea culture, on land now waste and unsuitable for tea. It may be that future discoveries with regard to improved methods of growth by means of tapping the plants annually without injury, or growing of a larger number of healthy heavily yielding plants on the same area, may alter the opinion above expressed.[17]

Mann understood that, whereas a tea garden yielded a return relatively quickly, it was doubtful if the 'enthusiasts of private enterprise' would have the patience for the maturation of rubber plantations for the benefits of their grandchildren. A recurring theme in all the government reports was that a lack of local labour had significantly hindered the successful operation of timber cultivation. Yet workers could have been attracted with proper wages. In lower Assam, A. P. Aylmer, assistant conservator of forests, succeeded in working extensive plantations of teak, rubber, *toon* and *sissu* entirely with local labour. By paying an attractive rate to every worker and giving the men perfect liberty to leave when they wished, Aylmer was able to secure as much assistance as he needed. It appeared that apathy on the part of the officials concerned was also responsible for the decline of rubber production in the province. Had their owners been provided with more assistance, rubber plantations had the potential to be developed as extensively as tea. Moreover, no attempt was made to process the material in Assam and the entire quantity of rubber produced in the province was exported from the region in a raw state.[18]

Jute and Rhea

The trade in jute had been important since the start of the East India Company for the manufacture of cords and ropes. Until about 1830 the production of gunny bags and jute cloth had been the monopoly of the Bengal handloom weaver. Thereafter, an active manufacturing industry had sprung up in Dundee and it was found more profitable to export the raw Indian jute than to produce gunnies on the handloom. The importance of jute as a raw material increased rapidly when, as a result of the Crimean War, supplies of Russian hemp were severed and within a few years the Bengal jute handloom industry was decimated as the entire quantity of jute was exported in a raw state to feed the mills in England.[1]

The Government of India began to look beyond the borders of Bengal to extend jute production and two regions of the Brahmaputra Valley were found to be suitable for the current methods of cultivation: one in high and dry tracts beyond the reach of annual floods, and the other in alluvial land which was more or less flooded during the rains. In the former areas, in upper Assam jute cultivation on a commercial scale had a slow start and was grown in small patches on homestead lands or on the periphery of rice-growing fields. In these tracts, the land under cultivation was not held for more than three years in succession, after which it was abandoned for a fresh plot. However, in the latter area jute cultivation expanded rapidly after 1880 in the riverine region of the western portion of Goalpara district among communities such as the Rabhas and Cacharis who were capable of producing a superior quality of fibre, and by 1897 some 35,022 acres were under jute cultivation.[2] The jute fibre was transported in small bundles called *paties* and *moras* and later rolled into bundles of 10 lbs for purchase by local *beparis* or traders who visited the remoter areas by boats and bullock carts.[3] Jute passed first through the primary or village markets known as *haats*, secondly the mofussil or secondary markets situated near trunk roads, steamer ghats and railway stations, and thirdly to the Bengal baling factories of Sirajganj and Narayanganj to be transported to Calcutta by steamer or large native boats.[4] The Moffatt Mills Report stated that 20,000 *maunds* of jute were exported from Goalpara to Calcutta in 1853, whereas in 1896–97 the total yield from the region was more than 3,48,332 *maunds*.[5] However, although the cultivation of jute was twice as profitable than that of *ahu* (autumn) rice, it required significantly more labour. Since labour in Bengal was cheaper than in Assam, both capitalists and government were unwilling to undertake a major financial commitment to the crop, giving maximum attention to the tea industry. Although it was suggested by the Department of Agriculture that the *ryots* could double their income with a little extra labour if they substituted jute for *ahu* rice, it was feared that that the promotion of jute at the expense of rice cultivation could lead to food scarcity.[6]

In 1898, F. J. Monahan, assistant director of the Assam Land Records and Agriculture Department, in an exhaustive report on the possibility of jute production in Assam stated that as Assamese peasants would not expand their jute acreage, some of the low-lying tracts in the western and central parts of the valley should be opened up to jute cultivation by Bengali immigrants who had worked similar soil in a similar climate.[7] By the end of the nineteenth century, with the reclamation of Assamese wasteland by land-hungry peasants from the crowded neighbouring districts of East Bengal, Assam became prominent as one of the principal jute-growing areas of the subcontinent. With the encouragement of the chief commissioner of Assam, Sir Henry Cotton, measures were adopted for the distribution of seeds to cultivators and the supply of information regarding methods of planting and the preparation of jute fibre, although it was categorically stated that any cultivation on a commercial scale should be the concern of private entrepreneurs, suggesting that the government at that time had doubts about the viability of the industry. Unlike the need for major transport links to bring workers into the tea plantations, the movement of East Bengalis into the districts of western Assam required at the most a few days of walking upland across rivers and wetlands. With their arrival, jute was encouraged on a minor scale in the plains' districts and the lower part of the Garo Hills, but produced on a commercial scale for export mainly in the districts of Goalpara and Sylhet, which adjoined the jute-growing areas of Bengal. Jute-producing regions in Assam increased from less than 500 acres before 1901 to over 6,000 acres by 1911, providing the product in a raw state to feed jute mills in Britain.[8]

Attempts to grow the rhea (or ramie) fibre (*Bohmeria nivea*) for the requirements of the British shipping industry for canvas, sailcloth, lines, ropes and cables proved less successful. In Assam the plant either grew wild at the foot of hills or was cultivated in small patches by fishermen to make nets. Manure, moisture and shade were essential for the quick growth of rhea in order to enable it to grow to a height of 8 feet from which a fibre stock of 6 feet could be separated. As early as 1803, Dr William Roxburgh of the Calcutta Botanic Gardens had written that it was 'one of the strongest fibres' and could be easily propagated, and the botanist Dr Forbes Royle, who was despatched to Assam to ascertain the properties and value of the product, observed that rhea and chinagrass were identical and that 'it appears to be likely to prove one of the most valuable products of India, for in strength it exceeds the best Hemp and in firmness it rivals superior kinds of Flax'.[9] It was pointed out that rhea could be produced and sold with profit 'at as cheap a rate as Russian Hemp' and would speedily undersell all other fibres, as four or five crops could be obtained within the year from the same plant. It was hoped that Assamese rhea would not only meet the British demand to a large extent but could be exported to other countries.

With a view to developing the cultivation of the rhea plant as an industry, during the 1870s the Government of India offered a series of prizes to the inventor of the best machine capable of 'producing by animal, water or steam power, a ton of dressed fibre of a quality which shall average not less than 45 pound sterling a ton in the English market'. The machinery was to be simple, strong, durable and inexpensive, and suitable for erection in plantations where rhea was grown. Seven machines were presented for trial but none of the fibres produced came up to the prescribed standard and the government concluded that it was unwise to invest in rhea plantations until it was shown that the cultivation of the plant could be undertaken with profit. However, since a real need had arisen for an improved method of producing the fibre, to aid private entrepreneurs a plot of land of about 3 acres was kept at the Botanic Gardens at Howrah to supply roots to prospective growers. Samples of both rhea and jute grown at the base of the Himalayas from Assam to the Sutlej River appeared at the International Exhibition of 1876 in Philadelphia, where it was noted that a 'proper mode of treatment seems to be all that is necessary to render them of great value as textile and paper-making materials'.[10]

Silk

Although basically an agricultural people, the Assamese combined agriculture with other trades. During the Ahom period there were references to weavers, spinners, goldsmiths, potters and workers in ivory, bamboo, wood, hide and cane.[1] Most of these craftsmen were self-employed and seldom worked for hire, and each village was a socio-economic unit containing persons skilled in various trades. One of the most prominent industries was silk and its manufacture. The Ahom greatly encouraged sericulture and grants of land were conferred upon the *jogis* or weavers. Three varieties of silkworm were reared: the *eri polu*, *pat polu* and *muga polu*. The *eri* worms were fed on the castor oil plant and yielded a thread which was not reeled but spun by hand. The *pat* worms were akin to the silkworms of Europe and were fed on mulberry leaves and reared in considerable quantities. The *muga* worms were found only in Assam and reared on *sum* trees. The silk from the *muga* was considered the most valuable and was the prescribed attire of the high officers of government.[2] All the upper-class women in the Assam Valley dressed largely in silk, even the least affluent women always had one or two silk *mekhelas* for special occasions, and as a result 80 per cent of the output comprised home consumption. Production was confined to the household. As William Robinson stated, 'This manufacture, like most others, is carried on without capital, without division of labour, by single individuals, each of whom spins, weaves and dyes his own web. Some of the fabrics produced are notwithstanding very creditable indeed.'[3]

The process of *muga* silk production was demanding. After the cocoons selected for breeding purposes began to form, they were put in a closed basket and suspended from the roof of a hut. The day after hatching, the female moths were removed, tied to small wisps of thatching grass hung on a string to protect them from rats and lizards, and taken out morning and evening to be exposed to the rays of the sun. After the eggs of the moths had been laid and a few hatched in about ten days, the wisps were fastened to the *sum* trees where the caterpillars were positioned to feed on the leaves. The labour and expense of keeping a plantation of *sum* was trifling, but great care was needed in the breeding season to watch the trees by day to keep away crows and other birds, and by night to fend off owls, bats and rats. Before placing the worms on the trees, the trunks were daubed with treacle to attract ants, which, when collected in great numbers, were burnt.[4] When about to spin, the caterpillars crawled down the tree trunks where they were collected in baskets covered by branches of dry leaves in which they formed cocoons. In a *sum* tree forest the ground was kept extremely clean to find *muga* worms more easily when they dropped off the trees. The cocoons were not easily killed and were put over a slow fire and boiled for an hour in a solution of potash before the silk was wound off on 'the coarsest imaginable' instrument made of bamboo. The *muga* species gave five breeds a year and from the first and the last the best silk was produced. The total duration of a breed was from sixty to seventy days and 50,000 cocoons was a good return from an acre of forest, yielding 25 lbs of silk.[5]

As early as 1831 David Scott had written to the Government of India that of all the commodities available in Assam, he felt that silk would be the most profitable. It was a product that did not necessarily require European supervision and the Assamese were universally acquainted with the preparation of the material, unlike other regions of India where production was confined to a particular class. Previously China had been the principal source of silk and English manufacturers were largely dependent on Chinese suppliers. The prospect that Assam could 'contribute large quantities of an article which is produced with so much ease in the Valley of the Brahmaputra' was greeted with enthusiasm.[6] As a result, with the object of capturing a portion of the growing demand for silk in England, various experiments were made in different parts of Assam after 1834 to grow *eri* and *muga* silk on a large scale. Archibald Campbell, deputy commissioner of revenue in Nowgong and in charge of one of the most extensive projects, declared that the only way of successfully developing the industry in Assam was to involve villages over large tracts of country in cultivation in small patches to avoid the risk of disease to silkworms. But the results were disappointing, as were subsequent British efforts to practice sericulture on a commercial scale in the province. Disease of silkworms did not appear to be the main cause, as the threat of disease had been greatly reduced in Bengal and elsewhere. The expenditure and effort involved in training the local population was clearly one challenge together with the fact that, since sericulture was largely carried out by women, plans for commercialisation would have required their involvement outside the home which was seen as culturally unacceptable. However, a lack of information on scientific methods of rearing silkworms appeared to be the most likely cause for the failure of the venture.

Despite limited production, during the nineteenth century the trade in silk between Assam and England continued in two forms: the export of thread and the export of cocoons. Of the two the latter was preferred because indigenous reeling was in a relatively crude form and the product was regarded by most English manufacturers as 'unfit for employment for any purpose'.[7] The manufacture of silk plushes and similar fabrics out of waste cocoons imported from India and China was a flourishing branch of the silk industry in England. However, there continued to be some interest in unrefined thread from English manufacturers, one of whom wrote,

> I ask nothing of India that requires skilled labour or machinery; only to collect the raw material in a state in which it must be almost valueless in India, and let us by our superior mechanical devices make something of it here.[8]

This request was unsuccessful. In his 1899 study of the silk trade in Assam, Basil Allen observed that 'in spite of the high price at present obtainable for silk thread, the villagers find that it pays them better to grow produce for the market than to rear broods of silkworm'.[9] In 1908 it was reported that the entire export business in both raw silk and piece goods had fallen into the hands of a few Marwari merchants who had no interest in either the welfare of the weavers or in the introduction of any improvement in the weaving industry.[10] The cheaper silk material from other parts of India and imported fabrics from foreign countries supplanted much of the local silk in the markets and, although silk manufacturing remained a major occupation for Assamese women, there was no appreciable development in the indigenous industry.

Cotton

The production of Assamese cotton faced the same challenges as the silk industry. In the plains patches of cotton were grown mainly in the Lakhimpur, Nowgong and Sibsagar districts for domestic consumption. In some *mauzas*, or administrative divisions, of the northern frontier cotton was grown extensively on the lower slopes of the Bhutan Hills. There were two main varieties of cotton: the *bor kopah* and the *soru kopah*. The *bor kapah* was the large-balled, high-growing cotton with fewer seeds and could be ginned easily and normally cropped twice a year. The *soru kopah* was the small, round-balled species which was grown and plucked annually. The greater portion of the cotton of both varieties was short stapled. Cotton was generally grown on *jhum* forest clearings and the same clearing was not normally used again for ten years due to the easy availability of land. The whole process of preparing the cotton from plucking to spinning was carried out by those involved in its cultivation and each household processed as much as it required. The Mikirs, however, grew cotton not only for domestic consumption but also for export and boatloads of it could be seen travelling down the Kopili and Kallang rivers in the cold season. Throughout Assam, every household possessed a loom and for all castes the spinning and weaving of both cotton and silk was carried out by the women of the family, principally for personal garments, although the muslin and calico used by the more affluent Assamese was imported from Bengal.[1] The cotton thread for the weaver was spun on a very fine piece of bamboo with a ball of clay at one end, turned around with the left hand while the cotton was fed through with the right. For the coarser thread, the women used a wheel very like that used in England, although of a smaller construction. In some areas the art of making cloth cotton was highly refined and often the borders were finely woven with a lace of gold or silver thread. Like silk, some of it was exported to Bengal, or bartered for other articles with the hill tribes.[2]

Manufactured English cotton articles initially met with certain obstacles in Assam. The dress of the Assamese women tended to be peculiar to each region and not manufactured outside the area, and silk competed very highly in supplying the clothing of the people, especially the higher classes.[3] In addition, the sizing of English cotton goods and the manufacturing technique of producing cloth in England was said to make it less durable than homemade material.[4] However, over the course of time the pressure of competition and the introduction of new ideas slowly changed popular attitudes and both Assamese men and women began to use the cheaper Manchester cloth.[5] As rapid advances were made in the improvement and invention of machinery, British manufacturers were able to push their products in the local outlets. Almost every year from 1885 onwards, imported cotton piece goods and twist yarn exceeded the export of finished goods and yarn from the Brahmaputra Valley.[6] At the same time, as in the case of silk, almost the entire quantity of raw material was taken out of the province and exported in an unginned state to England though Chittagong and Calcutta. Assam, at one time self-sufficient in cotton products, had to resort to importing yarn even to meet its own requirements. The rapid increase in the export of cotton was helped by the fact that almost all the varieties of Assamese cotton had short, coarse staples which were in great demand in Europe for mixing with wool or *eri* silk to make products such as suiting, dress materials and blankets. Since all the weaving in Assam was done by hand, 'the cheapest of labour could not compete in quality or quantity with Lancashire mules or throstles' and, finding no market for their goods, the local people no longer attempted to rival British products. However, as Tirthankar Roy points out, although the import of cheap textiles ended many artisan livelihoods, it was of huge benefit to Indian consumers generally and to Indian merchants who transported and marketed these textiles to the interior.[7] The result was a steady rise in India's per capita consumption of cotton cloth, despite some decline in handlooms. Only in those places where communications were difficult did the local industry survive.[8]

Lac

With its connection to textiles, an Assamese industry which held considerable economic potential was the cultivation of lac or shellac, the complex resinous secretion of a small insect called *laccifer lacca* used mainly as a dye. One of the most ancient of the Indian minor industries, Tavernier recorded in his accounts that Assam produced an abundance of shellac of a red colour and of a very superior quality, of which large quantities were exported to China and Japan where they were used for lacquering cabinets and other furniture.[1] According to the Scottish physician Francis Buchanan-Hamilton, in the first decade of the nineteenth century Assam exported 10,000 *maunds* of lac to Bengal, valued at Rs 35,000,[2] and in the 1840s it was seen as a principal article of export, for the most part taken out of the country in its natural state.[3] The cultivation and collection of lac was almost entirely in the hands of tribal people and the methods of propagation and collection had remained unchanged for centuries. In Assam lac was reared to a varying extent in all districts, but Kamrup and Nowgong were the main areas of cultivation. A considerable quantity of lac was also obtained from the Garos who brought it down to their weekly markets.[4] The lac was collected from three main sources: trees beyond the British frontier, trees in government forests, and trees cultivated in *jhums* and, to a very small extent, on leased lands. There were usually two crops of lac a year. The main crop was put on the trees in April and gathered in September, and the second crop put in October and collected in April.

The lac insect was reared on several species of the *ficus* family and the Assamese *arhar*. Pieces of stick lac containing living insects were placed in baskets and tied on to the twigs of the tree on which the next crop was to be grown. After a few days the insects crawled on to the young branches and began to feed and secrete resin. They were left undisturbed for about six months when the twigs, encrusted with deposits of a translucent orange yellow gum in which the insects were embedded, were broken off a few days before the young larvae swarmed. Ants and the caterpillars of a small moth were able to do great damage to the insects, and a heavy storm at the time when they were spreading across the tree could completely destroy them.[5] The bulk of the produce was exported in the form of stick lac, from which the gum substance was scraped off the twigs and separated from the dead bodies of the insects. It was then melted, strained, cleaned and sold as shellac or button lac. From the residue a red dye was obtained for colouring the thread of cotton and *mega* or *eri* silk.[6]

With the introduction of synthetic dyes, lac dye gradually lost its commercial value, but this was more than offset by the discovery of new uses for shellac in Europe and America: as a varnish and polish for furniture and metal, as a stiffening material for hats, as an ingredient for lithographic ink, and as sealing wax. Between 1868 and 1900, the value of exports of lac dye from India fell from Rs 4,45,612 to nil, while those of shellac increased from Rs 18,41,491 to Rs 92,65,600.[7] However, lac cultivation in Assam was not handled scientifically due to a paucity of official interest. Although two experimental factories were set up in Sibsagar and Cachar with promising results, much of the lac continued to be collected from traditional sources and almost the entire quantity produced in Assam was bought up and exported in a raw state to Calcutta by Marwari merchants.[8] Edward Stebbing, who researched the lac insect, deeply regretted that 'the cultivation of lac has been so neglected in the province of Assam' and so few attempts had been made to set up factories for its manufacture.[9] The official report on industries in the province from 1907 to 1908 stated that the feasibility of such factories should be considered but no positive step was taken, although in that year alone lac valued at Rs 22,49,629 was exported.[10]

Sugar and Mustard

Prior to British rule, the cultivation of sugarcane had been carried out in small patches, the area of the field determined by the labour at the command of the cultivator. The manufacture of jaggery or *gur* was the only industry connected with sugarcane and was sufficient to meet the local demand. However, the situation changed rapidly in the second half of the nineteenth century, when the government encouraged the large-scale Nepalese cultivation of sugarcane 'especially in the backward tracts'. With the influx of Nepalese immigrants into the districts of Lakhimpur, Darrang and Sibsagar, jungle settlements emerged on the banks of rivers and sugarcane was grown by clearing the forest before subsequently moving on to a new site. The Nepalis produced a variety of jaggery with which the Assamese peasants could not compete and the latter subsequently abandoned sugarcane production, most notably in the Sibsagar area where the crop had been cultivated earlier to a considerable extent.[1] In 1886, ten sugar mill workers came from Bihar to train the cultivators in improved methods of sugar production. The Assamese peasants displayed total indifference to these efforts, but the Nepalis made extensive use of the mills in the district of Lakhimpur where sugar was extensively grown on a commercial basis.[2] Cultivation of sugar also increased in Cachar and Sylhet where time-expired labourers cleared jungle-covered lands. However, almost the entire quantity was exported in a raw state to be refined in British mills and by 1901–05 the amount of sugar imported into Assam had swollen to 101,409 *maunds*.[3]

The growing of mustard seed suffered the same fate as that of sugar. Under the Ahoms the production of mustard oil was not only sufficient to meet the local demands but was also exported though Bengal in considerable quantities. But the importance of mustard as a marketable crop was speedily overturned by the cultivation of opium, for which there was a rapidly expanding demand, deplored by Butler for its use 'by all classes high and low, rich and poor, old and young, women and even children'.[4] During the 1840s, the average after-harvest price of opium was 5 rupees per *seer*, but the retail price rose to 80 rupees during the lean months.[5] As a result, cash-strapped peasants were able to find money advances from Marwari trader-financiers to grow opium rather than mustard. By the middle of the nineteenth century, although the area under mustard cultivation in Assam was nearly 15,000 acres and the average outturn 4 cwt per acre, trade reports reveal that Assam had to import large quantities of mustard oil as the bulk of the seeds were sent out of the province to be milled elsewhere. Even at the beginning of the twentieth century there were only seven mustard oil mills in Assam. As Britain systematically converted the province into a territory devoted to the large-scale production of raw materials, resulting in the decline of indigenous industries, the *ryots* lost the subsidiary income from cash crops on which they had traditionally depended and became increasingly reliant upon the moneylender.

5

Education

Primary and Secondary Education

Education in Assam at the advent of the British consisted largely of a Sanskrit grammar and lexicon, and religious instruction in the *tols* (Sanskrit schools) under Brahmin teachers. As the non-Brahmin noblemen and merchants acquired wealth and power, they began to demand education for their families. With the growth of the *satras* (Vaishnavite monasteries) new centres of learning emerged in which there was not only spiritual and moral education but also training in the arts, such as music, dancing and painting, as well as wood and bamboo work. In the village, the *namghar* (Vaishnavite prayer house) was the centre of culture and learning, confined to the priestly class and a few other individuals connected to the government. Education was a wholly male preserve.[1] After the First Anglo-Burmese War and the Treaty of Yandabo in 1826, David Scott favoured the encouragement of local learning by improving the indigenous system of education. When the British administration was set up, local people were not sufficiently educated to take advantage of the employment opportunities, even in the clerical cadres, and the nobility were seen as incapable of acting as responsible revenue collectors and record keepers

Education

due to their 'indolence and incapacity'.² Major John Butler when principal assistant in Nowgong remarked that in 1838 perhaps no more than thirty educated individuals could be found in his district.³ To promote local participation in government, Scott set up eleven schools, mostly in lower Assam, where teaching in the *sastras* was imparted through the medium of Sanskrit. In addition, an elementary English school was founded in 1831 in Gauhati with the help of Adam White, the collector of Gauhati, and James Rae, a member of the Serampore mission in Bengal.

According to William Robinson (later appointed the inspector of schools in 1841), at this stage the state of education was, in general terms, 'deplorable in the extreme':

> Unlike the provinces of Bengal, where every village has its teacher supported by general contribution, never till lately was a provincial school known in Asam [sic]. In some places there are a few Brahmins who teach the arts of reading and writing; but even this elementary knowledge is by no means extensively diffused. All instruction is unattainable to the labouring poor, whose own necessities require the assistance of the children as soon as they are capable of the smallest labour. With the higher classes, and those that can afford to pay for a teacher, education usually ends at ten years of age, and never reaches further than reading, writing (a scarcely legible hand), and the simplest rules of arithmetic.⁴

In 1833 Scott's successor, Thomas Campbell Robertson, with the aid of the Moravian mission attempted to establish several institutions for more practical purposes such as carpentry and smithery but failed to succeed.⁵

Francis Jenkins, following Robertson as commissioner of Assam in 1834, recognised that the Assamese were by no means 'wanting in intelligence', but (making somewhat dubious assumptions) had become debased due to their conversion to Hinduism which had rendered them effeminate and consequently susceptible to superstitious beliefs. What was needed, therefore, was a 'civilising mission' controlled by the state which would purge them of undesirable leanings. In his view, government intervention was essential:

> To leave this matter to the people would be to commit a duty incumbent in my opinion upon us to those who are mostly incapable of judging themselves and who from universal poverty caused perhaps greatly by our mismanagement are unable from want of means and intelligence to accomplish any progress that would satisfy us ... To leave the natives alone would approach nearly to parental neglect of children.[6]

Jenkins proposed the establishment of several English schools at the stations of Goalpara, Gauhati, Nowgong, Darrang and Bishwanath. Gauhati Jila School opened in 1835 and in 1838 William Robinson was appointed as its headmaster. The school proved to be the template of educational success in Assam, with 366 students by 1839–40, and emphasis was laid on the study of English language and literature, philosophy and arithmetic. Jenkins intended that a number of Assamese youths should be sent to Calcutta for training as teachers and in the meantime men capable of teaching English and Bengali would be brought in from Bengal. School buildings could be constructed by convicts of the local jail at little expense. However, although officers like Jenkins saw the gravity of the situation, the government in general was lukewarm in its attitude towards educational progress.[7]

The introduction of new revenue measures in Assam in 1833–34, requiring the employment of a substantial number of junior officers, emphasised the need for basic education at a local level. The dearth of qualified personnel to deal with the administration resulted in the recruitment of men from Bengal to perform clerical tasks and in 1836 Bengali was made the official court language and subsequently the medium of instruction in all village schools, while a combination of English and Bengali existed in *sadr* (higher) schools. At the same time the introduction of written leases created a demand for the basic ability to read and write, armed with which the general populace could combat the frequently corrupt decisions of the Bengali *amlahs* (officials) of the court.[8] James Matthew, the collector of Kamrup, in 1838 suggested a scheme through which existing indigenous educational institutions could be developed. His first plan involved the opening of an Anglo-vernacular school at Dharampore, the most central point on the north bank of the Brahmaputra, where pupils would be instructed at first to acquire a perfect knowledge of the vernacular language before learning the rudiments of English, qualifying them for admission to the Gauhati school to complete their higher education. Secondly, twenty-one vernacular schools were to be established in villages in the principal parganas of Kamrup for the instruction of pupils through the medium of both Assamese and Bengali.[9] In these village schools, Matthew proposed that little more than the basics of reading, writing and arithmetic would be taught.

Matthew's plan received much support from educationalists such as Thomas Munro, Mountstuart Elphinstone and William Adam, who saw it as a strong foundation upon which higher education might evolve. However, the General Committee of Public Instruction in Bengal turned down the proposal on the grounds that it was at variance with the declared policy of the government under which education should spread from the upper to the lower levels of society, the 'Downward Filtration Theory'.[10] Eventually, on the strong recommendation of the president of the Council of India, Alexander Ross, Matthew's plans for village schools received the approval of the government as an 'experimental measure'. In 1838, twenty-one village schools were established in the district of Kamrup and similar schools were set up in the region in the next two years. By 1843 the growing demand for such institutions resulted in a rise in the total number of village schools to twelve in Nowgong, five in Darrang and twenty-two in Kamrup.[11]

In his famous minute, Thomas Babington Macaulay, the first law member of the governor-general's council, urged the reform of secondary education on utilitarian lines to deliver 'useful learning', a phrase that to Macaulay was synonymous with western culture.

The English Education Act of 1835, enacted under the tenure of Lord William Bentinck as governor-general of India, instructed that European literature and science should be promoted among the people of India through the medium of the English language. Since the Gauhati school was not easily accessible to the sons of the Ahom royal family and the local gentry of upper Assam, it was suggested that an English school be established also at Sibsagar, but due to a paucity of funds this was deferred until 1841. The importance attached to the study of English depended mainly on the lure of jobs which attracted most of the students. However, it soon emerged that the beginners found it extremely difficult to tackle English both as a subject and language of instruction. There was a rapid fall in enrolment which dwindled to such an extent that in 1844 the government thought it wise to make the teaching of English optional. The two schools in Gauhati and Sibsagar were converted into Anglo-vernacular establishments. As instruction in English continued to prove challenging, the local authorities directed their attention to the spread of purely vernacular schools, the number of which increased in 1852 to seventy-four with an enrolment of 4,025.[12]

Outwardly there appeared to be a steady increase in the number of scholars but the total was insignificant compared with the population of the province. In 1853 the percentage of educated people was 2.68 per cent. Out of 35,416 boys of school-going age, only 4,268 were attending an educational institution. The main obstacles were fairly obvious: firstly, children could not be spared from agricultural labour; secondly, the poverty of the people led to an expectation that the responsibility of providing education belonged to the government alone and the few government schools could accomplish little in the promotion of mass education; thirdly, for the first half of the nineteenth century only the populous and easily accessible areas of Assam were selected for the establishment of schools and the outlying areas were not taken into consideration; fourthly, the influential classes of Assam took little or no interest in local institutions, although they were expected to look after the general administration and repair of these buildings;[13] and, finally, the desire for education was based on its value in attaining government employment. When this ultimate object was not achieved for whatever reason, the general complaint was that the British government had diverted the attention and energy of the people under false pretences. The accusation was made, 'You have given us education under the promise of employment and unfitted us for an agricultural life.'[14]

In 1853 the Moffatt Mills report declared proudly that since the British occupation of Assam, education had spread widely through the province and achieved much that was commendable. In 1838 in the district of Nowgong, 'universal ignorance pervaded the whole community without exception, but in the course of thirteen years, hundreds of boys had emerged from the village schools with reasonable literacy'. Despite this apparent success, although the principal attraction of education was the possibility of government service, only sixty pupils from Kamrup, eighty-five from Nowgong and sixteen from Sibsagar had secured minor jobs in criminal and judicial departments. The people of Assam were debarred from higher government posts due partly to their insufficient grasp of English and partly to the keen competition from Bengali candidates. Moffatt Mills informed the government of Bengal of deterrents to educational progress, such as the inefficiency of masters, lack of suitable vernacular textbooks and the use of Bengali as the medium of instruction. As a remedy, he recommended gradual substitution of the Assamese language for Bengali, the publication of a series of popular works in Assamese, and the completion of the existing course of vernacular education in Assamese. Under this system, he felt that pupils would learn more in two than in four years, as learning through the mother tongue would minimise both the time and labour of pupils.[15]

Concurring fully with the views of Moffatt Mills, the sub-assistant of Nowgong and eminent publisher Anandaram Dhekial Phukan (son of Haliram Dhekial Phukan, the author of the first modern history of the state) was of the opinion that education of the Assamese was essential, 'to make the people intelligent, of good repute, steady in duty, faithful in trust, firm in character, obedient to the laws, useful to the country and serviceable to their kind'. However, he strongly criticised the government for treating the establishment of schools in Assam as an experimental measure and rapidly implanting English instruction, only to suddenly abolish it on the grounds of the general lack of intellect and enthusiasm of the pupils, with no reflection on a more suitable system. Anandaram considered that there was much confusion over the educational policy and the growth of education suffered not because of the intellectual inferiority of the people, but due to the defective methods of instruction adopted by the government. Agreeing with Mills over the use of Assamese over Bengali, he also suggested the establishment of 'normal schools' to train a body of teachers with increased salaries and the creation of a separate department for the study of Sanskrit, as he felt that the combination of a knowledge of Sanskrit with the vernacular would be readily accepted by both the literate members of the community and those who supported an indigenous education.[16]

On the renewal of the East India Company charter in 1853, the Court of Directors produced a report drawing up a comprehensive scheme of Indian education from primary to university level. The resulting despatch of 1854 by Charles Wood, president of the Board of Control, recommended that the Government of India work towards the dissemination of practical knowledge suitable for the vast majority of the population who were incapable of obtaining it through their own efforts. A scheme had been developed in the Northwest Frontier Province whereby emphasis was given to establishing primary schools of an indigenous nature to achieve such mass coverage. This was subsequently adopted by the government of Assam, who saw the encouragement of indigenous schools as the first step in spreading education among those Assamese who were too poor to overcome their illiteracy. However, the government was not in a position to provide adequate funds for such an ambitious project and, as far as circumstances permitted, efforts were made to establish indigenous and self-supporting schools on a grant-in-aid basis. In 1855–56 private indigenous schools were opened in regions of Assam such as Lakhimpur, Sibsagar, Darrang and Kamrup. These schools instructed a total number of

1,479 pupils. In the following year a subsidy system was adopted whereby rewards were made to those schools who attracted the highest number of boys receiving the basic requirements of an education, but the practicalities proved to be far from ideal: firstly, the grant of money was based on efficiency, but a true judgement of a school could not be made regularly by inspecting staff due to the restrictions of transport and communication during the rainy season; and, secondly, if the teachers were not paid their monthly salary regularly, they were tempted to take up other employment. Yet despite these difficulties, new schools began to spring up in places where none had existed before and it was a source of some satisfaction that a good number were making steady progress.

Despite this improvement, in 1859 a despatch by Lord Stanley, secretary of state for India, marked another abrupt change of government policy and the end of the subsidy system. The secretary of state bent to the will of some 7,000 Hindus and Muslims at a meeting in Madras requesting an end to grant-in-aid, most of which was paid to mission schools, and the establishment of more government schools. Each province was to follow a policy of its own in response to the latest despatch. In Assam, the inspector of schools, William Robinson, in collaboration with the commissioner, decided in 1860 to abolish fifty out of seventy-one government primary schools, with the intention of raising the standard of the remainder and distributing them through the province to be more readily available to those who boys who wished to pursue higher studies. In 1862–63, nineteen schools in Kamrup and ten in Nowgong were abolished, and twenty-one schools in Darrang, Sibsagar and Lakhimpur were deprived of government grant-in-aid. The abolition raised great dissatisfaction among many parents who complained to their respective district commissioners of the difficulties of sending children far away from their homes to receive an elementary education in government vernacular schools of a superior grade. Although, in compensation for the removal of primary schools, grant-in-aid was increased to a greater number of indigenous self-supporting schools, the progress of primary education was far from ideal, and it was hard to find even one in 200 pupils capable of reading and writing.[17]

Secondary education fared better in the wake of Wood's 1854 despatch, and larger sums were allocated to local authorities for a wider dissemination of knowledge among all classes of people, resulting not only in the multiplication of high, middle and elementary schools but also in the increased number of literates in the province. However, vocational training for older pupils was conspicuous by its absence and little attempt was made to train secondary school teachers, resulting in a dearth of qualified personnel. The government of Bengal often sent inferior men from Dacca or Calcutta to fill the higher posts in the schools and, for the lower classes, teachers with little more than the minimum of knowledge. The retention of Bengali as the medium of instruction in both primary and secondary education continued to produce poor results, and it was only after a long-drawn-out controversy that Sir George Campbell, lieutenant-governor of Bengal, in 1872 replaced Bengali with Assamese in the all the schools in the Brahmaputra Valley, resulting in a rapid growth in primary schools and a dramatic social regeneration in the plains.[18] Within a few years, achieving Sir George's goal to create 'intelligent labourers',[19] pupils were able to read and write letters, to survey the land they cultivated and to compute the rent they had to pay for it. From then onwards, petitions to the government from the local intelligentsia resulted in the establishment of not only many more schools but also a college at Gauhati and a medical college in Dibrugarh in 1900–01.

In 1882, viceroy Lord Ripon set up the first commission on education headed by William Hunter, which, in the light of the heavy financial pressure placed upon the Government of India by the Second Afghan War, the threatening attitude of Russia and the Third Burmese War, called for private support of educational institutions. The commission recommended that it should be the aim of the government to cease direct funding and where reasonable to help independent institutions under the control of private bodies on a grant-in-aid basis. It was anticipated that local enterprise would come forward to aid the expansion of education from primary to secondary level.[20] For the promotion of mass education, it recommended the rapid growth of indigenous schools (nurtured by local people only) which should be granted special allowances on condition that they imparted secular education up to the standard existing in the lower grade of primary schools or at least reading, writing and arithmetic in the vernacular. Religious schools such as *tols* and *maktabs* were not entitled to a government grant, and as a result there was a gradual decrease in their number. At the same time, it was considered necessary that the local government should sanction at least one model high school in each district.[21] In the course of the next twenty years the number of government high schools reached ten, with 2,411 students; government middle English schools numbered three, with 179; and government vernacular middle schools numbered fourteen, with 1,103 pupils.

In addition, the commission recommended that new schools be established in rural areas where the people were unable to accomplish this themselves. Under Ripon's 1882 resolution on local self-government, local and municipal boards were established throughout Assam. Primary education was to become their main concern. In 1883–84, the number of primary schools stood at 1,048 and rose to 1,259 in 1891–92. However, from 1897 to 1902 there was a rapid fall in such schools. Initially government officers dealt with the inhabitants of the populous and easily accessible areas of Assam, where the value of education was appreciated, but when their efforts were moved to the population in the interior they met with indifference. As a result, the government failed to give adequate aid to many local bodies while additional funds were spent on higher education. Although there was some expansion of education through private enterprise during the last decades of the nineteenth century, it was obvious that the lack of sufficient government control had left in its train various evils. Most of the schools conducted by private agencies were inefficient, ill-equipped and poorly staffed, and less centres of learning than coaching institutions. It was only at the start of the twentieth century, under the tenure of Lord Curzon, that there was a more positive move towards greater control and a general improvement.[22]

Higher Education

The educational agenda of the Assam government was focused upon the creation of a class of intelligent labour possessing some useful skills and practical knowledge. There was little room or financial means in this programme for the higher learning which would have the potential to create an enlightened community capable of challenging the British system of government, as existed in Bengal. Nevertheless, in 1861–62 the Gauhati and Sibsagar schools were affiliated to Calcutta University to send up candidates for the entrance examination, with limited success. Although three candidates in 1864 passed the examination, none availed themselves of the newly introduced junior scholarships. Their parents were reluctant to send their sons away to Calcutta where the families had no contacts, and the scholarship money was too meagre to meet student expenses in the presidency capital where the cost of living was considerably higher than Assam.

When the lieutenant-governor of Bengal, Cecil Beadon, visited Assam in 1862, William Robinson (at that time headmaster of the Gauhati school) proposed the establishment of a high school or college in Assam. It was suggested that, instead of providing an expensive college for the handful of students coming out of the two schools at Gauhati and Sibsagar, that the Gauhati school should be upgraded in 1865 to a collegiate school to the standard of the Faculty of Arts course at Calcutta University. However, enrolment was poor due to the few successful candidates at the entrance examination and during the years 1872–74 not a single candidate emerged successfully. As a result, Colonel Richard Keatinge, the first chief commissioner of Assam, abolished the collegiate section of the school in 1876.[1] In its absence several senior scholarships were established to enable students to pursue higher studies in colleges in Bengal. By 1883–84 there were forty-six junior students and eleven scholarship holders in Bengal preparing for Fine Arts and BA examinations respectively, and in 1899–1900 the total number of students from the province receiving a college education in Bengal reached nearly 300. In the last quarter of the nineteenth century there were further moves for the promotion of collegiate education in Assam which did not succeed until the intervention of Manik Chandra Baruah, general secretary of the Assam Association, who strongly advocated the establishment of a second-grade college in Gauhati.[2] The chief commissioner, Henry Cotton, endorsed the foundation of such a college in 1901, subsequently named after him and thereafter a significant part of Assam's academic life.

Female Education

Commenting on the depressed status of women in Assam in the nineteenth century, Robinson observed,

> A state of dependence more humiliating than that to which the weaker sex is here subject, cannot easily be conceived. Like most women in India, they are denied even the least portion of education and are excluded from every social circle ... every ray of mental improvement is kept away from the sex. As they are always confined to domestic duties, and excluded from the society of the other sex, the people see no necessity for their education.[1]

Due to the social and religious prejudices existing in Assam, the authorities in Calcutta only assumed responsibility for the education of women after the Wood despatch of 1854. The difficulties which faced the promoters of female advancement were formidable. Most challenging was the widely held view of the irrelevancy of education for girls as a means to a livelihood whereas, in the case of boys, material considerations had helped considerably to spread the desire for schools. In addition, the conservative values of upper- and middle-class parents resulted in apathy towards the education of their daughters, and the system of child marriage posed a great barrier by secluding girls at an age when their education began. Finally, there was a belief that the education of women might bring a social revolution. To most of the population, domestic duties were regarded as the sole objective of a woman's life.[2]

Nevertheless Wood's 1854 despatch emphasised the need for female education and advised the provision of large grants to achieve this end:

> The importance of female education in India cannot be overrated; and we have observed with pleasure the evidence which is now afforded of an increased desire on the part of many of the natives of India to give a good education to their daughters. By this means a far greater proportional impulse is imparted to the educational and moral tone of the people than by the education of men.[3]

In 1860–61 the first elementary school for girls was started in upper Assam, followed by more schools in the next two years in Sibsagar, Nowgong and Gauhati. Within fifteen years, forty-four schools were opened throughout the province with an enrolment of 552.[4] However, although private enterprise received some aid, government encouragement remained half-hearted and in 1874–75 the number of girls receiving primary education was only 875. The Hunter Commission of 1882 reported that the proportion of girls attending school for the entire female population of India was one in 843, whereas in Assam the figure was one in 2,236. With the recommendation of the commission that female education should have its legitimate share of the local, municipal and provincial funds, there was more interest in girls' schools and a gradual change in social outlook as, even among the orthodox community, social practices such as child marriage gradually lost their rigidity and prejudice against the education of women began to disappear.[5] Although the commission did not encourage mixed education other than for infants, it was found that in Assam mixed schools thrived (possibly because Assamese society was predominantly semi-tribal and the process of Hinduisation had been a gradual one).

In 1885–86 a scheme was introduced whereby each teacher in a lower primary school was given an additional 4 annas monthly for each girl who could read a little. This plan had the effect of doubling the number of girls in boys' schools; by 1889 the number

Education

of female pupils had risen to 2,414 in 185 co-educational schools, and by 1897–98, in the same number of schools, the female intake had increased to 3,823. However, even by the end of the century the great majority of the girls receiving education never progressed beyond primary school. A few were reading in upper primary schools, a smaller number in middle schools, and absolutely none in high schools.[6] Causing practical difficulties for those parents to whom a mixed school was undesirable, most girls' schools were in urban locations and out of the reach of families in rural areas, and a number were shut down for lack of pupils. In 1884–85, there were 154 girls' schools but by 1889–90 the number was down to 142.[7] In addition, many girls left without completing their course due to social and economic factors. Upper-class families seldom sent their daughters to school after they reached puberty. One of the greatest drawbacks was the dearth of female teachers in a climate in which respectable families could not be expected to send their daughters to a school where there were only male teachers. Yet social constraints and poor pay made it almost impossible for women teachers to live in places other than their own villages and under the protection of their families.[8]

Despite these setbacks, a determined group of social reformers supported the education of girls, despite being tied to their tradition and caste-Hindu social norms. Assamese elites such as Anandaram Dhekial Phukan, Gunabhiram Barua and Hemchandra Barua wished women to be educated and modernised, but at the same time to dedicate their lives to the service of their husband and to bear all the responsibilities of a respectable home. Anandaram taught his wife Mahindri Devi at home at home and started his daughter Padmavati's education at the age of five.[9] In 1884 Padmavati published the first Assamese fictional narrative in prose, *Sudhamar Upakhyam*, advocating the duty of a woman to develop her mind by learning to read and write while still maintaining a total submission of wife to husband. Gunabhiram Barua, a social reformer, also supported female education and in 1880 took his nine-year-old daughter Swarnalata to Calcutta to study, believing that it was the responsibility of parents to educate both boys and girls equally.[10]

However, in general few parents took the education of their girls seriously. In a province where even among the upper classes of society the education of a boy meant little unless it carried with it a certain financial value, the education of a girl was bound to remain a matter of public indifference. Often the establishment of a village girls' school was of little interest to the inhabitants, and it was difficult to give girls more than the merest rudiments of education in the light of early marriage. Tentative steps had been initiated by the government of Assam to promote female education, but they proved inadequate and fell far short of the basic requirement. In contrast, for missionaries working in the province the education of girls was a matter of priority.

Missions

Originally the East India Company sent chaplains to India to look after the spiritual welfare of its Christian employees and to spread the message of Christ among Indians. However, towards the end of the eighteenth century, the British government took the stance that 'in matters of religion the natives of India were particularly sensitive' and 'any interference ... would eventually ensure the total destruction of British power' in India.[1] Religious neutrality became a priority of the British authorities and their attitude towards the missionaries ranged from one of indifference to open hostility. When William Carey, the first British missionary, arrived in Calcutta in 1793, he was prohibited from preaching and forced to make his headquarters in the city of Serampore in Danish India.[2] However, in the early nineteenth century there was a vigorous move by evangelists such as William Wilberforce, in collaboration with the Church Missionaries Society, the Bible Society and other organisations, to send missionaries to India. By the publication of papers and pamphlets, they succeeded in winning favourable public opinion on their behalf. As a result, the Charter Act of 1813, renewing the charter granted to the East India Company, included a clause permitting missionaries to 'go out and reside in India under certain conditions'.[3] More English and American missionaries arrived in the subcontinent and a bishop was appointed in Calcutta. The governor-general was, however, enjoined to impress upon Company officials the need for strict religious neutrality.

The newly acquired freedom of movement granted by the Charter Act encouraged missionaries to venture into Assam, where there were three types of indigenous schools of a strictly religious character: the Hindu *tols* for teaching Sanskrit and the Vedas; the Muslim *maktabs*, teaching Arabic and the Koran; and the Khamti priests' schools, teaching Buddhism.[4] Krishna Pal, Carey's first convert, conducted his mission from headquarters at Pandua in the Sylhet district and by 1813 was said to have baptised seven more converts, of whom two were Khasis, in the presence of a large gathering including several tribal chiefs.[5] In 1829 a branch of the English Baptist Mission was set up at Gauhati by James Rae under the patronage of David Scott, and soon after assuming office in 1834 the agent to the governor-general, Francis Jenkins, suggested to the mission that an establishment in Sadiya might be opened in an effort to pacify the quarrelling Khamtis and Singphos. When no response was forthcoming, he extended an invitation to the American Baptists to undertake the task, in the knowledge that the foundation in 1810 of the American Board of Commissioners for Foreign Affairs, a Protestant agency, had improved the prospects for American proselytization.

When the proposal for Sadiya arose, the board, which had decided to 'enter into every unoccupied field and to extend their operations as widely as possible', instructed the reverends Nathan Brown and Oliver T. Cutter to move from Burma to set up the mission. An establishment in Assam was geographically important. It was hoped that, beneath the protection offered by the East India Company, the missionaries might join the caravans that traded yearly to the interior of China and, while the 'jealous mandarins' were excluding foreigners from the ports, missionaries could plant Christianity in the Chinese interior.[6] As a bonus, the British government proved useful to their activities in India:

> It lent prestige to their religion ... provided financial support for their institutions and gave them government–granted monopoly

on education in many areas, an invaluable instrument of influence far beyond anything that such a small group of people could have ordinarily have on an alien society.[7]

At Sadiya the American Baptists set up the first printing press in Assam, for which Francis Jenkins granted the mission Rs 1,000 yearly if they settled in the area.[8] Nathan Brown had studied the Shan language before leaving Burma and compiled a vocabulary of 3,000 words prior to printing the language in the Roman character. It was hoped that this would not only enable the missionaries to convert the frontier tribes to Christianity but also open an entry into China.

However, their plans failed to materialise. The resources of the Assam mission were small and the board felt that without a substantial increase in its revenue it must 'either recall some of the missionaries or go deeper into debt'.[9] Moreover the hostile attitude of the Khamtis and Singphos forced the missionaries to move to Jaipur and eventually to Sibsagar where the mission remained. In the light of the inaccessibility of the Shan country lying between Assam and Burma, all hopes to move on to China were dashed. The Sibsagar press, for many years the only one in Assam, issued most of the literature printed in the Assamese language: schoolbooks, tracts, portions of scripture, a hymnbook, and a monthly paper called *Orunodoi* or 'dawn of light'. In 1848 the entire New Testament translated by Nathan Brown from the Hebrew into Assamese was published and in 1850 there came a third edition. In 1848 Brown also published a treatise on the Assamese language, giving a strong boost to its introduction as the official language of the province.[10] Another American Baptist missionary, Miles Bronson, who was one of the early mission workers among the Nagas, edited the first Assamese–English dictionary in 1867 and thereafter worked tirelessly to reverse the imposition of the Bengali language on schools and courts in the valley of the Brahmaputra. Brown left Assam due to ill health after more than twenty years of work, but the translation of the Bible was carried on by his successors.[11] *Orunodoi*, for many years the only paper published in Assam, was widely circulated and read by those who understood the language. Great pains were taken by the early missionaries to make the publication both attractive and instructive, illustrating it with engravings by native Assamese. The government recognised its usefulness in spreading the gospel and 'imparting information on subjects of scientific and general interest, among an unenlightened people', however the popularity of the paper gradually declined, and the printing house finally closed in December 1880.[12]

One of the most important contributions of the American Baptist missions in Assam was education through the establishment of numerous village schools. The early missionaries found that the majority of the Assamese people were unable to read and believed that it was the intention of the Hindu priesthood to keep them in a state of ignorance.[13] It was hoped that mission schools could produce a new generation with an early understanding of the principles of Christianity, thereby armed with the means 'to launch an attack' on the Hindu *shastras*.[14] American Baptists were the pioneers of female education in Assam and only a few months after their arrival in 1836 they set up their first schools in Sadiya, with separate classes for girls and boys. The wives of Nathan Brown and Oliver Cutter established additional girls' schools in Sadiya in 1837 and 1838 and in Sibsagar in 1840. Miles Bronson, when founding the Nowgong Orphan Institute in 1843, the first co-educational establishment in the northeast,[15] stated that one purpose for starting the school was to introduce education to girls who, in his view, appeared to be wholly neglected. When a sufficient number of girls had been assembled, missionaries tended to adopt the boarding school system to cut the pupils off from 'heathen influences', and Bronson's wife created such a school with thirteen pupils.[16] Women were identified as one of the most important tools in the process of evangelisation as, following conversion, they were in a position to influence issues of religion and caste in the home. As a result, when the girls' schools failed to grow, female mission workers started what were called zenana classes, going door to door to encourage girls to study, but with little success.[17] Many people were critical of missionary activity and the impact of western influence which, they argued, resulted in the erosion of traditional values.

The British Takeover of Assam

By 1880, the American Baptist missionary Susan Ward numbered the congregation of the church in Sibsagar at about 200 and the Christian community of the town roughly twice that number. A large portion of the church members were migrants employed on the tea gardens, two of whom were employed by the mission to hold services for their fellow workers on Sundays, encouraged by some planters and vehemently opposed by others. Other than educational facilities set up by missionaries, a few liberal-minded and enthusiastic planters had organised private primary schools open to the public to cater to the educational need of the neighbouring areas. George Williamson, a senior administrative officer in Golaghat, 'bequeathed two lakhs of Rupees as a permanent fund for the establishment of schools for training the native young men of the province in mechanical skills such as carpentry, smithing and shoe-making' and the interest on this bequest supported such a school in Jorhat. However, few encouraging results were achieved from a 'generous effort to raise up a class of skilled artisans to meet a crying want everywhere'.[18] Elsewhere in the area schools for native boys and girls were sustained by the mission with the main objective of 'the proclamation of the gospel to the people of the village', and for several years there was a boarding school for Eurasian children overseen by Susan Ward. In addition, in the Sibsagar and Lakhimpur districts members of the German Lutheran mission had followed the large number of migrant workers moving to the tea plantations from Chota Nagpur where the mission was highly active.

The American Baptists also had two branches in the Naga Hills, one at Molong in the south and the other at Kohima, the civil station among the Angami Nagas. Ward reported that at the former station the Reverend Edwin W. Clark and his wife had lived for some years in the 1870s working among the Ao people,

> without Government protection, among a rude race of savages, learning an unwritten language, isolated from all European society; and in the rainy season shut up in the hills by swollen rivers and malarious paths, a journey to the plains being impracticable.[19]

However, the mission had the help of a 'most efficient' ordained Assamese preacher, Godhula Rufus Brown, who learnt the native language, compiled a large vocabulary, translated portions of scripture and other books, and composed several hymns in the vernacular. At Kohima, the Reverend Charles DeWitt King and his wife, Anna, working among the Angami Nagas, were more comfortably situated in a civil station where they were under the protection of British arms. A magistrate, surgeon and half a regiment of soldiers with officers were stationed in the area with telegraphic communication and there was 'a prosperous school of Naga youth, who give a willing ear to the gospel message, and attend Sabbath services'.[20] However, the progress of evangelisation was slow as, 'independent in bearing and exclusive in spirit', the Angamis not only refused to accept Christianity but also openly resisted the infiltration of the new faith, reluctant to abandon their habits of using opium and 'drinking to such an extent that no church could stand against its ravage'.[21] The Angami uprising forced the Kings to flee to Sibsagar in November 1879.

The goal of the missions in the Naga Hills was 'the introduction of civilisation and Christianity among a large class of people at present hopelessly buried in barbarism and superstition'.[22] This goal was not helped by the fact that the Nagas feared that American missionaries were Company agents, coming 'to spy out their roads, sources of wealth, number of slaves, amount of population, and means of defence, and the best methods of taking the country'.[23] The work was challenging in the extreme, as Naga Christian converts were naturally expected to participate in the defence of the village as well as its raids and 'their reluctance to do so as well as to participate in village festivities that involved drinking made them increasingly unpopular and objects of persecution'.[24] Missionary insistence on the prohibition of *azu* (rice beer) and the condemnation of the use of the Naga community *moorung*, on the grounds that it was a heathen establishment where unchristian conduct took place, were just two of the indigenous customs and practices which failed to meet the requirements for the salvation of the soul. The Austrian ethnologist Christopher Furer-Haimendorf regretted that, rather than bringing the Naga culture and Christianity into harmony, the missionaries set them at opposite poles, declaring that, 'seeing his own customs condemned by the missionaries, [the Naga] learnt to despise his own tribe and cultural inheritance'.[25] By the early 1920s, the British administrator and anthropologist John Henry Hutton noted the remarkable rapidity at which the Naga culture was being transformed in the cause of progress, declaring, 'Old beliefs and customs are dying, the number of Christians or quasi-Christians is steadily increasing, and the spirit of change is invading and pervading every aspect of village life.'[26]

Elsewhere in the province a chaplain was appointed by the Bishop of Calcutta for Gauhati and Shillong, dividing his time between the two towns to hold Sunday services. There was also a chaplain who served both Sibsagar and Dibrugarh who occasionally held services in some of the tea gardens. The American Baptists maintained a mission in Gauhati for over thirty years, supporting fourteen churches with 614 members and a girls' school, and more than 200 pupils in the village schools. However, the most successful mission in Assam was that of the Welsh Calvinistic society among the Khasis, because the work was with a people 'free from the trammels of caste' and the field was well supplied with missionaries. In the 1880s the work of the society spread into the hills and the Reverend T. J. Jones was appointed to Shillong, assisted by six other missionaries stationed in different places in the area, where ninety schools for boys and girls were scattered. A larger number of girls were under instruction in this district than in any other in Assam. Whereas it was possible to have mixed schools among the Khasis, this was unfeasible in the education of Hindus or Muslims. Connected to the mission were sixty-six churches, boasting over 2,000 members. The people were characterised as 'gentle in disposition, truthful and industrious, free from the prejudices of caste' and (welcome to evangelists) 'never idolaters', their worship consisting of sacrifices to evil spirits.[27]

The American Baptist Mission for several years also held property in the Goalpara region. In 1877 in order to be among the people the mission was moved to Tura, a civil station which had recently opened on the Garo Hills. The work began when two men of the Garo tribe who were in police service in Gauhati and stationed at one of the mission bungalows picked up a Christian tract, 'were interested, and sought further instruction'. Both men were ordained and subsequently actively engaged in proselytization among the tribesmen. The Bible was translated into the local language, a new dictionary was prepared and a monthly sheet, *The Garos' Friend*, was issued. Nine churches were formed at different villages with over 600 members, mostly administered by native preachers, six of whom were ordained. There was a girls' boarding school in Tura and in the villages thirty-five schools numbering 662 pupils, to which the government made a liberal grant of Rs 3,000 and 'the people also contribute liberally from their scanty means in aid of Christian work'. The Garo tribe numbered about 109,000 and it was evident in the 1880s that the work was still in an early stage. However, to the missionaries there was a certain consolation in observing the change that Christianity had wrought upon the 'nearly naked savages, filthy and barbarous in their habits and customs'.[28]

To the American Baptists working in Assam, the basic animistic practices of the hill tribes were considerably less fit for condemnation than 'the hoary system of idolatry' adopted by the Hindu religion which had been graphically described by the English pioneer missionary William Ward (husband of Susan), who founded the original Baptist college in Serampore. Ward's *A View of the History, Literature and Religion of the Hindoos* when published in 1811 immediately became the standard work on the Hindu religion for those interested in the spread of missions or in the missionary vocation itself. A mixture of academic detail and evangelical invective, the book ultimately concluded that Hinduism comprised 'the most puerile, impure and bloody, of any system of idolatry THAT WAS EVER ESTABLISHED ON EARTH'.[29] Denominational and missionary publications weighed in with their support of Ward and the inflammatory nature of his narration and lurid descriptions of alleged Hindu abominations underscored the urgent responsibility of Christians to evangelise Britain's Indian possession.³⁰ It was welcomed that only the great Hindu festivals brought the 'most devout' to the temple for worship and elsewhere temples 'were decaying, fit emblems of the system they represent … only here and there, a living stone falls out and is transferred to the temple of the true God'.³¹ Where temples did flourish, there was criticism of the Hindu priestly practice of taking donations from disciples which to the Baptists was regarded as 'robbery and oppression'. Bronson wrote,

> The temple subsists on the offerings of the people and the yearly payments of their disciples. They tax every man to the value of 50 cents a year and manage to get much more out of them. Collectors go annually to distant villages where the disciples live, and if any one [sic] refuses to pay, he is at once denounced and made to suffer as an outcaste.³²

Sharing a healthy disrespect for idolatry and the fortunes of the Hindu priestly classes, government officials maintained a largely mutual understanding with Christian missionaries during the first half of the nineteenth century. For evangelisation, physical security was essential and could be provided only by the colonial rulers. From a religious standpoint, the British supported missionary activities and aided missions with financial and moral support. However, following the transfer of power to the Crown in 1858 after the Revolt of 1857, the Government of India was instructed to revert to a policy of religious neutrality in education, in the belief that evangelical activity was to some extent responsible for the outbreak. Nevertheless, a sudden change was seen as unwise in the tribal areas of Assam, where teaching of the scriptures was considered neither objectionable nor dangerous, and grant-in-aid to schools was continued. The British also hoped that their work among the tribes would bring loyalty to the Crown, whereas military expeditions against the hill people only produced suspicion culminating in retaliation and revenge.

Although missionaries usually supported the government, they reacted strongly against those official moves which were seen to obstruct the process of conversion. Aware that a large number of Assamese were addicts (an opinion which was reinforced by the Moffatt Mills Report of 1853, which maintained that three-fourths of the population were opium eaters),[33] they welcomed the ban on poppy cultivation in May 1860, which was instigated largely by British tea planters who believed that the drug was responsible for making the Assamese too lazy to work on plantations. The subsequent government decision to sell imported opium from Malwa at retail outlets (steadily increasing the wholesale price of opium over the second half of the nineteenth century to raise revenue while reducing the number of vending licences issued) initially received widespread support from British officials, planters and missionaries. However, the downward trend in opium consumption did not occur. Revenue considerations did not permit drastic and frequent upward price revisions and prevented greater expenditure on anti-smuggling measures. Despite government acquisition of a monopoly over the opium trade, consumption intensified rather than reduced and contraband opium continued to circulate. Lower classes were said to be spending 10 to 20 per cent of their income on the drug and it was observed that in 1893 some veteran users in the district of Lakhimpur spent up to one-half. In 1864–65, the total quantity of *abkari* (excise) opium sold in the Brahmaputra Valley amounted to 1,939 *maunds* and the excise collected from the drug during the same period was almost 1,70,500 rupees more than land revenue collection.[34] The missionary Samuel Whiting wrote of his great dismay and that of his fellow evangelists that 'the government, as it maintains, in order to destroy the cultivation of the plant in Assam, and so gradually to discourage its use, introduces its own drug, and it is now sold from our Government treasuries. The result is, as might be expected, a perfectly alarming demand for the article.'[35]

In addition, in opposition to the government, mission activities furthered the cause of the Assamese people in their opposition to Bengali influence within the province. As has been stated above, the American Baptists were the precursors of the Assamese renaissance in language and literature; firstly, through their own writings and books published in Assamese at the mission press in Sibsagar and, secondly, by their insistence upon reinstating the Assamese language in the schools and courts of Assam. It is doubtful whether the government of Bengal would have conceded to the demands of the Assamese in the teeth of strong opposition had it not been for the protracted struggle carried on by the Baptists for over two decades. The renaissance occurred both in style and content; writings with a medieval emphasis on spiritual and supernatural themes were replaced by secular subjects and rational thinking, giving birth to western literary forms such as lyrics, sonnets, novels, short stories and biographies.

However, even a century after the arrival of the first missionaries, the membership of the American Baptist mission in the Brahmaputra Valley stood at only 845, of whom 496 were Garos and 43 Mikirs.[36] Considering the total population of the valley, the small percentage of converts was a sign of the failure of evangelisation in the plains. It was in the hills where, despite considerable hostilities and hardships, Christian missionary activity reaped its greatest rewards with animistic tribes who were not attracted by Hinduism. As far as the impact of missionaries on the hill tribes was concerned, opinions were divided. The anthropologist Verrier Elwin considered that 'the activities of the Baptist missionaries among the Nagas have demoralised the people, destroyed tribal solidarity and forbidden the joys and feastings, the decorations and romance of communal life'.[37] However, those in favour of mission work were convinced that with the inevitable changes brought about by colonial rule, such as developments in communication, a money economy and material benefits, it was western education and thought which was needed to rouse the tribesmen to assert their political, economic and cultural rights rather than being drawn into the contemporary mainstream in which they stood to be overwhelmed by Hindu numerical dominance. In the words of an eminent Naga scholar, Asoso Yonuo, Christian evangelisation pushed his people 'out of the thought of seclusion and isolation from which they were suffering for centuries into open ideas, ideals and civilizations of the peoples of the world'.[38] This search for a distinct identity inevitably opened the breach between the inhabitants of the hills and inhabitants of the plains into what became a yawning gulf.

Jawaharlal Nehru regretted the fact that, 'when a new political awareness dawned on India, there was a movement to encourage the people of the Northeast to form separate and independent States. Many foreigners (missionaries) resident in the area supported this movement.'[39] In fact, there was remarkably little evidence to show that missionaries made any organised move to encourage the tribesmen to raise the flag of revolt against the Indian government. In the opinion of the historian Herambakanta Barpujari it appeared much more likely that their inspiration came from insurrectionary movements over the borders; in Burma, Malaya or Indonesia, in the wake of Japanese invasions.[40] Yet schools and churches established by the missionaries did emerge as new sites of interactions among the tribes and new bonds contributed to the decline of clan identities and the development of broader tribal ethnic formations as Nagas, Mizos, Khasis and Garos. From within each of the tribes, a middle class developed with its base neither in land nor in business but formed of newly educated members working in modern professions and closely associated with the church. These emerging elites started socio-cultural organisations for the uplift of their communities and, by differentiating themselves from the people in the plains and from other native hill communities, played a key role in shaping the attitudes of their members to political developments taking place in the subcontinent during the last three decades of British rule in India.

Epilogue

The repercussions of policies instigated under British rule in Assam rolled on into the twentieth century. Following the resentment aroused by Curzon's 1905 partition of the Bengal Presidency and its subsequent annulment, the Assamese fear of losing identity continued into the following decades, as Bengali Hindus dominated the administration and professions and the many hard-working Bengali Muslims who occupied vacant land and put virgin areas under cultivation altered the demography of the province. With constitutional reforms, India began to advance towards democracy and the Muslim League emerged with its demand for partition on the basis of religion. A concerted effort was made by those in favour of Muslim-majority provinces to encourage the migration of Bengali Muslims into Assam in the hope that Bengal and Assam would be grouped together as one province in the east of India. However, with Gandhi's support, the chief minister of Assam, Lokapriya Gopinath Bordoloi, vehemently opposed the suggestion on the grounds that local representatives would lose significant power. Eventually partition was chosen as a permanent solution rather than grouping, with an international border separating Assam and East Pakistan. The population movement from East Pakistan continued, initially mostly of Hindu refugees fleeing from religious persecution. Unlike the west of India, where the population displacement lasted for only a few months, in the case

Epilogue

of the east this movement spread over several years as the number of Hindus in East Pakistan declined steeply and Muslim infiltrators continued to migrate to Assam for economic reasons. Anti-Bengali riots and violence in the wake of insurgency in the state largely arrested the influx of Hindu refugees, but the illegal migration of Muslims from the new nation of Bangladesh into Assam continued alongside significant legal migration from West Bengal, fuelling the fear that the indigenous people of Assam would be reduced to a minority in their home state. Their cultural survival appeared to be in jeopardy, their political control weakened, and their employment opportunities undermined.

After partition and the transfer of the huge Bengali Muslim district of Sylhet to East Pakistan, the Assamese middle class, composed of caste Hindus, came to power for the first time in a century. Through expanded educational programmes and the use of Assamese in universities, this newly acquired, electorally buttressed power was used to consolidate the party's position, not only against Bengali control of administrative services and professions but also over the political aspirations of the less educated Assamese and other non-Assamese groups, and the tribal peoples in both hills and plains who remained largely backward. The enforcement of the dominant position of the middle class and the associated response from disadvantaged sections of the population largely determined the politics of the region immediately after the departure of the British, as the limitations of a bourgeois democracy controlling an economically backward country became apparent. In the hills, a very small but significant group emerged among the Naga, Mizo and Khasi tribals as a result of their exposure to modern education, mainly at the hand of Christian missionaries. These individuals, with a sense of national identity which had been reinforced under the colonial isolation policy, became instigators of social and political change in their respective societies. The separate policies adopted by the British towards the Assam plains on the one hand and the hill areas on the other were continued by the government of independent India, whose provisions for tribal self-governance included extensive legislative as well as executive powers to protect land and traditions through a system of autonomous district and regional councils, mirroring the treatment of the very areas that were classified as Excluded and Partially Excluded territory under colonial rule.

However, whereas the British administrative mechanism was aimed at the development of the tribes in relative isolation, the aim of the Indian government was a gradual political, economic and administrative integration of tribal people into Indian society while preserving linguistic, religious and cultural features. The results of this intervention were far from satisfactory due to the structural implementation of the policy, and in the aftermath of the Chinese aggression of 1962 there was a significant change in approach towards the northeast when policies were driven more by security considerations than a development perspective. The earlier policy was replaced by an aggressive regime of cultural assimilation of tribal people to speed up their socio-economic development (with the loss of ethnic attributes) in order to maintain the territorial integrity of the region. The resulting alienation and antagonism produced insurgency in the Naga Hills in the early 1950s and in the Lushai Hills in the mid-1960s, resulting in the uncritical granting by the central government of political autonomy, which in some cases took the form of the birth of states along ethnic lines. The state of Nagaland was created in 1963, the United Khasi–Jaintia Hills district and the Garo Hills district combined to become the state of Meghalaya in 1970, and the state of Mizoram (the Lushai Hills) emerged in 1987. These entities created their own problems when ethnic minorities within the newly formed boundaries claimed that their rights and resources were being violated and demanded political autonomy of their own, paving the way for further divisions of the existing territories and a setback to the prospects of economic and social growth in the region which were already precarious in the wake of Indian independence.

Following the departure of the British, Indian capitalists were given a decisive role in developing and modernising the post-colonial economy of the subcontinent. This path of development generated severe regional disparities and capitalists seeking a maximisation

Epilogue

of profit proved to be wary of investing in an area which did not assure the anticipated return. In the second half of the twentieth century the problems of the northeast were painfully apparent: its geographical location in a strategically sensitive region near the border of four foreign countries (China, Bangladesh, Bhutan and Burma); perennial flood and political disturbances; a severely underdeveloped infrastructure of roads, railways, communication systems, power delivery and institutional facilities; and abject poverty with low indigenous capital formation. As a result, there was a failure to draw significant private investment and the pace of development in Assam was extremely slow and lethargic compared to that of more modernised regions of India. The legacy of the colonial economy lived on, and the raw supplier status of Assam barely changed as it remained an agriculturally and industrially backward state despite its rich water, forest and mineral resources. The promotion by the British of immigration from other parts of India, especially East Bengal, fuelled a rapid growth of population in the first decades of the twentieth century that severely increased the pressure on available land.[1] Moreover, the colonial failure to control the flow of the Brahmaputra and other rivers and to encourage farmers to adopt better technology was still painfully evident. The average size of operational landholding and per capita cultivable land were significantly less than the all-India average. As a result of the Green Revolution in the second half of the twentieth century, states such as Punjab, Haryana, Tamil Nadu and Maharashtra produced high crop yields, yet in Assam factors such as a low use of fertiliser and limited power in farming practice resulted in a virtually stagnant agricultural growth which increased Assam's dependence upon other states for food grains.

In the immediate post-colonial era, tea remained the major industry of Assam. Although tea estates were transferred to influential non-resident Indians, British capital maintained a strong position within the industry. The most profitable estates in the area were still controlled from Calcutta and London, employing a managerial cohort largely recruited from outside the state, and it was alleged that both Indian and foreign capitalists concealed a major share of their profits, thus robbing the state government of its due share of revenue and taxes.[2] The labour force, which continued to toil under severe exploitation, remained largely culturally backward and economically immobile, with an increase in the number of temporary, adolescent and child labourers. In the energy sector, until the 1970s Assam continued to produce half of the total crude oil and half of the total natural gas of India. As under colonial rule, British capital dominated the oil industry until the major oil companies were nationalised by the Government of India in 1981. This change proved of little benefit to the Assamese population, who observed that the exploitation of their resources continued under the control of the Indian government, with no increase in the refining capacity of the state despite much local protest. Such protest was given added weight by a repeated plea for adequate royalties on the crude product. The gains from natural gas were also marginal, with millions of cubic feet being flared up each day in upper Assam, an appalling waste for a region which had the potential to be one of the richest states for power generation and production of industrial goods such as types of rubber, plastics, nylon, polyester fibres, paint, dyes, pesticides and other chemicals.

In the textile sector, despite being one of the major jute-producing areas of India, there was little opportunity to manufacture jute textiles on an industrial scale in Assam with only one jute mill in 1978. Similarly, not a single silk or art silk mill with more than twenty-four power looms existed to process the large production of raw silk in the state, although weaving continued to be an important occupation for the women of the region. In the timber industry the processing capability of the state was more promising. By the 1980s the great richness in forest resources enabled Assam to feed two large paper mills, five match factories and fifty-two plywood factories, providing employment directly to 6,000 and indirectly to 25,000 labourers. However, most of the plywood industry was owned and managed by major Indian capitalists such as the Birlas. Not one factory was owned by the Assamese, and all large sales depots with their significant tax revenue were located outside the state. Moreover, it was evident that due to the extractive nature of the industry, which followed the colonial pattern of maximising profits with a healthy disregard for the environment, the ecological balance of the region continued to be seriously affected.[3]

The communication system in Assam, although having made some improvement during the post-colonial period, remained precarious and low investment in infrastructure failed to provide adequate support to the economy of the region. In the wake of Partition and the creation of East Pakistan, Assam became dangerously landlocked and connected to the rest of India only through a narrow strip of land, the Siliguri corridor, where a disruption could severely affect the entire northeast. The long-distance water-transport system within Assam virtually collapsed after independence and water transport was used solely to cross the rivers at various points in the Brahmaputra Valley. The history of neglect in building bridges over the vast river system was matched by a failure to build highways and the state remained significantly behind the all-India average of surfaced road. In the case of railways, apart from a 350-kilometre line built in the north of the state in the 1960s in the wake of Chinese aggression, until the 1980s there was no substantial construction of lines to expand the British metre-gauge railway which had been built to serve the tea belts, a route which failed to touch most of the important towns and villages of Assam. The poor state of road and rail connectivity, apart from hindering the general mobility of the population, retarded the growth of both the agricultural and industrial sectors by increasing the difficulties of accessing markets both for finished commodities and material inputs for production, and hindering the movement of labour. Moreover, even after two decades of independence and the existence of Assam as a separate state, the pattern of employment in the railways and other services echoed the situation which existed during British rule, with a large percentage of workers coming from East and West Bengal to the detriment of the Assamese locals.

At the time of independence Assam's per capita income stood above the national average, but this decreased substantially during the immediate post-colonial period compared to its sister states in the northeastern region. The 1981 National Committee on the

Development of Backward Areas found that, other than the upper Assam region containing the oil, tea and forest industries, all the remaining districts (with 76 per cent of the total population of the state) were failing to advance industrially, their occupants barely contributing to the local economy as any savings tended to be spent on consumer goods imported from outside Assam. Nevertheless, despite this bleak evidence of a stalling in financial growth, there was a significant expansion in the field of education during the post-colonial period. Gauhati University was established in 1948, Dibrugarh University in 1964 and Assam Agricultural University in 1968, spawning affiliated colleges with major diversification and specialisation. Assam's literacy rate became near equal to the all-India average, even with the educational inequalities which existed among various social groups in the province. But given the listless state of Assam's agriculture and a rapid population growth without corresponding growth in industry, the widening of the education band produced in its wake a large army of educated, semi-educated and illiterate unemployed, resulting in the popular action against illegal immigrants, the Assam Movement, whose activists fought from 1979 to 1985 to protect and provide constitutional, legislative and administrative safeguards to the indigenous Assamese people.

While the foreign nationals' issue, primarily centred around the ownership of land, gained most traction in the poverty-ridden rural areas, the urban populace saw the problem as one of industrial underdevelopment as had been the case under the British, resulting in poverty and large-scale unemployment. That Assam was nothing but a 'pseudo-colonial hinterland' to provide raw materials for the industrial centres of India became the theme of most writings and public speeches of the Assamese intelligentsia involved in the movement.[4] This growing consciousness among the Assamese middle class was further heightened by provocative and insensitive statements made by the central government, seen as evidence of the hostile attitude of the Indian ruling class towards the northeastern region, whose inhabitants saw themselves as the victims of a colonial pattern of plunder and dependency. By the

Epilogue

end of the twentieth century, it appeared that the central Indian government with its vested interests in the more affluent regions of the republic was following the British precedent of denying Assam the opportunity to reap the benefits of its resources.

As a postscript, *An India Economic Strategy to 2035* (2018), exploring the possibilities of an economic partnership between India and Australia, noted that Assam's first global investor summit in February 2018 had, alongside those industries fostered under colonial rule, concentrated on several new areas such as pharmaceuticals, tech start-ups, the sugar sector, solar energy and biotechnology. To deal with the infrastructure of the state, which was widely acknowledged to be inadequate, a number of new bridges over the Brahmaputra were proposed, along with a significant expansion of the rail network and industrial corridors along the river. Although both rural and urban poverty remained higher than the national average, these potentially transformative propositions appeared to place Assam's prospects on a more optimistic footing. However, the impact of the 2020 twin disasters of the Covid-19 pandemic and the unusually severe flooding in the region, with the related job losses of around 70 per cent of the population whose livelihood depended upon agriculture, was bound to be a major setback to the economic advancement of the state in the immediate future. Yet the subject of flood and erosion, and the resultant internal displacements of 'marginalised' people, repeatedly fails to feature as a central issue in state elections. A recent proposal for a study of the political economy of land and development in Assam stresses that flood-free areas are needed on the one hand for the autonomous development of the large numbers of tribal and indigenous peoples who inhabit the state, and on the other for land-hungry economic activity. Until this conflict is reconciled, any sense of economic achievement will exist in the shadow of the poverty and communal stress of the region.

Endnotes

Introduction
1. John McCosh, *Topography of Assam* (Calcutta: Bengal Military Orphan Press, 1837), p. 2.
2. Jayeeta Sharma, A Historical Perspective. https://www.india-seminar.com/2005/550/550 per cent20jayeeta per cent20sharma.htm
3. Ibid.
4. Sangamitra Misra, *Space, Borders and Histories: Identity Construction in Colonial Goalpara* (London: University of London, 2004), p. 107.
5. Amalendu Guha, *Planter-Raj to Swaraj: Freedom Struggle and Electoral Politics in Assam, 1826-1947* (New Delhi: Tulika Books, 1977), p. 40.
6. A. Mackenzie, *History of the Relations of the Government with the Hill Tribes of the Northeast Frontier of Bengal* (Calcutta: The Home Department Press, 1884), p. 7.
7. Quoted Mackenzie, *History of the Relations of the Government with the Hill Tribes*, pp. 89-90.
8. Sanjib Baruah, *India Against Itself: Assam and the Politics of Nationality* (Pennsylvania: University of Pennsylvania Press, 1999), p. 29.
9. Peter Robb, 'The Colonial State and Constructions of Indian Identity: An Example on the Northeast Frontier in the 1880s', *Modern Asian Studies*, 31, 2 (1997), p. 276.
10. Bipan Chandra, *Nationalism and Colonialism in Modern India* (New Delhi: Orient Blackswan, 1984), p. 122.

Endnotes

1 History

Ahom Rule
1. http://www.assam.org/node/977.
2. The Koch dynasty ruled territory in the eastern part of the Indian subcontinent, mainly in Assam and Bengal. It emerged as the dominant ruling house in the Kamata kingdom in 1515 after the fall of the Khen dynasty in 1498.
3. E. A. Gait, *A History of Assam* (Calcutta: Thacker Spink and Co., 1906), pp. ii-iii.
4. Susan R. Ward, *A Glimpse of Assam* (Calcutta: City Press, 1884), pp. 18-19.
5. L. W. Shakespear, *History of the Assam Rifles* (Gauhati: Spectrum Publications, 1929), p. 3.

The Burmese War of 1824–26
1. Gait, *History of Assam*, pp. 57-58.
2. Quoted H. K. Barpujari, *Assam in the Days of the Company:1826-1858* (Gauhati: Spectrum Publications, 1980), p. 13.
3. Major John Butler, *Travels and Adventures in the Province of Assam* (London: Smith, Elder, 1855), pp. 247-49.
4. It was reported that 'it was dangerous for a beautiful woman to meet a Burmese even on the public road. Brahmans were made to carry loads of beef, pork and wine ... the Gosains were robbed of all their possessions'. Eyewitness account of Maniram Dewan quoted Barpujari, *Assam in the Days of the Company*, p. 11.
5. Gait, *History of Assam*, pp. 274-278.
6. J. Erroll Gray, an enterprising tea planter, narrated how during a visit to the hills an Assamese woman told him how she had been captured by Singphos who raided her village and took all the inhabitants into slavery. In the course of time, she married a Singpho and had two sons by him. Even after fifty years, she had not forgotten her mother tongue nor her memories of the plains. J. Erroll Gray, 'Diary of a Journey to the Bor Khamti Country, 1892-3' in Verrier Elwin ed., *India's North East Frontier in the Nineteenth Century* (Bombay: Oxford University Press, 1959), p. 416.
7. Despatch to Court of Directors, dated 20 July 1823, quoted Gait, *History of Assam*, p. 281.
8. Captain Robert Boileau Pemberton's *Report on the Eastern Frontier of British India* was first published in 1835 (Calcutta: Baptist Mission Press) as a result of the survey undertaken by Pemberton on the northeast frontier under the order of Lord William Bentinck in 1832. The report covers the physical, anthropological, economic and political conditions in a large area including Assam, Manipur and

Burma and also incorporates valuable data on military affairs and commercial routes between Assam, Burma and Bhutan. Pemberton expressed his unbelief at the extent of British ignorance of the 'whole frontier' at the start of the Burmese War which neutralised any efforts 'to preserve the integrity of our dominions', p. 2.
9. Gait, *History of Assam*, p. 282.
10. Anandaram Dhekial Phukan, 'Observations on the Administration of the Province of Assam' in A. G. Moffatt Mills, *Report on the Province of Assam* (Calcutta: Thomas Jones, 1854), p. 290.
11. Despite suffering defeat and substantial loss of territory in its war with the British in the first Anglo-Burmese War of 1824–26 and the Second Anglo-Burmese War of 1852–53, Burma posed a significant threat to the region's security up to 1885 and was suspected of sponsoring numerous raids into British territory by frontier tribes. Ian Heath, *The North-East Frontier, 1837-1901* (Oxford: Osprey, 1999), p. 3.

Annexation
1. Gait, *History of Assam*, p. 287.
2. Robinson, *Descriptive Account of Asam*, p. 210.
3. Gait, *History of Assam*, p. 288. Each *thana* contained one *daroga*, one *jemadar* and a number of constables.
4. The *paik* system was a type of *corvee* labour system on which the economy of the Ahom kingdom depended, under which adult able males were under obligation to render service to the state and form its militia, in return for which they received a piece of land for cultivation. Every male in the Ahom kingdom between the ages of sixteen and fifty who was not a noble, a priest, a member of a high caste or a slave was a *paik*. The *paiks* were organised into four-member groups called *gots* and each *got* sent one member by rotation for public works. The *paiks* were grouped into divisions called *khels*.
5. Gait, *History of Assam*, p. 288.
6. Gait, *History of Assam*, p. 292.
7. Gait, *History of Assam*, pp. 294.
8. Gait, *History of Assam*, p. 295-96.
9. Gait, *History of Assam*, p. 300.
10. The act of removing the raja and the seizure of his property was seen by the hill people as an act of treachery and twenty-five years later their resentment to British rule was expressed in rebellion.
11. Gait, *History of Assam*, p. 309.
12. Robinson, *Descriptive Account of Asam*, p. 211.
13. *Calcutta Gazette*, 1842 p. 683 quoted Gait, *History of Assam*, p. 305.
14. Assamese was only restored to its rightful position when Sir George Campbell became lieutenant-governor of Bengal in 1871.
15. Gait, *History of Assam*, p. 306.

Post 1857

1. Ward, *Glimpse of Assam*, p. 67.
2. Maniram Dutta Baruah was an Assamese nobleman. He was appointed dewan of the Assam Company in 1839 and became the first Indian planter to grow tea commercially in Assam. Apart from the tea industry, Maniram ventured into iron smelting, gold prospecting, salt production and a multitude of other business activities. His hostility to the British stemmed from his suspension from the Assam Company in about 1842 on charges of diverting seed and labour for his own use. He subsequently maintained that numerous administrative obstacles had been placed before him by competing European planters to thwart his establishment of private tea plantations. Maniram's 1852 petition to Andrew Moffatt Mills criticising British economic policies in Assam and recommending the reinstatement of Ahom rule was dismissed as a 'curious document' by Mills. After his execution, both of his tea gardens were taken over by the British. Maniram's death was widely mourned in Assam.
3. Gait, *History of Assam*, pp. 328-9.
4. Gait, *History of Assam*, p. 332.
5. Fitzwilliam Thomas Pollok, *Sport in British Burmah, Assam and the Cassyah and Jyntiah Hills*, Vol. II (London: Chapman and Hall, 1879), pp. 61, 78.
6. Gait, *History of Assam*, p. 335.
7. *The Assam Mission of the American Baptist Union: Papers and Discussions of the Jubiliee Conference held in Nowgong, 18-29 December 1886* (Calcutta: J. W. Thomas, Baptist Mission Press, 1887), p. 6.
8. Gait, *History of Assam*, p. 337.

2 Geography

1. Ward, *Glimpse of Assam*, p. 4.
2. Robinson was a missionary who was appointed as headmaster of the Gauhati Government Seminary in 1838 and the first inspector of schools in Assam in 1841.
3. Robinson, *Descriptive Account of Asam*, pp. 4-5.
4. George M. Barker, *A Tea Planter's Life in Assam* (Calcutta: Thacker, Spink, 1884), pp. 39-40.
5. T. Kinney, *Old Times in Assam* (Calcutta: Star Press, 1896), p. 108.
6. The lac, the cocoons of the insect *laccifer lacca*, was exported in its natural state, uncrusted on twigs of trees.
7. Ward, *Glimpse of Assam*, p. 58.
8. Robinson, *Descriptive Account of Asam*, pp. 54-55. The betelnut was 'about the size of a hen's egg, enclosed in a membraneous [*sic*] covering of a reddish yellow when ripe ... generally eaten green and

cut into slices ... wrapped up in the leaf of the betel-piper, to which is added a little quicklime. Thus prepared it is chewed and eaten by the natives as a universal luxury.'
9. Ward, *Glimpse of Assam*, p. 5.
10. Ward, *Glimpse of Assam*, p. 60.
11. Robinson, *Descriptive Account of Asam*, p. 287.
12. R. Wilcox, 'Memoir of a Survey of Assam, and the Neighbouring Countries, Executed in 1825-6-7-8', *Asiatic Researches*, XVII (1832), p. 464.
13. Ward, *Glimpse of Assam*, p. 63.
14. Lt. Col. P. R. T. Gurdon, *The Khasis* (London: Macmillan, 1914), pp. 7-8.
15. Ward, *Glimpse of Assam*, p. 64.
16. Robinson, *Descriptive Account of Asam*, p. 299. See also Capt. Edward Tuite Dalton, 'Notes on Assam Temple Ruins', *Journal of the Asiatic Society of Bengal*, XXIV (1855), pp. 1-24.
17. Butler, *Travels and Adventures in the Province of Assam*, pp. 231-32.
18. Ward, *Glimpse of Assam*, p. 5.
19. *Assam Mission of the American Baptist Missionary Union*, p. 2.
20. Altogether, a force of 1,135 of all ranks together with two mountain guns from Calcutta, Colonel James Johnstone's force of 2,000 Manipuri troops, 700 boats, 200 carts, 305 elephants (from Dhaka), 227 ponies and 405 coolies were pressed into service.
21. C. A. Elliott, Chief Commissioner, to Ripon, 22 March 1881, Add. Mss 43605, Asian and African Studies, British Library (AAS, BL), quoted Robb, 'The Colonial State and Constructions of Indian Identity', p. 274.
22. James Alban Wilson, *Sport and Service in Assam and Elsewhere* (London: Hutchinson & Co., 1924), p. 33.
23. Butler, *Travels and Adventures in the Province of Assam*, p. 24.
24. Hence the name of the town from Sib, the deity, and Sagar, meaning ocean.
25. Ward, *Glimpse of Assam*, pp. 68-70.
26. McCosh, *Topography of Assam*, p. 133.
27. Lt. E. T. Dalton, Junior Assistant Commissioner of Assam, 'Report of his visit to the Hills in the Neighbourhood of the Soobanshiri River', *Journal of the Asiatic Society of Bengal*, XIV, Pt. I (1845), p. 250.
28. Ward, *Glimpse of Assam*, pp. 71-72.
29. Kinney, *Old Times in Assam*, p.181.
30. Ward, *Glimpse of Assam*, pp. 86-95.
31. It is widely believed that the word 'cooly' or 'coolie' was derived from Tamil, in which the word '*kuli*' means wages. However, rather than being simply a term for a hired labourer, it usually described a worker who formed part of a system of indentured labour used

Endnotes

throughout the British colonies. The word became increasingly pejorative.
32. Ward, *Glimpse of Assam*, pp. 7-8.
33. Ibid.
34. Robinson, Descriptive Account of Asam, p. 20.
35. https://www.telegraphindia.com/states/north-east/an-european-s-account-of-assam/cid/443929
36. Ibid.
37. T. Pollok, W. S. Thom, *Wild Sports of Burma and Assam* (London: Hurst and Blackett, 1900), pp. 426, 429.
38. Ward, *Glimpse of Assam*, p. 10.
39. Ward, *Glimpse of Assam*, p. 11.
40. Robinson, *Descriptive Account of Asam*, pp. 15-16.
41. Gait, *History of Assam*, p. 345.
42. Roger Bilham, 'Tom La Touche and the Great Assam Earthquake of 12 June 1897. Letters from the Epicentre', *Seismological Research Letters*, 79, 3 (2008), pp. 426-37.
43. George Dunbar, *Other Men's Lives: A Study of Primitive Peoples* (London: Scientific Book Club, 1938), pp. 230-31.

3 *The Hill Tribes of Assam*
1. Gait, *History of Assam*, p. 8.
2. Jelle J. P. Wouters, 'Keeping the Hill Tribes at Bay: A critique from India's Northeast of James C. Scott's paradigm of state evasion', *European Bulletin of Himalayan Research*, 39 (2011), pp. 46-47.
3. Wouters, 'Keeping the Hill Tribes at Bay', p. 49.
4. Lord Dalhousie, 'Minutes as Regard to the Relations to be Maintained with the Angami Nagas', 20 February 1851, quoted Mackenzie, *History of the Relations of the Government with the Hill Tribes*, pp. 113-14.
5. N. N. Acharyya, *A Brief History of Assam: from earliest time to the year 1983* (New Delhi: Omsons, 1987), p. 252. See also R. G. Woodthorpe, 'A Punitive Expedition in 1875', *General Report of the Topographical Surveys of India 1874-5* (Calcutta: Govt. of India, 1876), p. 54.
6. Elwin, *India's North East Frontier*, pp. xv-xvi.
7. Sir James Johnstone, *My Experiences in Manipur and the Naga Hills* (London: Sampson Low, 1896), p. 43.
8. John Butler, *A Sketch of Assam with some account of the Hill Tribes, by an Officer* (London: Smith Elder, 1847), p. 81.

The Bhutanese
1. Robinson, *Descriptive Account of Asam*, p. 350.
2. L. W. Shakespear, *History of Upper Assam, Upper Burmah and North-Eastern Frontier* (Cambridge: Cambridge University Press, 1914), p. 92.

3. Quoted Shakespear, *History of Upper Assam*, pp. 91-92.
4. Peter Collister, *Bhutan and the British* (London: Serindia Publications, 1987), p. 77.
5. Gait, *History of Assam*, p. 307.
6. Ashley Eden, 'Report on the State of Bootan and the Progress of the Mission of 1863-64', *Political Missions to Bootan* (Calcutta: Bengal Secretariat Office, 1865), p. 108.
7. Eden, Report on the State of Bootan', p. 118.
8. Eden, Report on the State of Bootan', p. 124. See also Dr Sonam B. Wangyai, 'A Cheerless Change: Bhutan Dooars to British Dooars'. http://himalaya.socanth.cam.ac.uk/collections/journals/jbs/pdf/JBS_15_02.pdf p. 41.
9. Shakespear, *History of Upper Assam*, p. 96.
10. Gait, *History of Assam*, p. 316.
11. G. N. Mehra, *Bhutan, The Land of the Peaceful Dragon* (Delhi: Vikas Publishing House, 1974), p. 92.

The Aka

1. Mackenzie, *History of the Relations of the Government with the Hill Tribes*, p. 21. See also Reverend C. H. Hesselmeyer, 'The Hill Tribes of the Northern Frontier of Assam', *Journal of the Asiatic Society of Bengal*, XXXVII (1868), pp. 194-202.
2. Major C. R. Macgregor, 'Notes on Akas and Akaland', *Proceedings of the Asiatic Society of Bengal*, XI (1884), p. 198.
3. Also spelt *joom*. According to Gait, 'The hill tribes generally cultivate on the jhum system, i.e. they burn down part of the forest, the ashes of which make a valuable manure, and then dibble in various kinds of seeds all mixed together. After one or two years, cultivation becomes impossible on account of the choking weeds that spring up; the villagers then move on to a new clearance and the deserted fields remain unfit for cultivation until, after the lapse of some years, fresh forest growth has killed out the weeds.' Gait, *History of Assam*, p. 345.
4. Hesselmeyer, 'Hill Tribes of the Northern Frontier of Assam', p. 207.
5. R. S. Kennedy, 'Ethnological Report on the Akas, Khoas and Mijis and the Monbas of Tawang' (1914), Mss Eur F157/324/(h), AAS, BL, p. 5. See also Macgregor, 'Notes on Akas and Akaland', p. 202.
6. Macgregor, 'Notes on Akas and Akaland, p. 198.
7. Maxwell's Report, For. Dept. Ext. A Progs, October 1894, Nos. 41-116, quoted Birendra Chandra Chakravorty, *British Relations with the Hill Tribes of Assam* (Calcutta: Firma K. L. Mukhopadhyay, 1964), p. 23.
8. Quoted Elwin, *India's North East Frontier*, p. 454.

The Daflas

1. Robinson, *Descriptive Account of Asam*, p. 355.

Endnotes

2. W. Robinson, 'Notes on the Dophlas and the peculiarities of their Language', *Journal of the Asiatic Society of Bengal*, XX (1851), p. 129.
3. H. J. Harman, 'Narrative Report of Lt. H. J. Harman in charge of the Daphla Military Expeditionary Survey', *General Report on the Topographical Surveys of India, 1874-5* (Calcutta: Govt. of India, 1876), p. 87.
4. Robinson, 'Notes on the Dophlas', pp. 128-29. See also E. T. Dalton, *Descriptive Ethnology of Bengal* (Calcutta: Supt. Govt. Printing, 1872), p. 36.
5. Chakravorty, *British Relations with the Hill Tribes*, p. 6.
6. 'R. B. McCabe's Report of 1897' quoted Elwin, *India's North-East Frontier*, p. 202.
7. Shakespear, History *of Upper Assam*, p. 105.

The Miris
1. Chakravorty, *British Relations with the Hill Tribes of Assam*, p. 6.
2. Lt. E. T. Dalton, 'Report of his visit to the Hills in the Neighbourhood of the Soobanshiri River', *Journal of the Asiatic Society of Bengal*, XIV, Pt. 1 (1845), p. 260.
3. G. W. Dun, *Preliminary Notes on Miris* (Simla: 1897) quoted Elwin *India's North-East Frontier*, p. 163.
4. McCosh, *Topography of Assam*, p. 163.
5. Dalton, 'Report of his visit to the Hills', p. 263.
6. Ward, *Glimpse of Assam*, pp. 204-5.

The Abors
1. Judicial Progs. November 1863, No. 166 quoted Chakravorty, *British Relations with the Hill Tribes of Assam*, pp. 8-9.
2. Gait, *History of Assam*, p. 317.
3. Lt. E. T. Dalton, 'On the Meris and Abors of Assam', *Journal of the Asiatic Society of Bengal*, XIV, Pt. 1 (1845), pp. 426-27.
4. Chakravorty, *British Relations with the Hill Tribes of Assam*, pp. 8-9.
5. Ibid.
6. Yak tails, sometimes made into fly whisks.
7. 'Correspondence and Journal of Capt. Dalton, of his Progress in a late visit to a Clan of Abors on the Dihong River', *Selections from the Records of the Bengal Government*, XXIII (Calcutta, 1855), p. 160.
8. Ward, *Glimpse of Assam*, p. 203.
9. Father Nicholas Michael Krick in a letter dated 1 September 1851 noted this mark of a cross tattooed on the foreheads of the Bor Abors. The tribesmen were unable to explain the origin of the symbol but believed that any man marked with a cross was protected in this life and taken straight to heaven in the next. *Journal of the Asiatic Society of Bengal*, IX New Series (1913), p. 114.

10. Quoted Elwin, *India's North-East Frontier*, p. xvii.
11. J. McCosh, *Topography of Assam*, p. 142.
12. Father N. M. Krick, 'Account of an Expedition among the Abors in 1853', translated by Father A. Gille, S. J., *Journal of the Asiatic Society of Bengal*, IX New Series (1913), p. 108.
13. Mackenzie, *History of the Relations of the Government with the Hill Tribes*, p. 36.
14. G. W. Beresford, *Notes on the North-Eastern Frontier of Assam* (Shillong: Assam Secretariat Printing Office, 1881), p. 15.
15. Shakespear, *History of Upper Assam*, p. 115. The British colonial administration did not do away with the existing *posa* arrangements adopted by the Ahom but, under a policy advocated by Cecil Beadon, lieutenant-governor of Bengal, increasingly 'bought out' hill peoples' suzerainty over local plainspeople by providing them with annual stipends which were paid in cash. This policy was condemned as an admittance of government weakness by many officials (in particular, Henry Hopkinson, who became commissioner of Assam in February 1861) and a sense of embarrassment runs through colonial accounts about the payment of 'blackmail'. See also B. Kar 'When was the Postcolonial? A history of policing impossible lines', in S. Baruah ed., *Beyond Counter-Insurgency: Breaking the Impasse in Northeast India* (New Delhi: Oxford University Press, 2009), pp. 49-77.
16. Wilson, *Sport and Service in Assam*, pp. 104-107.

The Mishmis
1. Butler, *Sketch of Assam*, p. 115.
2. Ibid.
3. E. A. Rowlatt, 'Report of an Expedition into the Mishmee Hills to the north-east of Sudyah', *Journal of the Asiatic Society of Bengal*, XIV, Pt. 2 (1845), p. 488.
4. T. T. Cooper, *The Mishmee Hills* (London: H. S. King, 1873), p. 189.
5. Cooper, *Mishmee Hills*, p. 102.
6. Dalton, *Descriptive Ethnology of Bengal*, p. 18.
7. J. F. Needham, *Report on the Bebejiya Mishmi Expedition, 1899-1900* (Shillong: Assam Secretariat Printing Office, 1900), p. 16.
8. Butler, *Sketch of Assam*, p. 115.
9. This nettle fibre could be *Bohmeria nivea*. See Rhea under Agro-Industries.
10. Dalton, *Descriptive Ethnology of Bengal*, p. 18.
11. The semi-domesticated *mithun* is a bovine species of the north-eastern region of India, reared in hill forests. The *takin* is sometimes referred to as a goat antelope, but is closely related to sheep, and is found on high snow-covered ranges. Cooper, *Mishmee Hills*, p. 189.
12. Ward, *Glimpse of Assam*, p. 196.

13. Chakravorty, *British Relations with the Hill Tribes of Assam*, pp. 10-1. See also Beresford, *Notes on the North-Eastern Frontier of Assam*, p. 28.
14. Mackenzie, *History of the Relations of the Government with the Hill Tribes*, p. 49.
15. Needham, *Report on the Bebejiya Mishmi Expedition*, p. 16.

The Khamtis
1. Pemberton, *Report on the Eastern Frontier of British India*, p. 70.
2. Dalton, *Descriptive Ethnology of Bengal*, p. 6. See also Butler, *A Sketch of Assam*, p. 57.
3. Prince Henri d'Orleans, *From Tonkin to India*, translated by Hamley Bent (London: Methuen, 1898), p. 322.
4. Robinson, *Descriptive Account of Asam*, p. 372.
5. Shakespear, *History of Upper Assam*, p. 150.
6. Robinson, *Descriptive Account of Asam*, p. 372.
7. Cooper, *The Mishmee Hills*, p. 145.
8. Quoted Shakespear, *History of Upper Assam*, p. 150. See also S. E. Peal, Report on the Visit to the Nongyang Lake on the Burma Frontier, February 1879, *Journal of the Asiatic Society of Bengal*, L, Pt. 2 (1881), pp. 1-30.
9. Gait, *History of Assam*, pp. 303-5.

The Singphos
1. Dalton, *Descriptive Ethnology of Bengal*, p. 10.
2. Butler, *A Sketch of Assam*, p. 80. See also J. Errrol Gray, *Diary of a Journey to the Bor Khamti Country 1892-93* (Simla: G. C. Press, 1893).
3. Robinson, *Descriptive Account of Asam*, p. 377.
4. Dalton, *Descriptive Ethnology of Bengal*, p. 9.
5. Butler, *Sketch of Assam*, p. 80.
6. Ward, *Glimpse of Assam*, pp. 194-5.
7. The extreme point of British India's line was about 70 miles east of Sadiya. Ten miles further east Chinese influence was deemed to start. Chakravorty, *British Relations with the Hill Tribes of Assam*, p. 18.
8. The colonial officer Samuel Peal was astonished when, during an expedition to Singpho territory, he came across a village whose inhabitants were clearly not Singphos, but the descendants of Assamese who had been abducted some ninety years before and reduced to slavery. Peal, 'Report on the Visit to the Nongyang Lake', p. 99.
9. J. McCosh, 'Account of the Mountain Tribes on the Extreme N. E. Frontier of Bengal', *Journal of the Asiatic Society of Bengal*, V (1836), pp. 200-01.
10. Mackenzie, *History of the Relations of the Government with the Hill Tribes*, p. 61.

The Nagas

1. Lt. Col. R. G. Woodthorpe, 'Notes on the Wild Tribes inhabiting the so-called Naga Hills' in Verrier Elwin ed., *The Nagas in the Nineteenth Century* (Bombay: Oxford University Press, 1969), pp. 52-53.
2. Chakravorty, *British Relations with the Hill Tribes of Assam*, p. 13.
3. Wilson, *Sport and Service in Assam*, p. 236.
4. Butler, *Travels and Adventures in the Province of Assam*, p. 41.
5. Robinson, *Descriptive Account of Asam*, p. 39.
6. Shakespear, *History of Upper Assam*, pp. 198-99.
7. Ziipao, R. Raile, Tribes and Tribal Studies in North East India: Deconstructing the Politics and Colonial Methodology. https://www.academia.edu/6505077 pp. 8-9.
8. Woodthorpe, 'Notes on the Wild Tribes inhabiting the so-called Naga Hills', pp. 55-56.
9. Ward, *Glimpse of Assam*, p. 188. To further such celebrations a species of grass (*lachryma jobi*) was grown, from the grain of which the Nagas extracted an intoxicating liquor by an operation that closely resembled brewing. Robinson, *Descriptive Account of Asam*, p. 390.
10. Robinson, *Descriptive Account of Asam*, p. 392.
11. Ward, *Glimpse of Assam*, p. 187.
12. Moffatt Mills, *Report on the Province of Assam*, p. 290.
13. Captain John Butler, 'Rough Notes on the Angami', *Journal of the Asiatic Society of Bengal*, XLIV, Pt. I (1875), p. 293. Captain Butler, Bengal Staff Corps and political agent in the Naga Hills, died in January 1876 aged thirty-three near Golaghat in Assam from a spear wound received in an ambush by Lhota Naga tribesmen.
14. Ward, *Glimpse of Assam*, pp. 185-86.
15. John Owen, *Notes on the Naga Tribes in communication with Assam* (Calcutta: W. H. Carey, 1844), p. 15.
16. Dalton, *Descriptive Ethnology of Bengal*, p. 41.
17. Robinson, *Descriptive Account of Asam*, p. 395.
18. R. G. Woodthorpe, 'Notes Descriptive of the Country and People in Western and Eastern Naga Hills', *General Report of the Topographical Surveys of India 1874-5* (Calcutta: Govt. of India, 1876), p. 65.
19. Butler, *Travels and Adventures in the Province of Assam*, p. 143.
20. Ward, *Glimpse of Assam*, p. 188.
21. Robinson, *Descriptive Account of Assam*, p. 393.
22. Mackenzie, *History of the Relations of the Government with the Hill Tribes*, p. 101.
23. A fact that was not lost on the Nagas, as John Owen wrote in 1844, declaring that the Nagas held 'the impression that our wandering into their forests in search of the plant is a mere pretext to see their country, and if found to be plentifully supplied with valuable productions that appropriation will follow'. John Owen, *Notes on*

the Naga Tribes, in communication with Assam (Calcutta: W. H. Carey, 1844), p. 49.
24. S. K. Barpujari, *The Nagas: The Evolution of their History and Administration, 1832-1939* (Guwahati: Spectrum Publications, 2003), p. 68. See also S. Baruah, *Durable Disorder: Understanding the Politics of Northeast India* (Oxford: Oxford University Press, 2012), p. 104.
25. Butler, *Travels and Adventures in the Province of Assam*, p. 185. Butler eventually concluded that the government should abandon any attempt to administer the hills, considering that official intervention in internal disputes had been a failure.
26. Butler, *Travels and Adventures in the Province of Assam*, p. 207.
27. Butler, *Travels and Adventures in the Province of Assam*, p. 198. On all of his expeditions Butler took the precaution of carrying with him 'two windows, one for a sitting room and one for a bed-room' which he inserted in the reed walls of the thatched houses which were usually allotted to him.
28. Chakravorty, *British Relations with the Hill Tribes*, p. 100.
29. B. C. Allen, *Assam District Gazetteers,* IX, Naga Hills and Manipur (Calcutta: Baptist Mission Press, 1905), pp.15-16.
30. Butler, *Travels and Adventures in the Province of Assam*, pp. 103-04.
31. Barpujari, *The Nagas: The Evolution of their History and Administration*, p. 141.
32. Gait, *History of Assam*, p. 312.
33. Gait, *History of Assam*, p. 321.
34. S. E. Peal, 'Fading Histories', *Journal of the Asiatic Society of Bengal,* LXIII, Pt. 3 (1894), p. 11. Peal was an exceptional figure in the field of early Assam planters as a naturalist, ethnographer, ornithologist and geographer. A regular contributor to many journals, he was known for identifying the cause of tea blight as the tea mosquito bug, *Helopelta theovora,* and discovering the Peal palmfly or *Elymnias peali.* He also provided information on the rich deposits of coal and petroleum in the Makum region of upper Assam. His residence in Sibsagar was a rich and seemingly inexhaustible ecological laboratory that connected him to the world of tea, science, ethnography and entomology.

The Mikirs
1. Robinson, *Descriptive Account of Asam*, p. 308.
2. A. M. Meerwarth, *The Andamanese Nicobarese and Hill Tribes of Assam* (Calcutta: Spectrum Publications, 1919), p. 35.
3. Robinson, *Descriptive Account of Asam*, pp. 309-10.

The Jaintias and Khasis
1. Lt. Col. P. R. T. Gurdon, *The Khasis* (London: Macmillan, 1914), p. 27.
2. Gurdon, *The Khasis,* pp. 18, 59-60, 196.

3. Gurdon, *The Khasis*, p. 103. See also Gait, *History of Assam*, p. 301.
4. Gait, *History of Assam*, p. 326.
5. Ward, *Glimpse of Assam*, p. 179.
6. Quoted Gurdon, *The Khasis*, p. 6.
7. Gurdon, *The Khasis*, pp. 105, 144-155.
8. James Alban Wilson reported that the Khasis later resorted to dynamite to disturb the bees. *Sport and Service in Assam*, p. 5.
9. Lt. H. Yule, 'Notes on the Kasia Hills, and People', *Journal of the Asiatic Society of Bengal*, XIII, Pt. 2 (1844), p. 613.
10. Gurdon, *The Khasis*, pp. 25-33.

The Garos
1. Robinson, *Descriptive Account of Asam*, p. 415.
2. Ward, *Glimpse of Assam*, p. 176
3. Robinson, *Descriptive Account of Asam*, p. 416
4. Ward, *Glimpse of Assam*, pp. 176-78.
5. Quoted J. B. Bhatterjee, *Cachar under British Rule in North East India* (New Delhi: Radiant Publishers, 1977), pp. 159-60.
6. Gait, *History of Assam*, pp. 312-13.

The Lushais
1. Butler, *Travels and Adventures in the Province of Assam*, p. 90.
2. R. G. Woodthorpe, *The Lushai Expedition, 1871-72* (London: Hurst and Blackett, 1873), p. 79.
3. Mackenzie, *History of the Relations of the Government with the Hill Tribes*, pp. 514-16. See also Johnstone, *My Experiences in Manipur and the Naga Hills*, pp. 25-27.
4. Woodthorpe, *The Lushai Expedition*, p. 91.
5. Woodthorpe, *The Lushai Expedition*, pp. 88-93.
6. Dhriti Kanta Rajkumar, 'Raids made out by the Lushai Tribes in the Tea Gardens of Cachar during the Colonial Period', *Journal of Humanities and Social Science*, 9, 4 (2013), pp. 43-54.
7. Gait, *History of Assam*, pp. 113-14.

The Cacharis
1. See Sidney Endle, *The Kacharis* (London: Macmillan, 1911).
2. Robinson, *Descriptive Account of Asam*, pp. 294-5.
3. Ward, *A Glimpse of Assam*, pp. 180-81.

Government Policy towards Tribal People
1. Quoted Mackenzie, *History of the Relations of the Government with the Hill Tribes*, p. 242. Also J. Zorema, *Indirect Rule in Mizoram* (New Delhi: Mittal Publications, 2007), p. 6.
2. T. H. Lewin, *The Hill Tracts of Chittagong and the Dwellers Therein* (Calcutta: Bengal Printing Press, 1869), p. 118. See also Robert Lalremtluanga Ralte, 'Colonialism in Northeast India: An

Environmental History of Forest Conflict in the Frontier of Lushai Hills 1850-1900', *International Journal of Humanities and Social Science Invention*, 4, 1 (2015), pp. 67-75.
3. Peal, 'Report on the Visit to the Nongyang Lake', p. 25.
4. Gait, *History of Assam,* p. 331.
5. M. L. Bose, *History of Arunachal Pradesh* (New Delhi: Concept Publishing Co., 1997), p. 114.
6. Nikhlesh Kumar, 'Identity Politics in the Hill Tribal Communities in the North-Eastern India', *Sociological Bulletin*, 54, 2 (2005), p. 203.
7. Quoted David R. Syiemlieh, *British Administration in Meghalaya: Policy and Pattern,* (New Delhi: Heritage Publishers, 1989), p. 188.
8. Chandan Kumar Sharma, 'The State and the Ethnicisation of Space in Northeast India' in N. G. Mahanta and D. Gogoi eds., *Shifting Terrain: Conflict Dynamics in North East India* (Guwahati: DVS Publishers, 2012), p. 2. See also Sanjib Baruah, *Post-Frontier Blues: Towards a New Policy Framework for Northeast India* (Washington DC: East-West Center, 2007), p. 26.
9. Mackenzie, *History of the Relations of the Government with the Hill Tribes,* p. 101.
10. S. K. Chaube, *Hill Politics in Northeast India* (New Delhi: Orient Blackswan, 2012), p. 7.
11. Wouters, 'Keeping the Hill Tribes at Bay', p. 58.
12. Sanjib Baruah, 'Indigenous Peoples, Cultural Survival and Minority Policy in Northeast India', *Cultural Survival*, 13, 2 (1989), pp. 53-58.

4 *Trade and Industry*
1. Jean-Baptiste Tavernier, *Travels in India* Vol. II, translated V. Ball (London: Macmillan, 1889) p. 281. Tavernier, a French gem merchant best known for the discovery of the 116-carat Tavernier blue diamond that he subsequently sold to Louis XIV, made six voyages to Persia and India between 1630 and 1668. His account provides an invaluable source of material for the socio-economic history of India of the period.
2. There were brine springs in Sadiya and Borhat but the local salt, although of a better quality than the imported variety, was significantly more expensive due to the inability of the local people to work the mines efficiently. Almost 1,000,000 *maunds* of salt were imported annually from Bengal.
3. Morris D. Morris, 'Towards a Reinterpretation of Nineteenth Century Indian Economic History', *Journal of Economic History*, 23, 4 (1963), pp. 606-618.
4. Amiya Kumar Bagchi, 'Contextual political economy, not Whig economy', *Cambridge Journal of Economics*, 38, 3 (2014), pp. 545-562.
5. Thomas A. Timberg, *The Marwaris: from Traders to Industrialists* (New Delhi: Vikas Publishing House, 1978), p. 148.

6. Robinson, *Descriptive Account of Asam*, p. 45. In 1880 the province's annual report noted, 'The enterprise and endurance of the Marwaris is surprising. They live the whole year round in miserable houses, sometimes in mostly unhealthy situations and slowly store what they collect from the hill tribes and country produce for export.' *Assam Administrative Report, 1880-81*, p. 27.
7. Jayeeta Sharma, *Empire's Garden: Assam and the Making of India* (New Delhi: Permanent Black, 2012), p. 88.
8. Letter No 275 from Francis Jenkins, dated Gowhatty, 23 May 1853, in Moffatt Mills, *Report on the Province of Assam*, Appendix B, p. 61.
9. Tirthankar Roy, *How British Rule Changed India's Economy: The Paradox of the Raj* (London: Palgrave Macmillan, 2019), p. 61.

TEA
The Tea Trade
1. Kinney, *Old Times in Assam*, pp. 119-121.
2. Ward, *Glimpse of Assam*, pp. 98-100. The party travelled from Calcutta to Cachar and climbed the Khasi Hills, descending to the Brahmaputra at Gauhati to make the upward journey to eastern Assam, a road and boat journey of four and a half months.
3. Ward, *Glimpse of Assam*, pp. 102-3.
4. Robinson, *Descriptive Account of Asam*, pp. 140-42.
5. Robinson, *Descriptive Account of Asam*, p. 142.
6. Sanjib Bauruah, 'Clash of Resource Use Regimes in Colonial Assam: A Nineteenth Century Puzzle Revisited', *Journal of Peasant Studies*, 28, 3 (2001), pp. 111, 114.
7. J. N. Das, *An introduction to the land-laws of Assam* (Gauhati: Lawyers Book Stall, 1988), pp. 4-6.
8. Mohammed Abu B. Siddique, *Evolution of Land Grants and Labour Policy of Government: The Growth of the Tea Industry in Assam 1834-1940* (New Delhi: South Asian Publishers, 1990), pp. 19-26.
9. Ward, *Glimpse of Assam*, pp. 102-03.
10. Ward, *Glimpse of Assam*, pp. 103-04.
11. Sir Percival Griffiths, *The History of the Indian Tea Industry* (London: Weidenfeld and Nicholson, 1967), pp. 61-99.
12. Kinney, *Old Times in Assam*, p.105.
13. Rana P. Behal, 'Coolie Drivers or Benevolent Paternalists? British Tea Planters in Assam and the Indenture Labour System', *Modern Asian Studies* 44, 1 (2010) p. 35.
14. Barker, *Tea Planter's Life*, pp. 123-24.
15. Ward, *Glimpse of Assam*, p.116.
16. Behal, 'Coolie Drivers or Benevolent Paternalists?', p. 33.
17. Barker, *Tea Planter's Life*, p. 91

18. S. Barkataki, *Tribes of Assam* (New Delhi: National Book Trust, 1969), p. 118.

The Tea Garden
1. Ward, *Glimpse of Assam*, pp. 107-9.
2. Robinson, *Descriptive Account of Asam*, p. 132.
3. Barker, *Tea Planter's Life*, p. 118.
4. Ward, *Glimpse of Assam*, pp. 107-9.
5. Kinney, *Old Times in Assam*, pp. 135-6.
6. Barker, *Tea Planter's Life*, p. 135.
7. Barker, *Tea Planter's Life*, p. 136.
8. A *seer* weighs 2 lbs.
9. Barker, *Tea Planter's Life*, pp. 137-38.
10. Kinney, *Old Times in Assam*, pp. 36-37.
11. Bizarrely, the costliest part of getting machinery sent from England was the transport between Calcutta and Assam, considerably higher than the cost of transport between Calcutta and England.
12. Barker, *Tea Planter's Life*, p. 144.
13. Kinney, *Old Times in Assam*, pp. 37-39.

The Tea Planter
1. Kinney, *Old Times in Assam*, p. 177.
2. Ibid.
3. Kinney, *Old Times in Assam*, pp. 178-81.
4. One *maund* was standardised in the Bengal presidency in 1833 to a weight of 82.28 lbs.
5. Ward, *Glimpse of Assam*, p. 126.
6. Kinney, *Old Times in Assam*, pp. 138-39.
7. Barker, *Tea Planter's Life*, p. 171.
8. Barker, *Tea Planter's Life*, p. 173.
9. Ward, *Glimpse of Assam*, p. 125.
10. Barker, *Tea Planter's Life*, pp. 175, 181.
11. Barker, *Tea Planter's Life*, p. 69.
12. Kinney, *Old Times in Assam*, p. 21.
13. Barker, *Tea Planter's Life*, p. 109.
14. Kinney, *Old Times in Assam*, pp. 115-118.
15. Barker, *Tea Planter's Life*, p. 98.
16. Barker, *Tea Planter's Life*, pp. 103-104.
17. Ibid.
18. Ward, *Glimpse of Assam*, p. 128.
19. Kinney, *Old Times in Assam*, p. 36.
20. John Weatherstone, *The Pioneers 1825-1900: The Early British Tea and Coffee Planters and Their Way of Life* (London: Quiller Press, 1986), Ch. III.
21. Ward, *Glimpse of Assam*, p. 129.
22. Barker, *Tea Planter's Life*, pp. 216, 219.

23. Ward, *Glimpse of Assam*, pp. 129-131.
24. Ibid.
25. Ward, *Glimpse of Assam*, p. 133.

Tea Workers
1. Barker, *Tea Planter's Life*, p. 78.
2. The Times, 25 December 1841 quoted Jayeeta Sharma, '"Lazy" Natives, Coolie Labour and the Assam Tea Industry', *Modern Asian Studies* 43, 6 (2009), p. 1303.
3. Guha, *Planter Raj to Swaraj*, p. 45.
4. Barker, *Tea Planter's Life*, p. 147. Kinney, *Old Times in Assam*, p. 139.
5. Rana P. Behal, 'Forms of Labour Protest in Assam Valley Tea Plantations, 1900-1930', *Economic and Political Weekly*, 20, 4 (1985), p. 19.
6. Barker, *Tea Planter's Life*, p. 169. In his history of the Assam Company, H. A. Antrobus cites a cost in 1865 of £20,000 for 1,000 coolies (£1,000 a head at current prices). H. A. Antrobus, *A History of the Assam Company, 1839-1953* (Edinburgh: private printing T. and A. Constable, 1957), p. 146.
7. Barker, *Tea Planter's Life*, p. 165.
8. Kinney, *Old Times in Assam*, p. 137.
9. Letter of John Carnegie, 17 February 1866, Mss Eur C682, AAS, BL.
10. Barker, *Tea Planter's Life*, p. 168.
11. Anna Kay Scott, *Korno Siga, the Mountain Chief; or, Life in Assam* (Philadelphia: The American Sunday-School Union, c1889), p. 36.
12. Barker, *Tea Planter's Life*, p. 169.
13. Guha, *Planter-Raj to Swaraj*, p. 18.
14. https://www.telegraphindia.com/states/north-east/an-european-s-account-of-assam/cid/443929
15. Hardly a reasonable wage. The wage rate of able-bodied agricultural labourers in Lakhimpur, for example, was Rs 9.37 per month in 1873 and for most of the subsequent period until 1901 it remained within the range of Rs 7 to Rs 10. In the early 1880s an unskilled railway construction labourer in the province earned Rs 12 to Rs 16 a month. Guha, *Planter Raj to Swaraj*, p. 44.
16. Behal, 'Coolie Drivers or Benevolent Paternalists?', p. 3. See also Rana P. Behal, Marcel van der Linden eds., *Coolies, Capital and Colonialism: Studies in Indian Labour History* (Cambridge: Cambridge University Press, 2006), p. 165.
17. Barker, *Tea Planter's Life*, p. 173.
18. Barker, *Tea Planter's Life*, p. 154.
19. Quoted Charles Dowding, Introduction to the Hon. J. Buckingham's letter entitled *Tea-Garden Coolies in Assam* (Calcutta: Thacker, Spink, 1894), p. ix.
20. Quoted H. J. Cotton, *Indian and Home Memories* (London: T. Fisher Unwin, 1911), p. 264.

Endnotes

21. Behal, 'Forms of Labour Protest in Assam Valley Tea Plantations', p. 19.
22. Gabrielle LaFavre, 'The Tea Gardens of Assam and Bengal: Company Rule and Exploitation of the Indian Population during the Nineteenth Century', *The Trinity Papers*, 1, 1 (2013), p. 25.
23. A. Mackenzie, *Papers regarding the Tea Industry in Bengal with Notes by J. W. Edgar and Mr. Campbell* (Calcutta: Bengal Secretariat Press, 1873), p. xvi.
24. Kala-azar first came to the attention of western doctors in in 1824 in Jessore (now Bangladesh) where it was initially thought to be a form of malaria. It was identified as a disease caused by protozoan parasites transmitted by sandflies by Scottish doctor William Leishman, who observed the parasite in spleen smears of a soldier who died of the disease in Dumdum, Calcutta in 1901.
25. Griffiths, *History of the Indian Tea Industry*, pp 354-55.
26. Mackenzie, *Papers Regarding the Tea Industry in Bengal*, p. xxi.
27. *The Times*, 2 September 1902, p. 6.
28. Letter of Alexander Carnegie, 4 April 1866, Mss Eur C682, AAS, BL. See also Rana P. Behal and Prabhu P. Mohapatra, 'Tea and Money versus Human Life: The Rise and Fall of the Indenture System in the Assam Tea Plantations 1840-1908', *Journal of Peasant Studies*, 19 (1992), pp. 3-4. Nitin Varma, 'Coolie Acts and the Acting Coolies: Coolie, Planter and State in the Late Nineteenth and Early Twentieth Colonial Tea Plantations of Assam', *Social Scientist*, 33, 5/6 (2005), pp. 5-6.
29. Barker, *Tea Planter's Life*, p. 131.
30. Sir Bampfylde Fuller, *Some Personal Experiences* (London: J. Murray, 1930), pp. 118-119.
31. See Samita Sen, 'Questions of Consent: Women's Recruitment for Assam Tea Gardens, 1859-1900', *Studies in History* 2 (2002), pp. 231-60.
32. These articles have been published in book form in *Slavery in British Dominion*, compiled K. L. Chattopadhyay and edited Sris Kumar Kunda (Calcutta: Jijnasa, 1972).
33. See Mrs Emma Williams, 'Letter regarding abuses on the tea plantations of Assam', 22 October 1907, IOR/L/PJ/6/832, AAS, BL.
34. Cotton, *Indian and Home Memories*, p. 269.
35. Behal, 'Coolie Drivers or Benevolent Paternalists?', p. 44.
36. Cotton, *Indian and Home Memories*, p. 273.
37. Barker, *Tea Planter's Life*, pp. 161, 163.
38. Dowding, *Tea Garden Coolies in Assam*, pp. vi, 31.
39. Quoted Griffiths, *History of the Indian Tea Industry*, p. 377.
40. Guha, *Planter Raj to Swaraj*, pp. 46-7.
41. H. K. Barpujari, *Assam in the Days of the Company*, p. 167.
42. *Report on Labour Immigration into Assam for the Year 1888* (Shillong: Assam Secretariat Printing Office, 1889), Ch. I.
43. Cotton, *Indian and Home Memories*, pp. 262-65.
44. Cotton, *Indian and Home Memories*, pp. 267-68.

45. *The Englishman*, 14 January, 11 and 23 February, and 7 March 1901, and *Capital*, 21 February 1901, quoted Behal, 'Coolie Drivers or Benevolent Paternalists?', p. 47.
46. Cotton, *Indian and Home Memories*, p. 275.
47. Curzon to Cotton, 22 July 1901, Cotton Papers, Mss Eur D1202/2, AAS, BL.
48. Proceedings of the Central Legislative Council, 1901, Vol. XL, p. 139, quoted Behal, 'Coolie Drivers or Benevolent Paternalists?', p. 31.
49. Hamilton to Curzon, 26 August 1903, No. 59, Curzon Papers, Mss Eur F111/161, AAS, BL.
50. Cotton, *Indian and Home Memories*, p, 276.
51. Behal, 'Coolie Drivers or Benevolent Paternalists?', p. 51.

MINING

1. David Arnold, *Science, Technology and Medicine in Colonial India* (Cambridge: Cambridge University Press, 2004), pp. 44-46.
2. The Asiatic Society of Bengal played a significant role in popularising and institutionalising western science in colonial India.
3. Lt. R. Wilcox, 'Memoir of the Survey of Assam and the Neighbouring Countries, executed in 1825', *Asiatic Researches*, 17 (1832), p. 415.
4. T.H. Holland, 'Presidential Address', *Transactions of the Mineralogical and Geological Institutes of India*, 2 (1908), p. 13.

Gold

1. Barker, *Tea Planter's Life*, p. 75.
2. Jean-Baptiste Chevalier, *The Adventures of Jean-Baptiste Chevalier in Eastern India, 1752-65: Historical Memoir and Journal of Travels in Assam, Bengal and Tibet*, translated Caroline Dutta-Baruah and Jean Deloche (Guwahati: LBS Publishers, 2008).
3. Moneeram, Revenue Sheristadar, Bur Bundaree, 'Native Account of Washing for Gold in Assam', *Journal of the Asiatic Society of Bengal*, VII, Pt. 2 (1838), pp. 621-25.
4. E.T. Dalton and S.F. Hannay, 'Note on Recent Investigations Regarding the Extent and Value of the Auriferous Deposits of Assam', *Memoirs of the Geological Survey of India*, I, Pt. 1 (1856), pp. 94-98.
5. Rajen Saikia, *Social and Economic History of Assam* (New Delhi: Manohar, 2000), p. 60.
6. J. Malcolm Maclaren, 'The Auriferous Occurrences of Assam', *Records of the Geological Survey of India*, XXXI (1904), p. 232.

Oil

1. Wilcox, 'Memoir of a Survey of Asam', p. 415.
2. William Griffith, *Journals of Travels in Assam, Burma, Bootan, Afghanistan and the Neighbouring Countries* (Calcutta: Bishop's College Press, 1847), p. 63.

3. F. R. Mallet, 'On the Coal-Fields of the Naga Hills Bordering the Lakhimpur and Sibsagar Districts, Assam', *Memoirs of the Geological Survey of India*, XII (1876), p. 273.
4. S. F. Hannay, Proceedings of the Asiatic Society, 2 May 1838, *Journal of the Asiatic Society of Bengal*, VII, Pt. 1 (1838), p. 368.
5. C. F. H. Jenkins, Proceedings of the Asiatic Society, 7 February 1838, *Journal of the Asiatic Society of Bengal*, VII, Pt. 1 (1838), p. 169.
6. Mallet, 'On the Coal-Fields of the Naga Hills', p. 277.
7. Sir T. H. Holland, *Sketch of the Mineral Resources of India*, (Calcutta: Govt. of India, 1908), p. 24.
8. H. B. Medlicott, 'The Coal of Assam: Results of a Brief Visit to the Coal-fields of that Province in 1865; with Geological Notes on Assam and the Hills to the South of It', *Memoirs of the Geological Survey of India*, IV (1865), p. 415. Medlicott strongly opposed the employment of Indians in the GSI and was particularly scathing about the native guides who accompanied him on his survey of the Makum area, declaring, 'Every European traveller in India must encounter more or less of indigenous apathy, but in no part of India have I found this very natural propensity as prevalent as in Assam.' Ibid p. 387.
9. Mallet, 'On the Coal-Fields of the Naga Hills', p. 280.
10. R. A. Way, *Assam-Burma Connection Railway Surveys, Hukong Valley Route: Report and Approximate Estimate* (Calcutta: 1896), IOR/V/27/722/11, AAS, BL.
11. At the end of the nineteenth century the town of Makum was renamed Margherita after the Italian queen consort to honour the Italian chief engineer of one of the railway sections, Chevalier R. Paganini.
12. W. R. Gawthrop, *The Story of the Assam Railways and Trading Company Ltd. 1881-1951* (London: Harley Publishing Co., 1951), pp. 44-54.
13. S. N. Visvanath, *A Hundred Years of Oil: A Narrative Account of the Search for Oil in India* (Delhi: Vikas Publishing House, 1990), p. 31.
14. Assam State Records, Revenue and Agriculture, August 1894, Prog. 141, quoted Priyam Goswami, http://hdl.handle.net/10603/57147, p. 156.
15. *Batori* (in-house magazine of the Assam Oil Company) Silver Jubilee Edition, Digboi, September 1978, p. 2.
16. T. H. Holland, 'Sketch of the Mineral Resources of India', p. 24.
17. Antrobus, *A History of the Assam Company*, p. 72, n. 48.
18. *Batori*, Digboi, January 1956.

Coal
1. Wilcox, 'Memoir of a Survey of Asam', p. 420.
2. 'Report of the Coal Committee', *Journal of the Asiatic Society of Bengal*, IX (1840), p. 213.

3. John McClelland, *Reports of a Committee for investigating the Coal and Mineral Resources of India* (Calcutta: G. H. Huttman, 1838), Section VII, p. 14.
4. Lt. H. Bigge, 'Notice of the Discovery of Coal and Petroleum on the Namrup River', *Journal of the Asiatic Society of Bengal,* VI (1837), p, 243.
5. 'Report upon the Coal beds of Assam', *Journal of the Asiatic Society of Bengal,* VII, Pt. 2 (1838), pp. 951-54.
6. Medlicott, 'The Coal of Assam', p. 407.
7. Gawthrop, *Story of the Assam Railways,* pp. 26-32.
8. B. C. Allen, *Gazetteer of Bengal and North East India* (Delhi: Mittal, reprinted 1979), p. 190.
9. George Turner to Directors of the ARTC, May 1882, quoted Gawthrop, *Story of the Assam Railways,* pp. 26-27.
10. Ibid.
11. Gawthrop, *Story of the Assam Railways,* pp. 30-31.
12. Kinney, *Old Times in Assam,* pp. 157-58.
13. Kinney, *Old Times in Assam,* pp. 166-67.
14. Kinney, *Old Times in Assam,* p. 157.
15. Kinney, *Old Times in Assam,* pp. 157-58. The output of Assamese mines was 168,000 tonnes in 1894.
16. *The Friends of India and Statesman,* 8 May 1895.
17. Gawthrop, *Story of the Assam Railways,* p. 36.
18. Assam State Records, Revenue and Agriculture, August 1894, Prog. 141, letter 214G, 10 February 1894, quoted Goswami, http://hdl.handle.net/10603/57147, p. 133.
19. Gawthrop, *Story of the Assam Railways,* pp. 37-38.
20. Allen, *Gazetteer of Bengal and North East India,* p. 192.

Iron
1. Mallet, 'On the Coal-fields of the Naga Hills', p. 359.
2. S. F. Hannay, 'Notes on the Iron Ore Statistics and Economic Geology of Upper Assam', *Journal of the Asiatic Society of Bengal,* XXV (1856), p. 332.
3. Mallet, 'On the Coal-fields of the Naga Hills', p. 272.
4. Robinson, *Descriptive Account of Asam,* p. 34.
5. Hannay, 'Notes on the Iron Ore Statistics', p. 332.
6. Hannay, 'Notes on the Iron Ore Statistics', p. 330.
7. Priyam Goswami, *Assam in the Nineteenth Century: Industrialisation and Colonial Penetration* (Guwahati: Spectrum Publications,1999), p. 139.
8. G. N. Gupta, *A Survey of the Industries and Resources of Eastern Bengal and Assam for 1907-8* (Shillong: Assam Secretariat Printing Office, 1908), p. 43.
9. Gupta, *Survey of the Industries and Resources of Eastern Bengal,* p. 44.

Endnotes

10. H. Z. Darrah, *Report on the River-Borne Trade of the Province of Assam for the Year 1892-3* (Shillong: Assam Secretariat Printing Office, 1893), p. 16.

TRANSPORTATION
Railways

1. To follow the rise and progress of the Assam Railway and Trading Company see IOR/L/AG/46/2, AAS, BL.
2. Kinney, *Old Times in Assam*, pp. 142-44.
3. Gawthrop, *Story of the Assam Railways*, p. 12
4. Kinney, *Old Times in Assam*, pp. 144-45.
5. Gawthrop, *Story of the Assam Railways*, p. 13.
6. Kinney, *Old Times in Assam*, p. 146.
7. Kinney, *Old Times in Assam*, p. 147.
8. Kinney, *Old Times in Assam*, pp. 147-48.
9. Kinney, *Old Times in Assam*, pp. 149-55.
10. Gawthrop, *Story of the Assam Railways*, p. 16.
11. Kinney, *Old Times in Assam*, pp. 161-62.
12. Kinney, *Old Times in Assam*, p. 171.
13. Kinney, *Old Times in Assam*, p. 156.
14. 'Brief History of the Assam Bengal Railway', *The Assam Review and Tea News*, XVIII, V, p. 213.
15. H. K. Barpujari, *The American Missionaries and North-East India, 1836-1900 A. D.: A Documentary Study* (Guwahati: Spectrum Publishers, 1986), p. 90.
16. Gait, *History of Assam*, p. 342.

Waterways

1. H. A. Antrobus, *A History of the Jorehaut Tea Company Ltd, 1859-1946* (London: Tea and Rubber Mail, c. 1947), p. 66, n. 48.
2. McCosh, *Topography of Assam*, p. 82.
3. Antrobus, *History of the Assam Company*, p. 420.
4. Antrobus, *History of the Assam Company*, p. 349.
5. Antrobus, *History of the Assam Company*, pp. 349-57.
6. Antrobus, *History of the Assam Company*, p. 353, n. 60.
7. Goswami, *Assam in the Nineteenth Century*, p. 146.
8. Moffatt Mills, *Report on the Province of Assam*, p. 22-3.
9. B. C. Allen, *Assam District Gazeteers*, VI, Nowgong (Calcutta: City Press, 1905), pp. 167-68.
10. Goswami, *Assam in the Nineteenth Century*, p. 147.
11. Ibid.
12. Quoted Allen, *Assam District Gazetteers*, VI, p. 169.
13. Oscar Flex, *Asom 1864*, translated by Dr Salim M. Ali (Guwahati: G. L. Publications, 2012), pp. 20-22.

14. Quoted H. K. Barpujari (ed) *The Comprehensive History of Assam*, Vol. IV (Guwahati: Assam Publication Board, 1992), p. 306.
15. Assam State Records, Home Proceedings A, May 1881, 114-15, quoted Goswami, http://hdl.handle.net/10603/57147, p. 191.
16. Barker, *Tea Planter's Life*, p. 44.
17. Barker, *Tea Planter's Life*, pp. 41-42.
18. Kinney, *Old Times in Assam*, p. 96.
19. Barker, *Tea Planter's Life*, p. 49.
20. Barker, *Tea Planter's Life*, pp. 49, 53.
21. Barker, *Tea Planter's Life*, pp. 52-53. Also McCosh on miasma, *Topography of Assam*, p. 100.
22. S. B. Mehdi, *Transport System and Economic Development in Assam* (Guwahati: Publication Board, 1978), p. 22.
23. Mehdi, *Transport System and Economic Development in Assam*, p. 32.
24. Arupjyoti Saikia, *The Unquiet River: A Biography of the Brahmaputra* (New Delhi: Oxford University Press, 2019), pp. 458-503.

Roadways
1. Kinney, *Old Times in Assam*, p. 141.
2. Quoted Barjupari (ed.) *Comprehensive History of Assam*, Vol. IV, p. 291.
3. Anandaram Dhekiyal Phukan, 'Observations on the Administration of the Province of Assam' in Moffatt Mills, *Report on the Province of Assam*, Appendix J.
4. Moffatt Mills, *Report on the Province of Assam*, p. 108.
5. W. W. Hunter, *A Statistical Account of Assam*, Vol. I (London: Trubner and Co. 1879), p. 228.
6. Robinson, *Descriptive Account of Asam*, pp. 317-18.
7. Ward, *Glimpse of Assam*, p. 77.
8. Derived from the Latin '*metallum*' which means both mine and quarry. Road metal later became the term for stone chippings mixed with tar to form the road-surfacing material tarmac.
9. Moffatt Mills, *Report on the Province of Assam*, pp. 22-23.
10. Barker, *Tea Planter's Life*, p. 150.
11. Antrobus, *History of the Assam Company*, p. 369, n. 60.
12. Antrobus, *History of the Assam Company*, p. 55.
13. P. H. Moore, *Twenty years in Assam* (Rochester, NY: self-published, 1901), p. 86.
14. Allen, *Gazetteer of Bengal and North East India*, p. 90.
15. Ward, *Glimpse of Assam*, p. 129.
16. Lipokmar Dzuvichu, 'Roads and the Raj: the politics of road building in colonial Naga Hills, 1860s-1910s', *Indian Economic and Social History Review*, 50 (2013), p. 474.
17. Dzuvichu, 'Roads and the Raj', pp. 480-81

18. Quoted Dzuvichu, 'Roads and the Raj', p. 482. See also Sanghamitra Misra, 'The Nature of Colonial Intervention in the Naga Hills, 1840-80', *Economic and Political Weekly*, 33, 51 (1998), p. 3274.
19. Dzuvichu, 'Roads and the Raj', pp. 482-83.
20. Johnstone, *My Experiences in Manipur and the Naga Hills*, p. 13.
21. Robb, 'The Colonial State and Constructions of Indian Identity', p. 261.
22. R. G. Woodthorpe, 'Notes on the Wild Tribes inhabiting the so-called Naga Hills, on our North-East Frontier of India, Part 1', *The Journal of the Anthropological Institute of Great Britain and Ireland*, XI (1882), pp. 63-64.
23. *Annual Administration Report of the Manipur Agency, 1873-74*, p. 17 quoted Dzuvichu, 'Roads and the Raj', p. 485.
24. *Assam Administration Report, 1887-88* quoted Dzuvichu, 'Roads and the Raj', p. 485.
25. Kinney, *Old Times in Assam*, p. 141.
26. Dzuvichu, 'Roads and the Raj', pp. 486-89.
27. *Assam Administration Report, 1887-88* quoted Dzuvichu, 'Roads and the Raj', p. 486.
28. *Imperial Gazetteer of India: Eastern Bengal and Assam* (Calcutta: Supt. of Govt. Printing, 1909), p. 478.

FORESTRY

1. Wilhelm Schlich, Memorandum on Forest Operations in Assam, quoted Arupjyoti Saikia, *Forests and Ecological History of Assam* (New Delhi: Oxford University Press, 2011), p. 56. The Indian Forest Service was not established until 1864 and its department did not function satisfactorily for several years. The Government of India surprisingly decided that there were no Britons capable of heading the department, and appointed a German, Herr Dietrich Brandis, as inspector-general of forests. Brandis was succeeded by Wilhelm Schlich who became a British citizen and was knighted for his achievements. David Gilmour, *The British in India* (London: Allen Lane, 2018) p. 83. See also S. F. Hannay, 'Observations on the quality of Principal Timber Trees growing in the Vicinity of Upper Assam, *Journal of the Agricultural and Horticultural Society of India*, IV (1845), pp. 116-133.
2. McCosh, *Topography of Assam*, p. 28.
3. Gustav Mann, *Progress Report of Forest Administration in the Province of Assam* (Shillong: Assam Secretariat Printing Office, 1874-75), p. 1.
4. Gustav Mann (1836–1916) was employed by William Hooker in 1859 at the Royal Botanic Gardens in Kew. In October of that year, he was sent to replace the British naturalist Charles Barter as botanist on the ill-fated Niger expedition of Captain Baikie, making stopovers

at the Canary Islands and Sierra Leone to collect specimens. Mann worked extensively in the tea and cinchona plantations of Darjeeling and Assam, aiming to improve the commercial cultivation of cash crops in northern India.

5. E. P. Stebbing, *The Forests of India*, Vol. 1 (London: Bodley Head, 1922), p. 3.
6. Ralte, 'Colonialism in Northeast India', pp. 72-73.
7. Barker, *Tea Planter's Life*, p. 150.
8. Mackenzie, *Papers Regarding the Tea Industry in Bengal*, p. 61.
9. B. C. Allen, *Assam District Gazetteers*, Vol. VIII, Lakhimpur (Calcutta: City Press, 1905), pp. 567, 595.
10. R. Handique, *British Forest Policy in Assam* (New Delhi: Concept Publishing Company, 2004), p. 96.
11. Gawthrop, *Story of the Assam Railways*, pp. 17-18. The rapidity with which sleepers were cut and prepared astonished the local inhabitants.
12. Srijani Bhattacharjee, 'The Coming of British Forestry in Assam in the Nineteenth and Early Twentieth Century: Initiatives and Problems' in Sajal Nag ed., *Playing with Nature: History and Politics of Environment in North-East India* (London: Routledge, 2018), pp. 113-132.
13. Bhattacharjee, 'The Coming of Britsh Forestry in Assam', pp. 113-132.
14. Arupjyoti Saikia, *Forests and Ecological History of Assam, 1826-2000* (New Delhi: Oxford University Press, 2011), p. 39.
15. Bhattacharjee, 'The Coming of British Forestry in Assam', pp. 113-132.

AGRICULTURE
1. Hunter, *A Statistical Account of Assam*, Vol. I, p 371.
2. Ward, *Glimpse of Assam*, p. 105
3. Hunter, *A Statistical Account of Assam*, Vol. I, p. 54.
4. Ibid.

AGRO-INDUSTRIES
Rubber
1. D. Morris, 'Sources of Commercial India-Rubber', *Journal of the Society of Arts*, XLVI (August 1898), p. 785.
2. Used extensively for the waterproof coating for cloth in Macintosh raincoats. By the time of William Griffith's report in 1838, every kind of coat was exported from Britain with rubberised fabric, including riding coats, and coats supplied to the British Army, the British railways and police forces.
3. Robinson, *Descriptive Account of Asam*, p. 57.
4. William Griffith, 'Report on the Caoutchouc Tree of Assam', *Journal of the Asiatic Society of Bengal*, VII, Pt. 1 (1838), pp. 132-42.

Endnotes

5. Gupta, *Survey of the Resources and Industries of Eastern Bengal*, p. 80. See also Goswami, *Assam in the Nineteenth Century*, p. 169.
6. W. Schlich, 'Memorandum on Forest Operations in Assam', 1873, quoted Goswami, http://hdl.handle.net/10603/57147, p. 222.
7. Goswami, *Assam in the Nineteenth Century*, p. 171.
8. Although in 1848 the Charduar forests of Darrang were halved and leased out to two European companies, Martin and Co. and Ritchie and Co., for a period of fifteen years. The long duration of such leases gave way to six or seven years and in 1869 the system of annual leases was put in place.
9. Bodhisattava Kar, 'Historia Elastica: A Note on the Rubber Hunt in the North-Eastern Frontier of British India', *Indian Historical Review*, 36, 1 (2009), p. 139.
10. Aparajita Majumdar, 'The Colonial State and Resource Frontiers: Tracing the Politics of Appropriating Rubber in the Northeastern Frontier of British India, 1810-84', *Indian Historical Review*, 43, 1 (2016), p. 6. See also Aparajita Majumdar, '"Objects" of Appropriations: Locating material efficacies of rubber in the northeastern resource frontier of British India, 1810-1906' in Lipokmar Dzuvichu, Manjeet Baruah eds., *Objects and Frontiers in Modern Asia: Between the Mekong and the Indus* (London: Taylor and Francis, 2019), pp. 43-67.
11. Majumdar, 'Colonial State and Resource Frontiers', p. 8. See also Goswami, *Assam in the Nineteenth Century*, p. 171.
12. Quoted Aparajita Majumdar, '"Objects" of Appropriations', pp. 43-67.
13. Aparajita Majumdar, 'Colonial State and Resource Frontiers', p. 3.
14. Kar, 'Historia Elastica', p. 135-36. Meghraj Kothari was one of the most significant traders in rubber in the region. His father, Mahasingha Kothari, came from Bikaner to work as a servant and between 1818 and 1838 established around 80 *golas* (operating as provision stores for the army) between Goalpara and Dibrugarh, made possible from the profit on selling opium at a high price. Meghraj consolidated his father's business and established more shops near the tea gardens which were also involved in the trans-border trade in ivory and timber.
15. James Collins, *Report on the Caoutchouc of Commerce* (London: W. H. Allen, 1872), p. 41. See also Edward Stebbing, *The Forests of India*, Vol. 3 (London: Bodley Head, 1926), pp. 220-21.
16. Collins, *Report on the Caoutchouc of Commerce*, p. 39.
17. Quoted Gupta, *A Survey of the Resources and Industries of Eastern Bengal*, p. 81.
18. 'Report on the Forest Resources of Assam', 1908, p. 20 quoted Priyam Goswami, http://hdl.handle.net/10603/57147, p. 227.

The British Takeover of Assam

Jute and Rhea
1. Priyam Goswami, *Indigenous Industries of Assam: Retrospect and Prospect* (New Delhi: Akansha Publishing House, 2005), p. 43.
2. H. C. Kerr, *Report on the Cultivation of and Trade in Jute in Bengal, and on Indian Fibres* (Calcutta: Bengal Secretariat Press, 1874), pp. xlviii-xlix.
3. H. R. Carter, *Jute and its Manufacture* (London: John Bale, Sons and Danielsson Ltd, 1909), p. 13.
4. Sarah Hilaly, *The Railways in Assam, 1885-1947* (Varanasi: Pilgrims Publishing, 2007), p. 229.
5. Moffatt Mills, *Report on the Province of Assam*, p. 282.
6. Priyam Goswami, *The History of Assam, from Yandabo to Partition: 1826-1947* (New Delhi: Orient Blackswan, 2012), p. 182.
7. Ibid.
8. Arupjyoti Saikia, *A Century of Protests: Peasant Politics in Assam since 1900* (New Delhi: Routledge, 2014), pp. 48-49.
9. John Forbes Royle, *The Fibrous Plants of India fitted for Cordage, Clothing and Paper* (London: Smith Elder, 1855) p. 349.
10. *International Exhibition, 1876*, Vol. 5 (Washington: US Govt. Printing Office, 1880), pp. 562-63.

Silk
1. Barpujari, *Assam in the Days of the Company*, p. 212.
2. Hunter, *Statistical Account of Assam*, Vol. I, p. 138.
3. Robinson, *Descriptive Account of Asam*, p. 227.
4. Ward, *Glimpse of Assam*, p. 91.
5. Robinson, *Descriptive Account of Asam*, pp. 229-232.
6. E. Stack, 'Silk in Assam', *Notes on some industries of Assam from 1884 to 1895* (Shillong: Assam Secretariat Printing Office, 1896), p. 3.
7. Ibid.
8. Stack, 'Silk in Assam', p. 4.
9. B. C. Allen, *Monograph on the Silk Cloths of Assam* (Shillong: Assam Secretariat Printing Office, 1899), pp. 166-180.
10. Gupta, *Survey of the Industries and Resources of Eastern Bengal*, p. 28.

Cotton
1. Hunter, *Statistical Account of Assam*, Vol. I, p. 57.
2. H. F. Samman, *Monograph on the Cotton Fabrics of Assam* (Calcutta: Supt. Government Printing, 1897), p. 28.
3. Goswami, *Assam in the Nineteenth Century*, pp. 47-48.
4. E. W. Collin, *Report on the Existing Arts and Industries in Bengal* (Calcutta: Bengal Secretariat Press, 1890), p. 10.
5. Gupta, *Survey of the Industries and Resources of Eastern Bengal*, p. 7.

6. F. C. Henniker, *Report on the River and Rail-Borne Trade of the Province of Assam for the Year ending 31st March 1901* (Shillong: Assam Secretariat Printing Office, 1901).
7. Tirthankar Roy, *How British Rule Changed India's Economy*, p. 46.
8. H. Z. Darrah, *Cotton in Assam*, 1885, IOR/V/27/631/27, AAS, BL.

Lac

1. Lac S. K. Bhuyan, *Anglo-Assamese Relations, 1771-1826* (Gauhati: Dept. of Historical and Antiquarian Studies, Assam, 1949), p. 61.
2. Francis Buchanan-Hamilton, *An Account of Assam: first compiled in 1807-1814*, S. K. Bhuyan ed. (Gauhati: Dept. of Historical and Antiquarian Studies, Assam, 1940), p. 46.
3. Robinson, *Descriptive Account of Asam*, p. 238.
4. Gupta, *Survey of the Resources and Industries of Eastern Bengal*, p. 82.
5. B. C. Allen, *Assam District Gazetteers*, Vol. X (Allahabad: Pioneer Press, 1906), p. 86.
6. E. P. Stebbing, 'A Note on the Lac Insect (Tachardia lacca): its life history, propagation and collection', *The Indian Forest Records*, Vol. 1, Pt. 1 (Calcutta: Supt. Govt. Printing, 1909), p. 2.
7. Gupta, *Survey of the Resources and Industries of Eastern Bengal*, p. 81.
8. Early in the twentieth century, Nepalese immigrants challenged the Marwari monopoly in both the rubber and lac trade by not only procuring the products themselves, but also selling directly to Calcutta firms.
9. Quoted Goswami, *Assam in the Nineteenth Century*, p. 182.
10. Gupta, *Survey of the Resources and Industries of Eastern Bengal*, pp. 83-4.

Sugar and Mustard

1. H. K. Barpujari, *The Comprehensive History of Assam*, Vol. V (Guwahati: Publication Board, 1990), p. 61. See also Monimala Devi, 'Economic History of Nepali Migration and Settlement in Assam', *Economic and Political Weekly*, 42, 29 (2007), p. 3006.
2. A. S. Sinha, T. B. Subba eds., *The Nepalis in Northeast India* (New Delhi: Indus Publishing Company, 2007), p. 187.
3. Gupta, *Survey of the Resources and Industries of Eastern Bengal*, pp. 65-66.
4. Butler, *Travels and Adventures in the Province of Assam*, p. 244. The poppy seed was sown in November and March. When the poppy heads had grown to a suitable size, diagonal incisions were made in the pod, and the juice collected on strips of coarse cloth (kanees), about 3 inches wide. When fully saturated and

dried, the cloth was tied up into little bundles. The cloth was then infused in water and chewed like tobacco. Alternatively, the opium could be smoked in a pipe, using small balls formed from the infused water and treated betel leaves. Robinson, *Descriptive Account of Asam*, pp. 72, 272.
5. Sharma, '"Lazy" Natives, Coolie Labour', p. 1295.

5 Education
Primary and Secondary Education
1. Bina Lahkar, *Development in Women* [sic] *Education: Study of Assam* (Guwahati: Omson's, 1987), p. 1.
2. Nirode K. Barroah, *David Scott in North East India, 1802-1831: A Study in British Paternalism* (New Delhi: Munshiram Manoharlal, 1970), p. 149.
3. Moffatt Mills, *Report on the Province of Assam*, p. 27.
4. Robinson, *Descriptive Account of Asam*, p. 277.
5. H. K. Barpujari, ed, *Political History of Assam*, Vol. I, 1826-1919 (Gauhati: Govt. of Assam, 1977), p. 104.
6. Quoted Madhumita Sengupta, *Becoming Assamese: Colonialism and New Subjectivities in Northeast India* (New Delhi: Routledge, 2016), p. 112.
7. Archana Chakravarty, *History of Education in Assam*: 1826-1919 (Delhi: Mittal Publications, 1989), pp. 9-11.
8. These officials had replaced the local aristocracy when the latter proved incapable of discharging their duties under British rule, since towards the later stage of Ahom rule, the criteria for holding high official positions was not merit but birth into certain families.
9. Barpujari, *Political History of Assam*, p. 107.
10. H. Sharp, *Selection from Educational Records, 1781-1839*, Part 1 (Calcutta: Supt. Govt. Printing, 1920), pp. 130-31.
11. Barpujari, *Political History of Assam* I, p. 107.
12. Moffatt Mills, *Report on the Province of Assam*, pp. 8-17.
13. Major John Butler, when principal assistant of Nowgong, suspected that the upper classes intended to suppress the rising generation in order to exercise their influence over them. In addition, in Butler's view the priesthood used 'most oppressive modes of keeping the people in subjection to themselves ... Possessed of great power over the minds of the people, bigoted, ignorant, and avaricious, they do not promote, in the smallest degree, through the means at their disposal, the education of the people'. Butler, *Travels and Adventures in the Province of Assam*, pp. 240-42.
14. Moffatt Mills, *Report on the Province of Assam*, p. 27.
15. Moffatt Mills, *Report on the Province of Assam*, pp. 20-28, 106.

16. Anandaram Dhekiyal Phukan, 'Observations on the administration of the province of Assam' in Moffatt Mills, *Report on the Province of Assam,* Appendix F, pp. xli-xlii.
17. Hunter, *Statistical Account of Assam,* Vol. I, p. 273.
18. Sir George Campbell's Resolution, 30 September 1872, quoted W. W. Hunter, *Report of the Indian Education Commission* (Calcutta: Supt. Govt. Printing, 1883), pp. 98-100.
19. Madhumita Sengupta, 'Orienting Progress? Some Aspects of Education in Nineteenth Century Assam', *Economic and Political Weekly,* 47, 29 (2012), p. 55.
20. Hunter, *Report of the Indian Education Commission,* p. 255. See also A. Croft, *Review of Education in India in 1886, with Special Reference to the Report of the Education Commission* (Calcutta: Supt. Govt. Printing, 1888), p. 6.
21. Hunter, *Report of the Indian Education Commission,* p. 254.
22. Aparna Basu, *The Growth of Education and Political Development in India, 1898-1920* (Delhi: Oxford University Press, 1974), pp. 8, 11.

Higher Education
1. H. K. Barpujari, *A Short History of Higher Education in Assam, 1826-1900: Golden Jubilee Volume, Cotton College* (Gauhati, 1952), p. 15.
2. Ibid, p. 23.

Female Education
1. Robinson, *Descriptive Account of Asam,* pp. 274, 277.
2. *Report on the Progress of Education in Eastern Bengal and Assam, 1901-2* (Calcutta: Bengal Secretariat Book Depot, 1902), p. 82.
3. Quoted Y. B. Mathur, *Women's Education in India, 1813-1966* (Bombay: Asia Publishing House, 1973), p. 29.
4. Barpujari ed., *Comprehensive History of Assam,* Vol. V, p. 201.
5. Hunter, *Report of the Indian Education Commission,* pp. 545-48.
6. W. Booth, *General Report on Public Instruction in Assam* (Shillong: Assam Secretariat Printing Office, 1904).
7. Lahkar, *Development in Women* [sic] *Education,* p. 24.
8. Niharika Moran, 'History of female education in Assam', *International Journal of Humanities and Social Science Invention,* 8, 7 (2019), pp. 40-42.
9. Anandaram Dhekial Phukan was a true representative of the spirit of the Bengal Renaissance in Assam. During his stay in Calcutta (1850–52) he became a member of the Bethune Society which was devoted to the cause of female education. On his return to Assam, he was instrumental in establishing the Jnan-Pradayini Sabha at Nowgong which worked for the development of the

society. He believed that women could only be liberated through education.
10. Moran, 'History of female education in Assam', p. 41. See also Ajit Konwar, 'Women, Society and Patriarchy in 19th Century Assam', *International Journal of Interdisciplinary Research in Social Science and Culture*, 3, 1 (1917), pp. 116-119.

Missions
1. H. H. Dodwell, *The Cambridge History of the British Empire*, Vol. V (Cambridge: Cambridge University Press, 1932), p. 124.
2. H. K. Barpujari, *The American Missionaries and North East India, 1836-1900* (Guwahati: Spectrum, 1986), pp. xi-xii.
3. Ibid.
4. Ward, *Glimpse of Assam*, p. 22.
5. N. Natarajan, *The Missionary among the Khasis* (New Delhi: Sterling, 1977), p. 60.
6. W. Gammell, *A History of American Baptist Missions in Asia, Africa, Europe and North America* (Boston: Kendall and Lincoln, 1850), p. 211.
7. F. S. Downs, *The Mighty Works of God: a brief history of the Council of Baptist Churches in North East India* (Gauhati: Christian Literature Centre, 1971), p. 279.
8. Letter from Francis Jenkins 10 March 1835 to the Bengal civil servant Charles Edward Trevelyan, quoted M. Saikia, 'Historical Writings on North-East India and the American Baptist Missionaries', *Proceedings of the Indian History Congress*, 72, Pt. 1 (2011), p. 909.
9. *The Baptist Missionary Magazine*, Vols. 17-18 (Boston: John Putnam, 1837-38), p. 261.
10. Nathan Brown, *Grammatical Notes on the Assamese Language* (Sibsagor [sic]: American Baptist Mission Press, 1848).
11. Ward, *Glimpse of Assam*, p. 208.
12. Ward, *Glimpse of Assam*, pp. 209-10.
13. *Report of the Assam Mission*, 1851 (Sibsagar, 1852), p. 21.
14. *Report of the Assam Mission*, p. 23.
15. Largely for homeless and destitute children, as native parents were unwilling to commit their children to the care of Christian missionaries. The idea was to make them competent teachers and assistants who would be useful for the mission.
16. Anupama Ghosh, 'Conversions, Education and Linguistic Identity in Assam: The American Baptist Missionaries, 1830s-1890', *Proceedings of the Indian History Congress*, 72, 1 (2011), pp. 868-869.
17. Barpujari ed., *Comprehensive History of Assam*, Vol. V, p. 218.
18. Ward, *Glimpse of Assam*, p. 22.
19. Ward, *Glimpse of Assam*, pp. 210-211.
20. Ward, *Glimpse of Assam*, p. 212

Endnotes

21. Barpujari, *American Missionaries and North East India*, p. xxiii.
22. Barpujari, *The Nagas: The Evolution of their History and Administration*, p. 60.
23. 'Journal of Mr. Bronson', January 1839, *The Baptist Missionary Magazine*, Vols. 19-20 (Boston: Board of Managers, Baptist General Convention, 1836-1849), p. 283. The Assamese evangelist Godhula was suspected at first of being 'a Company man'. Mary Mead Clark, *A Corner in India* (Philadelphia: American Baptist Publication Society, 1907), p. 10.
24. Downs, *Mighty Works of God*, p. 66.
25. Christoph von Furer-Haimendorf, *The Naked Nagas* (London: Methuen and Co., 1939), p. 49.
26. J. H. Hutton, *The Angami Nagas, with some notes on Neighbouring Tribes* (London, Macmillan and Co., 1921), p. vii.
27. Ward, *Glimpse of Assam*, pp. 214-15.
28. Ward, *Glimpse of Assam*, pp. 216-17.
29. William Ward, *A View of the History, Literature and Religion of the Hindoos*, Vol. II (Serampore: Mission Press, 1811), p. 89. Drawing on the three characteristics he imputed to Hinduism – sacrifice, idolatry and eroticism – Ward produced a concrete image of Hinduism as cruel, irrational and licentious and concluded that 'there is not a vestige of real morality in the whole of the Hindu system'. Vol 1, p. 216. Ward died of cholera at Serampore in March 1823.
30. See Brian K. Pennington. 'Reverend William Ward and his legacy for Christian (Mis)perception of Hinduism', *Journal of Hindu-Christian Studies*, 13, Article 6 (2000).
31. Ward, *Glimpse of Assam*, pp. 218-19.
32. Journal of Miles Bronson, Kullung River, June 28, 1852, quoted Barpujari, *American Missionaries and North East India*, pp. 208-09.
33. Anandaram Dhekial Phukan in his addendum to the Moffatt Mills Report of 1853 declared, 'The universal use of opium has converted the Assamese, once a hardy, industrious and enterprising race into an effeminate, weak, indolent and a degraded people.' Anandaram Dhekial Phukan, 'Observations on the Administration of the Province of Assam' in Moffatt Mills, *Report on the Province of Assam*, Appendix J.
34. Amalendu Guha, 'Imperialism of Opium: its Ugly Face in Assam (1773-1921)', *Proceedings of the Indian History Congress*, 37 (1976), pp. 340, 343. See also Anirudh Deshpande, 'An Historical Overview of Opium Cultivation and Changing State Attitudes towards the Crop in India, 1878-2000 AD', *Studies in History*, 25, 1 (2009), p. 121.

35. Letter from Whiting to Home Board, 6 April 1858, cited in Barpujari, *American Missionaries and North-East India,* p. 97.
36. Downs, *The Mighty Works of God,* pp. 82-3.
37. Elwin Verrier, 'The Aboriginals', *Oxford Pamphlets on Indian Affairs,* No. 14 (London: Oxford University Press, 1943) quoted Asoso Yonuo, *The Rising Nagas* (Delhi: Manas Publications, 1948), p. 120.
38. Ibid.
39. *The Adivasis* (Delhi: Ministry of Information and Broadcasting, Government of India, 1955), p. 4.
40. H. K. Barpujari, *Problem of the Hill Tribes: North-East Frontier,* Vol. 3, 1873-1962 (Guwahati: Spectrum, 1981), pp. 335-6.

Epilogue

1. Susanta Krishna Dass has observed that Assam's rate of population growth during 1901–51 was the second highest in the world, exceeded only by Brazil. In 1901, Assam's population constituted only 1.38 per cent of India's total population, but by 1971 Assam's share nearly doubled (2.67 per cent). 'Immigration and Demographic Transformation of Assam, 1891-1981', *Economic and Political Weekly,* 15, 19 (May 1980), p. 850.
2. Tilottoma Misra, 'A Colonial Hinterland', *Economic and Political Weekly,* 15, 32 (August 1980), p. 1359.
3. Misra, 'A Colonial Hinterland', pp. 1361-62.
4. Misra, 'A Colonial Hinterland, p. 1364.

Bibliography

Acharyya, N. N. *A Brief History of Assam: from earliest time to the year 1983*. New Delhi: Omsons, 1987.

Allen, B. C. *Assam District Gazetteers*, IX, Naga Hills and Manipur. Calcutta: Baptist Mission Press, 1905.

Allen, B. C. *Assam District Gazetteers*, VI, Nowgong. Calcutta: City Press, 1905.

Allen, B. C. *Assam District Gazetteers*, VIII, Lakhimpur. Calcutta: City Press, 1905.

Allen, B. C. *Assam District Gazeteers*, X, The Khasi and Jaintia Hills, the Garo Hills and the Lushai Hills. Allahabad: Pioneer Press, 1906.

Allen, B. C. *Gazetteer of Bengal and North East India*. Delhi: Mittal, reprinted 1979.

Antrobus, H. A. *A History of the Jorehaut Tea Company Ltd, 1859-1946*. London: Tea and Rubber Mail, 1948.

Antrobus, H. A. *A History of the Assam Company, 1839-1953*. Edinburgh: private printing T. and A. Constable, 1957.

Arnold, David. *Science, Technology and Medicine in Colonial India*. Cambridge: Cambridge University Press, 2004.

Assam Mission of the American Baptist Union: Papers and Discussions of the Jubilee Conference held in Nowgong, 18-29 December 1886. Calcutta: J. W. Thomas, Baptist Mission Press, 1887.

Bagchi, Amiya Kumar. *The Political Economy of Underdevelopment*. Cambridge: Cambridge University Press, 1982.

Bagchi, Amiya Kumar. *Colonialism and India Economy*. New Delhi: Oxford University Press India, 2010.

Barkataki, S. *Tribes of Assam*. New Delhi: National Book Trust, 1969.

Barker, George M. *A Tea Planter's Life in Assam*. Calcutta: Thacker, Spink, 1884.

Barpujari, H. K. *A Short History of Higher Education in Assam, 1826-1900: Golden Jubilee Volume, Cotton College.* Gauhati, 1952.

Barpujari H. K. ed. *Political History of Assam,* Vol. I, 1826-1919. Gauhati: Govt. of Assam, 1977.

Barpujari, H. K. *Assam in the Days of the Company: 1826-1858.* Gauhati: Spectrum, 1980.

Barpujari, H. K. *Problem of the Hill Tribes: North-East Frontier,* Vol. 3, 1873-1962. Guwahati: Spectrum, 1981.

Barpujari, H. K. *The American Missionaries and North-East India, 1836-1900 A. D.: A Documentary Study.* Guwahati: Spectrum, 1986.

Barpujari H. K. ed. *The Comprehensive History of Assam,* Vol. IV. Guwahati: Assam Publication Board, 1992.

Barpujari, H. K. ed. *The Comprehensive History of Assam,* Vol. V. Guwahati: Publication Board, 1993.

Barpujari, S. K. *The Nagas: The Evolution of their History and Administration, 1832-1939.* Guwahati: Spectrum, 2003.

Barroah, Nirode K. *David Scott in North East India, 1802-1831: A Study in British Paternalism.* New Delhi: Munshiram Manoharlal, 1970.

Baruah, Maniram Dutta. 'Native Account of Washing for Gold in Assam'. *Journal of the Asiatic Society of Bengal,* VII, Pt. 2 (1838): 621-25.

Baruah, Sanjib. 'Indigenous Peoples, Cultural Survival and Minority Policy in Northeast India'. *Cultural Survival Quarterly,* 13, 2 (1989): 53-58.

Baruah, Sanjib. *India Against Itself: Assam and the Politics of Nationality.* Pennsylvania: University of Pennsylvania Press, 1999.

Baruah, Sanjib.'Clash of Resource Use Regimes in Colonial Assam: A Nineteenth Century Puzzle Revisited'. *Journal of Peasant Studies,* 28, 3 (2001): 109-124.

Baruah, Sanjib. *Post-Frontier Blues: Towards a New Policy Framework for Northeast India.* Washington DC: East-West Center, 2007.

Baruah, Sanjib, ed. *Beyond Counter-Insurgency: Breaking the Impasse in Northeast India.* New Delhi: Oxford University Press, 2009.

Baruah, Sanjib. *Durable Disorder: Understanding the Politics of Northeast India.* Oxford: Oxford University Press, 2012.

Basu, Aparna. *The Growth of Education and Political Development in India, 1898-1920.* Delhi: Oxford University Press, 1974.

Batori, Silver Jubilee Edition. Digboi: September 1978.

Behal, Rana P. 'Forms of Labour Protest in Assam Valley Tea Plantations, 1900-1930'. *Economic and Political Weekly,* 20, 4 (1985): 19-26.

Behal, Rana P. and Prabhu P. Mohapatra. 'Tea and Money versus Human Life: The Rise and Fall of the Indenture System in the Assam Tea Plantations 1840-1908'. *Journal of Peasant Studies,* 19, 3-4 (1992): 142-172.

Bibliography

Behal, Rana P., Marcel van der Linden eds. *Coolies, Capital and Colonialism: Studies in Indian Labour History*. Cambridge: Cambridge University Press, 2006.

Behal, Rana B. 'Coolie Drivers or Benevolent Paternalists? British Tea Planters in Assam and the Indenture Labour System'. *Modern Asian Studies* 44, 1 (2010): 29-51.

Beresford, G. W. *Notes on the North-Eastern Frontier of Assam*. Shillong: Assam Secretariat Printing Office, 1881.

Bhatterjee, J. B. *Cachar under British Rule in North East India*. New Delhi: Radiant Publishers, 1977.

Bhattacharjee, Srijani. 'The Coming of British Forestry in Assam in the Nineteenth and Early Twentieth Century: Initiatives and Problems' in Sajal Nag, ed. *Playing with Nature: History and Politics of Environment in North-East India*. London: Routledge, 2018.

Bhuyan, S. K. *Anglo-Assamese Relations, 1771-1826*. Gauhati: Dept. of Historical and Antiquarian Studies, Assam, 1949.

Bigge, H. 'Notice of the Discovery of Coal and Petroleum on the Namrup River'. *Journal of the Asiatic Society of Bengal,* VI (1837): 243.

Bilham, Roger. 'Tom La Touche and the Great Assam Earthquake of 12 June 1897. Letters from the Epicentre'. *Seismological Research Letters*, 79, 3 (2008): 426-437.

Booth, W. *General Report on Public Instruction in Assam*. Shillong: Assam Secretariat Printing Office, 1904.

Bose, M. L. *History of Arunachal Pradesh*. New Delhi: Concept Publishing Co., 1997.

Brown, Nathan. *Grammatical Notes on the Assamese Language*. Sibsagor: American Baptist Mission Press, 1848.

Buchanan-Hamilton, Francis. *An Account of Assam: first compiled in 1807-1814*. Gauhati: Dept. of Historical and Antiquarian Studies, Assam, 1940.

Buckingham J., *Tea-Garden Coolies in Assam*. Calcutta: Thacker, Spink, 1894.

Butler, John. *A Sketch of Assam with some account of the Hill Tribes, by an Officer*. London: Smith Elder, 1847.

Butler, John. *Travels and Adventures in the Province of Assam*. London: Smith, Elder, 1855.

Butler, John (son of above). 'Rough Notes on the Angami'. *Journal of the Asiatic Society of Bengal*, XLIV, Pt. I (1875): 307-350.

Carnegie Papers. Mss Eur C682, AAS, British Library.

Carter, H. R. *Jute and its Manufacture*. London: John Bale, Sons and Danielsson Ltd, 1909.

Cederlof, Gunnel. *Founding an Empire on India's North-Eastern Frontiers, 1790-1840: Climate, Commerce, Polity*. New Delhi: Oxford University Press India, 2013.

Chakravarty, Archana. *History of Education in Assam: 1826-1919.* Delhi: Mittal Publications, 1989.

Chakravorty, B. C. *British Relations with the Hill Tribes of Assam.* Calcutta: Firma K. L. Mukhopadhyay, 1964.

Chandra, Bipan. *Nationalism and Colonialism in Modern India.* New Delhi: Orient Blackswan, 1984.

Chaube, S. K. *Hill Politics in Northeast India.* New Delhi: Orient Blackswan, 2012.

Chevalier, Jean-Baptiste. *The Adventures of Jean-Baptiste Chevalier in Eastern India, 1752-65: Historical Memoir and Journal of Travels in Assam, Bengal and Tibet,* translated by Caroline Dutta-Baruah and Jean Deloche. Guwahati: LBS Publishers, 2008.

Clark, Mary Mead. *A Corner in India.* Philadelphia: American Baptist Publication Society, 1907.

Collin, E. W. *Report on the Existing Arts and Industries in Bengal.* Calcutta: Bengal Secretariat Press, 1890.

Collins, James. *Report on the Caoutchouc of Commerce.* London: W. H. Allen, 1872.

Collister, Peter. *Bhutan and the British.* London: Serindia Publications, 1987.

Cooper, T. T. *The Mishmee Hills.* London: H. S. King, 1873.

Cotton, H. J. *Indian and Home Memories.* London: T. Fisher Unwin, 1911.

Croft, A. *Review of Education in India in 1886, with Special Reference to the Report of the Education Commission.* Calcutta: Supt. Govt. Printing, 1888.

Curzon Papers. Mss Eur F111/161, AAS, British Library.

Dalton, Edward Tuite. 'Report of his visit to the Hills in the Neighbourhood of the Soobanshiri River'. *Journal of the Asiatic Society of Bengal,* XIV, Pt. I (1845): 150-267.

Dalton, Edward Tuite. 'On the Meris and Abors of Assam'. *Journal of the Asiatic Society of Bengal,* XIV, Pt. I (1845): 426-430.

Dalton, Edward Tuite. 'Notes on Assam Temple Ruins'. *Journal of the Asiatic Society of Bengal,* XXIV (1855): 1-24.

Dalton. Edward Tuite and S. F. Hannay, 'Note on Recent Investigations Regarding the Extent and Value of the Auriferous Deposits of Assam'. *Memoirs of the Geological Survey of India,* I, Pt. 1 (1856): 94-98.

Dalton, Edward Tuite. *Descriptive Ethnology of Bengal.* Calcutta: Supt. Govt. Printing, 1872.

Darrah, H. Z. *Cotton in Assam,* 1885. IOR/V/27/631/27, AAS, British Library.

Darrah, H. Z. *Report on the River-Borne Trade of the Province of Assam for the Year 1892-3.* Shillong: Assam Secretariat Printing Office, 1893.

Bibliography

Das, J. N. *An introduction to the land-laws of Assam*. Gauhati: Lawyers Book Stall, 1988.

Dass, Susanta Krishna. 'Immigration and Demographic Transformation of Assam, 1891-1981', *Economic and Political Weekly*, 15, 19 (May 1980): 850-859.

Deshpande, Anirudh. 'An Historical Overview of Opium Cultivation and Changing State Attitudes towards the Crop in India, 1878-2000 AD'. *Studies in History*, 25, 1 (2009): 109-143.

Devi, Monimala. 'Economic History of Nepali Migration and Settlement in Assam', *Economic and Political Weekly*, 42, 29 (2007): 3005-3007.

Dodwell, H. H. *The Cambridge History of the British Empire*, Vol. V. Cambridge: Cambridge University Press, 1932.

Downs, F.S. *The Mighty Works of God: a brief history of the Council of Baptist Churches in North East India*. Gauhati: Christian Literature Centre, 1971.

Dun, G. W. *Preliminary Notes on Miris*. Simla: 1897.

Dutta, Tarun. *Road Communication in North East India and Beyond: Bridging Culture and People*. New Delhi: Concept Publishing, 2018.

Dzuvichu, Lipokmar. 'Roads and the Raj: the politics of road building in colonial Naga Hills, 1860s-1910s'. *Indian Economic and Social History Review*, 50 (2013): 473-494.

Eden, Ashley. 'Report on the State of Bootan and the Progress of the Mission of 1863-64' in *Political Missions to Bootan*. Calcutta: Bengal Secretariat Office, 1865.

Elliott, C. A. to Ripon, 22 March 1881. Add Mss 43605, AAS, British Library.

Elwin, Verrier, 'The Aboriginals'. *Oxford Pamphlets on Indian Affairs*, No. 14. London: Oxford University Press, 1943.

Elwin, Verrier, ed. *India's North East Frontier in the Nineteenth Century*. Bombay: Oxford University Press, 1959.

Elwin, Verrier, ed. *The Nagas in the Nineteenth Century*. Bombay: Oxford University Press, 1969.

Flex, Oscar. *Asom 1864*, translated by Dr Salim M. Ali. Guwahati: G. L. Publications, 2012.

Fuller, Sir Bampfylde. *Some Personal Experiences*. London: J. Murray, 1930.

Gait, E. A. *A History of Assam*. Calcutta: Thacker Spink and Co., 1906.

Gammell, W. *A History of American Baptist Missions in Asia, Africa, Europe and North America*. Boston: Kendall and Lincoln, 1850.

Gawthrop, W. R. *The Story of the Assam Railways and Trading Company Ltd. 1881-1951*. London: Harley Publishing, 1951.

Ghosh, Anupama. 'Conversions, Education and Linguistic Identity in Assam: The American Baptist Missionaries, 1830s-1890'. *Proceedings of the Indian History Congress*, 72, 1 (2011): 863-874.

Gilmour, David. *The British in India*. London: Allen Lane, 2018.

Giri, Helen. *The Khasi under British Rule, 1824-1947*. New Delhi: Regency Publications, 1998.

Goswami, Priyam. 'Industrialisation and Colonial Penetration in the Assam in the Nineteenth Century: A Sectoral Analysis of the Tea, Coal and Oil Industries'. PhD North-Eastern Hill University, Shillong, 1993. http://hdl.handle.net/10603/57147

Goswami, Priyam. *Assam in the Nineteenth Century: Industrialisation and Colonial Penetration*. Guwahati: Spectrum, 1999.

Goswami, Priyam. *The History of Assam, from Yandabo to Partition: 1826-1947*. New Delhi: Orient Blackswan, 2012.

Gray, J. Erroll. *Diary of a Journey to the Bor Khamti Country, 1892-93*. Simla: G. C. Press, 1893.

Griffith, William. 'Report on the Caoutchouc Tree of Assam'. *Journal of the Asiatic Society of Bengal*, VII, Pt. 1 (1838): 132-142.

Griffith, William. *Journals of Travels in Assam, Burma, Bootan, Afghanistan and the Neighbouring Countries*. Calcutta: Bishop's College Press, 1847.

Griffiths, Sir Percival. *The History of the Indian Tea Industry*. London: Weidenfeld and Nicholson, 1967.

Guha, Amalendu. 'Imperialism of Opium: its Ugly Face in Assam (1773-1921)'. *Proceedings of the Indian History Congress*, 37 (1976): 338-346.

Guha, Amalendu. *Planter-Raj to Swaraj: Freedom Struggle and Electoral Politics in Assam, 1826-1947*. New Delhi: Tulika Books, 1977.

Gupta, G. N. *A Survey of the Industries and Resources of Eastern Bengal and Assam for 1907-8*. Shillong: Assam Secretariat Printing Office, 1908.

Gurdon, P. R. T. *The Khasis*. London: Macmillan, 1914.

Handique, R. *British Forest Policy in Assam*. New Delhi: Concept Publishing Company, 2004.

Hannay, S.F. 'Proceedings of the Asiatic Society, 2 May 1838'. *Journal of the Asiatic Society of Bengal*, VII, Pt. 1 (1838): 364-369.

Hannay, S. F. 'Observations on the quality of Principal Timber Trees growing in the Vicinity of Upper Assam'. *Journal of the Agricultural and Horticultural Society of India*, IV (1845): 116-133.

Hannay, S. F. 'Notes on the Iron Ore Statistics and Economic Geology of Upper Assam'. *Journal of the Asiatic Society of Bengal*, XXV (1856): 330-344.

Harman, H. J. 'Narrative Report of Lt. H. J. Harman in charge of the Daphla Military Expeditionary Survey'. *General Report on the Topographical Surveys of India, 1874-5*. Calcutta: Govt. of India, 1876.

Hasnu, Santosh. 'Disciplining the Hill Tribes into Coolie Labour for Road Construction' in Gwyn Campbell and Alessandro Stanziani eds. *The*

Bibliography

Palgrave Handbook of Bondage and Human Rights in Africa and Asia. New York: Palgrave Macmillan, 2020.

Hasnu, Santosh. 'Coolie Labour, Tea Planters, and Transport in Colonial India' in Andrea Komlosy and Goran Music eds. *Global Commodity Chains and Labour Relations*. Leiden/Boston: Brill, 2021.

Heath, Ian. *The North-East Frontier, 1837-1901*. Oxford: Osprey, 1999.

Henniker, F. C. *Report on the River and Rail-Borne Trade of the Province of Assam for the Year ending 31st March 1901*. Shillong: Assam Secretariat Printing Office, 1901.

Hesselmeyer, C. H. 'The Hill Tribes of the Northern Frontier of Assam'. *Journal of the Asiatic Society of Bengal*, XXXVII (1868): 192-208.

Hilaly, Sarah. *The Railways in Assam, 1885-1947*. Varanasi: Pilgrims Publishing, 2007.

Holland, T. H. *Sketch of the Mineral Resources of India*. Calcutta: Govt. of India, 1908.

Hunter, W. W. *A Statistical Account of Assam*, Vol. I. London: Trubner and Co., 1879.

Hunter, W. W. *Report of the Indian Education Commission*. Calcutta: Supt. Govt. Printing, 1883.

Hutton, J. H. *The Angami Nagas, with some notes on Neighbouring Tribes*. London, Macmillan and Co., 1921.

Imperial Gazetteer of India: Eastern Bengal and Assam. Calcutta: Supt. of Govt. Printing, 1909.

International Exhibition, 1876, Vol. 5. Washington: US Govt. Printing Office, 1880.

Jenkins, C. F. H. 'Proceedings of the Asiatic Society, 7 February 1838'. *Journal of the Asiatic Society of Bengal*, VII, Pt. 1 (1838): 169-170.

Johnstone, Sir James. *My Experiences in Manipur and the Naga Hills*. London: Sampson Low, 1896.

Kapal, Yuimirin. 'Spatial Organisation of Northeast India: Colonial Politics, Power Structure and Hills-Plains Relationship'. *Indian Historical Review*, 47, 1 (2020): 150-169.

Kar, Bodhisattva. 'Historia Elastica: A Note on the Rubber Hunt in the North-Eastern Frontier of British India'. *Indian Historical Review*, 36, 1 (2009): 131-150.

Kennedy, R. S. 'Ethnological Report on the Akas, Khoas and Mijis and the Monbas of Tawang' (1914). Mss Eur F157/324/(h), AAS, British Library.

Kerr, H. C. *Report on the Cultivation of and Trade in Jute in Bengal, and on Indian Fibres*. Calcutta: Bengal Secretariat Press, 1874.

Kinney, T. *Old Times in Assam*. Calcutta: Star Press, 1896.

Konwar, Ajit. 'Women, Society and Patriarchy in 19th Century Assam'. *International Journal of Interdisciplinary Research in Social Science and Culture*, 3, 1 (2017): 113-129.

Krick, N. M. 'Account of an Expedition among the Abors in 1853', translated by A. Gille. *Journal of the Asiatic Society of Bengal*, IX (1913): 107-122.

Kumar, Niklesh. 'Identity Politics in the Hill Tribal Communities in the North-Eastern India'. *Sociological Bulletin*, 54, 2 (2005): 195-217.

Kunda, Sris Kumar. *Slavery in British Dominion*. Calcutta: Jijnasa, 1972.

LaFavre, Gabrielle. 'The Tea Gardens of Assam and Bengal: Company Rule and Exploitation of the Indian Population during the Nineteenth Century'. *The Trinity Papers*, 1, 1 (2013): 17-31.

Lahiri-Dutt, Kuntala. *The Coal Nation: Histories, Economies and Politics of Coal in India*. London: Routledge, 2014.

Lahkar, Bina. *Development in Women [sic] Education: Study of Assam*. Guwahati: Omson's, 1987.

Lewin, T. H. *The Hill Tracts of Chittagong and the Dwellers Therein*. Calcutta: Bengal Printing Press, 1869.

Macgregor, C. R. 'Notes on Akas and Akaland'. *Proceedings of the Asiatic Society of Bengal*, XI (1884): 198-212.

Mackenzie, A. *Papers regarding the Tea Industry in Bengal with Notes by J. W. Edgar and Mr. Campbell*. Calcutta: Bengal Secretariat Press, 1873.

Mackenzie, A. *History of the Relations of the Government with the Hill Tribes of the Northeast Frontier of Bengal*. Calcutta: The Home Department Press, 1884.

Maclaren, J. Malcolm. 'The Auriferous Occurrences of Assam'. *Records of the Geological Survey of India*, XXXI (1904): 170-232.

MacWhirter Papers, Box 6, Centre of South Asian Studies, Cambridge.

Mahanta, N. G. and D. Gogoi eds. *Shifting Terrain: Conflict Dynamics in North East India*. Guwahati: DVS Publishers, 2012.

Majumdar, Aparajita. 'The Colonial State and Resource Frontiers: Tracing the Politics of Appropriating Rubber in the Northeastern Frontier of British India, 1810-84'. *Indian Historical Review*, 43, 1 (2016): 25-41.

Majumdar, Aparajita.'"Objects" of Appropriations: Locating material efficacies of rubber in the northeastern resource frontier of British India, 1810-1906' in Lipokmar Dzuvichu and Manjeet Baruah, eds. *Objects and Frontiers in Modern Asia: Between the Mekong and the Indus*. London: Taylor and Francis, 2019.

Mallet, F. R. 'On the Coal-Fields of the Naga Hills Bordering the Lakhimpur and Sibsagar Districts, Assam'. *Memoirs of the Geological Survey of India*, XII (1876): 269-362.

Bibliography

Mann, Gustav. *Progress Report of Forest Administration in the Province of Assam*. Shillong: Assam Secretariat Printing Office, 1874-75.

Mathur, Y. B. *Women's Education in India, 1813-1966*. Bombay: Asia Publishing House, 1973.

McClelland, John. *Reports of a Committee for investigating the Coal and Mineral Resources of India*. Calcutta: G. H. Huttman, 1838.

McCosh, John. 'Account of the Mountain Tribes on the Extreme N. E. Frontier of Bengal'. *Journal of the Asiatic Society of Bengal*, V (1836): 193-208.

McCosh, John. *Topography of Assam*. Calcutta: Bengal Military Orphan Press, 1837.

Medlicott, H. B. 'The Coal of Assam: Results of a Brief Visit to the Coal-fields of that Province in 1865; with Geological Notes on Assam and the Hills to the South of It'. *Memoirs of the Geological Survey of India*, IV (1865): 387-442.

Meerwarth, A. M. *The Andamanese Nicobarese and Hill Tribes of Assam*. Calcutta: Spectrum Publications, 1919.

Mehdi, S. B. *Transport System and Economic Development in Assam*. Guwahati: Publication Board, 1978.

Mehra, G. N. *Bhutan, The Land of the Peaceful Dragon*. Delhi: Vikas Publishing House, 1974.

Mills, A. G. Moffatt. *Report on the Province of Assam*. Calcutta: Thomas Jones, *Calcutta Gazette* Office, 1854.

Misra, Sangamitra. 'The Nature of Colonial Intervention in the Naga Hills, 1840-80'. *Economic and Political Weekly*, 33, 51 (1998): 3273-3279.

Misra, Sangamitra. *Space, Borders and Histories: Identity Construction in Colonial Goalpara*. London: University of London, 2004.

Misra, Tilottoma. 'A Colonial Hinterland'. *Economic and Political Weekly*, 15, 32 (August 1980): 1357-1364.

Moore, P. H. *Twenty years in Assam*. Rochester, NY: self-published, 1901.

Moran, Niharika. 'History of female education in Assam'. *International Journal of Humanities and Social Science Invention*, 8, 7 (2019): 40-42.

Morris, D. 'Sources of Commercial India-Rubber'. *Journal of the Society of Arts*, XLVI (August 1898): 785-796.

Morris, D. 'Towards a Reinterpretation of Nineteenth Century Indian Economic History'. *Journal of Economic History*, 23, 4 (1963): 606-618.

Nag, Sajal ed. *Playing with Nature: History and Politics of Environment in North-East India*. London: Routledge, 2018.

Naoroji, Dadabhai. *Poverty and Un-British Rule in India*. London: Swan Sonnenschein, 1901.

Natarajan, N. *The Missionary among the Khasis.* New Delhi: Sterling, 1977.
Needham, J. F. *Report on the Bebejiya Mishmi Expedition, 1899-1900.* Shillong: Assam Secretariat Printing Office, 1900.
Orleans, Prince Henri. *From Tonkin to India,* translated by Hamley Bent. London: Methuen, 1898.
Owen, John. *Notes on the Naga Tribes in communication with Assam.* Calcutta: W. H. Carey, 1844.
Pachuau, Joy. *Being Mizo: Identity and Belonging in Northeast India.* New Delhi: Oxford University Press, 2014.
Peal, S. E. 'Report on the Visit to the Nongyang Lake on the Burma Frontier, February 1879'. *Journal of the Asiatic Society of Bengal,* L, Pt. 2 (1881): 1-30.
Peal, S. E. 'Fading Histories'. *Journal of the Asiatic Society of Bengal,* LXIII, Pt. 3 (1894): 10-27.
Pemberton, Robert Boileau. *Report on the Eastern Frontier of British India.* Calcutta: Baptist Mission Press, 1835.
Pennington, Brian K. 'Reverend William Ward and his legacy for Christian (Mis)perception of Hinduism'. *Journal of Hindu-Christian Studies,* 13, Article 6 (2000): 1-7.
Phukan, Anandaram Dhekiyal. 'Observations on the administration of the province of Assam'. Appendices F and J in A. J. Moffatt Mills, *Report on the Province of Assam.* Calcutta: Thomas Jones, *Calcutta Gazette,* 1854.
Pollok, Fitzwilliam Thomas. *Sport in British Burmah, Assam and the Cassyah and Jyntiah Hills,* Vol. II. London: Chapman and Hall, 1879.
Pollok, Fitzwilliam Thomas and W. S. Thom. *Wild Sports of Burma and Assam.* London: Hurst and Blackett, 1900.
Rajkumar, Dhriti Kanta. 'Raids made out by the Lushai Tribes in the Tea Gardens of Cachar during the Colonial Period'. *Journal of Humanities and Social Science,* 9, 4 (2013): 43-54.
Ralte, Robert Lalremtluanga. 'Colonialism in Northeast India: An Environmental History of Forest Conflict in the Frontier of Lushai Hills 1850-1900'. *International Journal of Humanities and Social Science Invention,* 4, 1 (2015): 67-75.
'Report upon the Coal beds of Assam'. *Journal of the Asiatic Society of Bengal,* VII, Pt. 2 (1838): 951-54.
'Report of the Coal Committee'. *Journal of the Asiatic Society of Bengal,* IX, Pt. 1 (1840): 198-214.
Report on the Administration of the Province of Assam 1880-81. Shillong: Assam Secretariat Press, 1882.
Report on Labour Immigration into Assam for the Year 1888. Shillong: Assam Secretariat Printing Office, 1889.
Report on the Progress of Education in Eastern Bengal and Assam, 1901-2. Calcutta: Bengal Secretariat Book Depot, 1902.

Bibliography

Robb, Peter. 'The Colonial State and Constructions of Indian Identity: An Example on the Northeast Frontier in the 1880s'. *Modern Asian Studies,* 31, 2 (1997): 245-283.

Robinson, W. *Descriptive Account of Asam* [sic]. Delhi: Mittal, 1841.

Robinson, W. 'Notes on the Dophlas and the peculiarities of their Language'. *Journal of the Asiatic Society of Bengal,* XX (1851): 126-137.

Rowlatt, E. A. 'Report of an Expedition into the Mishmee Hills to the north-east of Sudyah'. *Journal of the Asiatic Society of Bengal,* XIV (1845): 477-495.

Roy, Tirthankar. *How British Rule Changed India's Economy: The Paradox of the Raj.* London: Palgrave Macmillan, 2019.

Roy, Tirthankar. *An Economic History of India 1707-1857.* Abingdon: Routledge, 2021.

Royle, John Forbes. *The Fibrous Plants of India fitted for Cordage, Clothing and Paper.* London: Smith Elder, 1855.

Saikia, Arupjyoti. *Forests and Ecological History of Assam.* New Delhi: Oxford University Press, 2011.

Saikia, Arupjyoti. 'Imperialism, Geology and Petroleum: History of Oil in Colonial Assam'. *Economic and Political Weekly,* 46, 12 (2011): 48-55.

Saikia, Arupjyoti. *A Century of Protests: Peasant Politics in Assam since 1900.* New Delhi: Routledge, 2014.

Saikia, Arupjyoti. *The Unquiet River: A Biography of the Brahmaputra.* New Delhi: Oxford University Press, 2019.

Saikia, M. 'Historical Writings on North-East India and the American Baptist Missionaries'. *Proceedings of the Indian History Congress,* 72, Pt. 1 (2011): 906-912.

Saikia, Rajen. *Social and Economic History of Assam.* New Delhi: Manohar, 2000.

Samman, H. F. *Monograph on the Cotton Fabrics of Assam.* Calcutta: Supt. Government Printing, 1897.

Scott, Anna Kay. *Korno Siga, the Mountain Chief; or, Life in Assam.* Philadelphia: The American Sunday-School Union, c.1889.

Selections from the Records of the Bengal Government, XXIII. Calcutta, 1855.

Sengupta, Madhumita. 'Orienting Progress? Some Aspects of Education in Nineteenth Century Assam'. *Economic and Political Weekly,* 47, 29 (2012): 53-60.

Sengupta, Madhumita. *Becoming Assamese: Colonialism and New Subjectivities in Northeast India.* New Delhi: Routledge, 2016.

Shakespear, L. W. *History of Upper Assam, Upper Burmah and North-Eastern Frontier.* Cambridge: Cambridge University Press, 1914.

Shakespear, L. W. *History of the Assam Rifles.* Gauhati: Spectrum Publications, 1929.

Sharma, Jayeeta. A Historical Perspective. https://www.india-seminar.com/2005/550/550 per cent20jayeeta per cent20sharma.htm

Sharma, Jayeeta. '"Lazy" Natives, Coolie Labour and the Assam Tea Industry'. *Modern Asian Studies* 43, 6 (2009): 1287-1324.

Sharma, Jayeeta. *Empire's Garden: Assam and the Making of India*. New Delhi: Permanent Black, 2012.

Sharp, H. *Selection from Educational Records, 1781-1839*, Part 1. Calcutta: Supt. Govt. Printing, 1920.

Siddique, Mohammed Abu B. *Evolution of Land Grants and Labour Policy of Government: The Growth of the Tea Industry in Assam 1834-1940*. New Delhi: South Asian Publishers, 1990.

Sinha, A. S. and T. B. Subba eds. *The Nepalis in Northeast India*. New Delhi: Indus Publishing Company, 2007.

Stack, E. 'Silk in Assam' in *Notes on Some industries of Assam from 1884 to 1895*. Shillong: Assam Secretariat Printing Office, 1896.

Stebbing, E. P. 'A Note on the Lac Insect (Tachardia lacca): its life history, propagation and collection'. *The Indian Forest Records,* Vol. 1, Pt. 1. Calcutta: Supt. Govt. Printing, 1909.

Stebbing, E. P. *The Forests of India*, Vol. 1. London: Bodley Head, 1922.

Stebbing, E. P. *The Forests of India*, Vol. 3. London: Bodley Head, 1926.

Syiemlieh, David R. *British Administration in Meghalaya: Policy and Pattern*. New Delhi: Heritage Publishers, 1989.

Tavernier, Jean-Baptiste. *Travels in India*, Vol. II, translated by V. Ball. London: Macmillan, 1889.

The Adivasis. Delhi: Ministry of Information and Broadcasting, Government of India, 1955.

'The Assam Railways and Trading Company'. IOR/L/AG/46/2, AAS, British Library.

The Baptist Missionary Magazine, Vols. 17-18. Boston: Putnam and Hewes, 1837-38.

The Baptist Missionary Magazine, Vols. 19-20. Boston: Putnam and Hewes, 1839.

The Friends of India and Statesman, 8 May 1895.

The Telegraph (India), 1 May 2022. https://www.telegraphindia.com/states/north-east/an-european-s-account-of-assam/cid/443929

Timberg, Thomas A. *The Marwaris: from Traders to Industrialists*. New Delhi: Vikas Publishing House, 1978.

Tomlinson, B. R. *The Economy of Modern India: from 1860 to the Twenty-First Century*. Cambridge: Cambridge University Press, 2013.

Transactions of the Mineralogical and Geological Institute of India, 2. The Institute, 1908.

Varma, Nitin. 'Coolie Acts and the Acting Coolies: Coolie, Planter and State in the Late Nineteenth and Early Twentieth Colonial Tea Plantations of Assam'. *Social Scientist*, 33, 5/6 (2005), 49-72.

Bibliography

Visvanath, S. N. *A Hundred Years of Oil: A Narrative Account of the Search for Oil in India*. Delhi: Vikas Publishing House, 1990.

Von Furer-Haimendorf, Christoph. *The Naked Nagas*. London: Methuen and Co., 1939.

Wangyai, Sonam B. 'A Cheerless Change: Bhutan Dooars to British Dooars'. http://himalaya.socanth.cam.ac.uk/collections/journals/jbs/pdf/JBS_15_02.pdf

Ward, Susan R. *A Glimpse of Assam*. Calcutta: City Press, 1884.

Ward, William. *A View of the History, Literature and Religion of the Hindoos*, Vol. II. Serampore: Mission Press, 1811.

Way, R. A. *Assam-Burma Connection Railway Surveys, Hukong Valley Route: Report and Approximate Estimate*. Calcutta: 1896. IOR/V/27/722/11, AAS, British Library.

Weatherstone, John. *The Pioneers 1825-1900: the Early British Tea and Coffee Planters and Their Way of Life*. London: Quiller Press, 1986.

Wilcox, R. 'Memoir of a Survey of Assam, and the Neighbouring Countries, Executed in 1825-6-7-8'. *Asiatic Researches*, XVII (1832): 314-469.

Williams, Emma. 'Letter regarding abuses on the tea plantations of Assam', 22 October 1907. IOR/L/PJ/6/832, AAS, British Library.

Wilson, James Alban. *Sport and Service in Assam and Elsewhere*. London: Hutchinson & Co., 1924.

Woodthorpe R. G. *The Lushai Expedition, 1871-72*. London: Hurst and Blackett, 1873.

Woodthorpe, R. G. 'A Punitive Expedition in 1875'. *General Report of the Topographical Surveys of India 1874-5*. Calcutta: Govt. of India, 1876.

Woodthorpe, R. G. 'Notes Descriptive of the Country and People in Western and Eastern Naga Hills'. *General Report of the Topographical Surveys of India 1874-5*. Calcutta: Govt. of India, 1876.

Woodthorpe, R. G. 'Notes on the Wild Tribes Inhabiting the So-Called Naga Hills, on Our North-East Frontier of India'. *Royal Anthropological Institute of Great Britain and Ireland*, 11 (1882): 56-73.

Wouters, Jelle J. P. 'Keeping the Hill Tribes at Bay: A critique from India's Northeast of James C. Scott's paradigm of state evasion'. *European Bulletin of Himalayan Research*, 39 (2011): 41-65.

Yonuo, Asoso. *The Rising Nagas*. Delhi: Manas Publications, 1948.

Yule, H. 'Notes on the Kasia Hills, and People'. *Journal of the Asiatic Society of Bengal*, XIII, Pt. 2 (1844), 612-630.

Ziipao, R. Raile. *Tribes and Tribal Studies in North East India: Deconstructing the Politics and Colonial Methodology*. https://www.academia.edu/6505077 pp. 8-9.

Zorema, J. *Indirect Rule in Mizoram*. New Delhi: Mittal Publications, 2007.

Index

Abors, 51, 52, 58, 62, 64, 65, 66, 67, 68, 70, 187

Ahom, 9, 10, 12, 14, 15, 16, 17, 18, 21, 22, 38, 42, 51, 52, 102, 127, 140, 174, 183, 189, 200, 214

Akas, 52, 58, 59, 60, 61, 194, 196

AOC (Assam Oil Company), 144, 147

ARTC (Assam Railways and Trading Company), 144, 145, 148, 149, 153, 162, 173

Assam Company, 43, 107, 111, 122, 148, 165, 166, 176

Barker, George, 36, 120, 121, 125, 126, 127, 128, 131, 133, 135, 170, 172, 173, 176

Baruah, Maniram Dutta, 28, 140

Bayley, Steuart, 31, 158

Beadon, Cecil, 95, 220

Bengal, 9, 11, 14, 15, 16, 17, 20, 22, 24, 27, 29, 30, 32, 33, 35, 36, 50, 55, 56, 57, 88, 92, 94, 95, 102, 127, 132, 133, 136, 140, 150, 156, 157, 166, 169, 176, 177, 184, 188, 191, 197, 199, 202, 204, 206, 208, 211, 212, 213, 215, 218, 220, 234, 236, 239, 241

Bentinck, William, 81, 105, 165, 166, 214

Bhutan, 10, 11, 15, 35, 37, 55, 57, 58, 59, 204, 239

Bhutanese, 55, 56, 57, 58, 65, 105

Bihar, 32, 33, 127, 152, 208

Bordoloi, Gopinath, 34, 236

Brahmaputra, 9, 10, 11, 13, 15, 16, 17, 18, 19, 21, 22, 23, 27, 29, 31, 32, 35, 37, 39, 40, 41, 42, 43, 44, 45, 51, 53, 55, 63, 64, 70, 72, 98, 105, 111, 122, 127, 129, 141, 147, 154, 156, 157, 158, 161, 163, 165, 166, 168, 169, 171, 173, 176, 177, 182, 183, 184, 185, 187, 189, 190, 202, 205, 213, 218, 226, 239, 243

Bruce, Robert and Charles, 105, 106, 142, 147, 155, 193

Burma, 9, 15, 18, 21, 35, 43, 45, 74, 75, 90, 143, 164, 178, 186, 225, 226, 235, 239

Butler, John, 68, 74, 77, 78, 80, 81, 83, 178, 208, 211

Cachar, 18, 20, 22, 25, 29, 30, 35, 49, 76, 84, 85, 90, 92, 93, 105, 163, 175, 177, 178, 184, 207, 208

Index

Cachar Hills, 84, 85, 98
Cacharis, 20, 84, 93, 100, 126, 132, 198
Calcutta, 9, 11, 28, 33, 36, 37, 45, 56, 87, 104, 105, 107, 109, 111, 113, 118, 121, 123, 128, 130, 132, 137, 147, 148, 154, 156, 157, 163, 164, 165, 166, 167, 169, 170, 186, 187, 192, 193, 196, 198, 205, 207, 212, 218, 220, 221, 223, 224, 239
Campbell, Archibald, 56, 202
Carnegie, John and Alexander, 129, 133
Chandra, Gobind, 17, 22, 25
China, 10, 35, 43, 45, 62, 69, 72, 75, 105, 106, 110, 116, 164, 202, 203, 206, 225, 226, 239
Chittagong, 17, 28, 33, 90, 92, 137, 163, 164, 205
Cooper, Thomas, 69, 73
Cotton, Henry, 32, 134, 135, 136, 137, 138, 199, 221
Curzon, Lord, 33, 137, 138, 219, 236

Daflas, 51, 58, 61, 62, 65
Dalhousie, Lord, 53, 82
Dalton, Edward Tuite, 44, 66, 69, 74, 79, 141, 143
Damant, Guybon Henry, 82
Darrang, 24, 30, 56, 93, 185, 192, 194, 196, 208, 212, 213, 216, 217
Dhekial Phukan, Anandaram, 174, 215, 223
Dhubri, 36, 37, 164, 170, 177
Dibang River, 64, 67, 69
Dibrugarh, 27, 28, 29, 40, 45, 64, 66, 71, 148, 157, 158, 161, 163, 165, 167, 169, 170, 173, 175, 218, 230, 242
Digboi, 144, 146
Dihang River, 63, 64, 65
Dihing River, 19, 74, 142, 145, 147, 149, 150, 163, 185
Dimapur, 41, 178, 179

d'Orleans, Henri, 72
Dunbar, George, 50

East India Company, 9, 10, 17, 22, 25, 28, 47, 53, 106, 139, 140, 197, 216, 224, 225
Eden, Ashley, 56, 58, 71
Endle, Sidney, 93

Flex, Oscar, 47, 49, 130, 169
Forest Department, 184, 185, 186, 187

Gait, Edward, 51, 86
Ganguli, Dwarkanath, 134
Garo Hills, 22, 30, 35, 88, 98, 181, 199, 238
Garos, 53, 88, 89, 90, 102, 206, 234, 235
Gauhati, 9, 16, 18, 27, 37, 38, 39, 40, 49, 57, 60, 164, 165, 166, 167, 168, 177, 211, 212, 213, 214, 218, 220, 225, 230, 231, 242
Goalpara, 18, 21, 22, 24, 30, 37, 50, 56, 57, 88, 89, 93, 177, 198, 199, 212, 230
Goalundo, 36, 128, 157, 169, 170, 173
Government of India, 24, 29, 30, 31, 33, 39, 89, 111, 138, 144, 158, 169, 177, 184, 186, 189, 197, 200, 202, 216, 218, 232, 240
Government of India Act, 33, 98, 100
Gray, J. Errol, 73
Griffith, William, 106, 142, 148, 192
GSI (Geological Survey of India), 139, 143, 146, 148
Gurkhas, 31, 179

Hannay, Samuel, 141, 142, 148, 154, 155
Himalayas, 35, 37, 41, 44, 46, 58, 140, 200
Holroyd, Charles, 28

291

Hopkinson, Henry, 89, 95, 108, 168, 182
Hunter, William, 189, 190, 218, 222

IGSNC (Indian General Steamer Navigation Company), 167, 168, 170, 173
Indian National Congress, 33, 136
Inner Line, 97, 99, 100, 101, 149, 181, 182, 184, 195

Jaintia, 26, 28
Jaintia Hills, 18, 27, 84, 85, 98, 238
Jaintias, 85, 86, 87
Jenkins, Francis, 24, 25, 81, 106, 142, 148, 167, 176, 211, 212, 225, 226
Johnstone, James, 54, 82, 179, 181

Kamrup, 24, 26, 30, 56, 88, 93, 184, 190, 192, 194, 206, 213, 215, 216, 217
Kamrupa, 15
Keatinge, Richard, 30, 169, 220
Khamtis, 51, 71, 72, 73, 74, 163, 225, 226
Khasi Hills, 31, 39, 41, 88, 155
Khasi-Jantia Hills, 30
Khasis, 85, 87, 179, 225, 230, 235
Kinney, Thomas, 109, 113, 115, 117, 118, 129, 151, 162, 181
Kohima, 41, 82, 178, 179, 180, 181, 182, 228, 229
Kokilamukh, 43, 130, 157, 169
Koliabar, 18, 19, 40, 41
Krick, Nicholas, 66, 71
Kukis, 84, 90, 100

Lakhimpur, 27, 29, 30, 43, 45, 62, 63, 76, 93, 136, 141, 153, 163, 167, 186, 189, 192, 194, 204, 208, 216, 217, 228, 233
La Touche, Tom, 50
Lushai Hills, 35, 90, 92, 97, 98, 100, 184, 238
Lushais, 53, 90, 91, 92

Mackenzie, Alexander, 81, 83, 91
Makum, 142, 143, 144, 145, 146, 148, 149, 150, 155, 158, 159, 162, 163, 173, 186
Manipur, 10, 20, 21, 22, 25, 29, 34, 58, 76, 80, 82, 90, 178, 180
Mann, Gustav, 184, 187, 195, 196
Marwaris, 32, 39, 104, 151, 194
Matak, 22, 24, 27
McCosh, John, 44, 63, 66, 87, 165, 183
Mijis, 58, 59
Mikir Hills, 29, 84, 85, 98
Mikirs, 84, 193, 204, 234
Miris, 52, 62, 63, 64, 65, 67, 102, 196
Mishmis, 35, 65, 67, 68, 69, 70, 72, 73
Moffatt Mills Report, 78, 175, 198, 215, 233
Montagu Chelmsford reforms, 33

Naga Hills, 30, 34, 35, 41, 42, 54, 81, 82, 83, 96, 97, 98, 142, 178, 179, 181, 182, 229, 238
Nagas, 52, 53, 65, 68, 76, 78, 80, 81, 82, 83, 84, 97, 100, 102, 111, 126, 145, 149, 150, 155, 161, 163, 178, 181, 226, 228, 229, 234, 235
Naoroji, Dadabhai, 14
Nepalis, 32, 191, 208
Nigriting, 41
Noctes, 52
Nowgong, 18, 24, 26, 29, 40, 42, 48, 76, 84, 136, 177, 192, 202, 204, 206, 211, 212, 213, 215, 217, 222, 227

Peal, Samuel, 83, 96, 97, 143
Pemberton, Robert, 20, 55, 56, 58, 81
Pollok, Fitzwilliam Thomas, 39, 47

Reid, Robert, 34, 99
Robertson, Thomas Campbell, 24, 211

Index

Robinson, William, 23, 36, 37, 61, 74, 77, 79, 88, 107, 112, 155, 175, 201, 211, 212, 217, 220, 221
Roy, Tirthankar, 104, 205
RSNC (Rivers Steam Navigation Company), 168, 170, 173

Sadiya, 22, 24, 27, 37, 45, 55, 64, 69, 70, 71, 72, 73, 74, 75, 105, 106, 158, 165, 174, 177, 225, 226, 227
Sadulla, Syed Muhammad, 34
Samaguting, 82, 178, 181
Scott, David, 18, 20, 22, 23, 24, 147, 202, 210, 211, 225
Shakespear, Leslie, 17, 55, 67, 77
Sharma, Jayeeta, 9
Shillong, 31, 33, 38, 39, 41, 49, 98, 158, 177, 230
Sibsagar, 9, 27, 28, 30, 41, 42, 43, 76, 155, 167, 175, 192, 204, 207, 208, 214, 215, 216, 217, 220, 222, 226, 227, 228, 229, 230, 234
Silchar, 26, 142
Singha, Gaurinath, 16, 17, 74
Singh, Gambhir, 20, 21
Singh, Purander, 17, 24, 27, 28, 94, 161

Singh, Ram, 22
Singphos, 20, 51, 68, 74, 75, 76, 142, 143, 148, 163, 225, 226
Subansiri River, 65, 141
Sylhet, 20, 22, 25, 26, 29, 30, 32, 35, 49, 92, 105, 163, 175, 177, 192, 199, 208, 225, 237

Tezpur, 16, 40, 133, 163, 193, 194
Tibet, 10, 11, 50, 58, 62, 64, 65, 69, 70, 71

Vetch, Hamilton, 27, 45, 66, 155, 165

Ward, Susan, 40, 46, 78, 113, 126, 175, 228
Wasteland Rules, 107
White, Adam, 45, 73, 142, 211
White, John Berry, 157, 158, 159, 161
Wilcox, Richard, 142, 147
Wilson, Alban, 67
Wood, Sir Charles, 14, 216, 221
Woodthorpe, Robert, 76, 77, 79, 90, 91, 92, 180

Yunnan, 10